WORLD CUP
CRICKET'S CLASH OF THE TITANS

WORLD CUP
CRICKET'S CLASH OF THE TITANS

P E T E R   B A X T E R

ANDRE
DEUTSCH

Edited by Phil McNeill

Designed by Robert Kelland

With thanks to
Louise Dixon, Tim Forrester, Claire Richardson
Dave Crowe, Catherine McNeill, Mark Peacock, Audrey Todd and Eve Cossins

Special thanks to Patrick, Jan and Lynda at Patrick Eagar Photography,
to Mark Goldsmith at Allsport and to Julian Guyer at Hayters for the statistics

First published in Great Britain in 1999 by André Deutsch Ltd
76 Dean Street, London W1V 5HA
www.vci.co.uk

Text copyright © Generation Publications and Peter Baxter 1999

A catalogue record for this title is available from the British Library

ISBN 0 233 99664 8

Printed and bound in Great Britain by Jarrold Book Printing, Thetford

PHOTOGRAPHIC ACKNOWLEDGEMENTS

All photographs by Patrick Eagar Photography unless specified below

Allsport, pages: 4, 83, 84, 85, 87, 88, 89, 107, 114, 118, 119, 121, 135, 137, 138, 139, 141, 142, 144 (right), 148, 149

Page 2: Roy Fredericks hooks Dennis Lillee for six, before falling on his wicket in the 1975 Final
Page 3: Kiran More tries to ignore Javed Miandad's wardance in a 1992 group match
Above: Groundstaff prepare Australia's practice pitch during the 1996 World Cup

CONTENTS

Aravinda de Silva catches Steve Waugh
in the 1996 World Cup Final

ONE DAY THAT CHANGED CRICKET FOREVER

The Prudential World Cup 24 years on by the captain of the
West Indies team that won the first two World Cups

Spring is usually green and full of promise, but there appeared to be nothing promising about the cold, snowy wetness that dominated the weather on the eve of the 1975 World Cup tournament. It certainly bore no hint of the apocalypse that was to have affected the tradition of international cricket for ever as the season unfolded.

In my view, the inaugural Prudential World Cup was cricket's first authentic make-over, that in effect tickled the fancy of the free spirit and prodded the passionless purists into the 20th century. And little did the die-hards know that they had not seen anything yet.

The one-day final at Lord's this year will bear only limited likeness to the West Indies/Australia Prudential epic of June 21 1975 that gave one-day international cricket its imprimatur. A quarter of a century ago, the one-day game seemed tailor-made for the West Indies. And so, not many observers would have been too surprised that we notched the first liens on that elegant trophy, in 1975 and 1979, and almost took it back home to the Caribbean for good in 1983. After all, we were generally regarded as having a patented cavalier flamboyance and an unorthodox flair that, in the early days, did not consistently win us many Test series, but was naturally suited to the limited-overs genre. But our early success in the World Cup was not that simple. As is wont to happen in a

CLIVE LLOYD

tournament that showcases the world's best cricketers, all of our matches were quite demanding.

In fact, a funny thing almost happened on the way to Lord's in 1975. If memory serves, it was West Indies versus Pakistan at Edgbaston. Pakistan had posted a challenging 266 for seven, considered very gettable for me and my heavy-hitters. But mainly through excellent out-cricket, with a few controversial decisions thrown in, the Pakistanis, led by Asif Iqbal, had us perilously positioned at 203 for nine, still needing 64 for an unlikely victory, with wicketkeeper Deryck Murray and one of the best fast bowlers ever to play the game, Andy Roberts, at the wicket. Earlier, I had been the victim of a bad decision, caught behind off the bowling of a young man named Javed Miandad. After the match, Pakistan wicketkeeper Wasim Bari apologised to me for the wrongful verdict.

When Roberts joined Murray, it appeared to be all over bar the shouting. But, as I nervously paced the dressing room, my accountant told me that he had just placed a small wager that West Indies would get the runs. He assured me he was investing his own money. That was reassuring, but I must say that I appreciated the faith he had in our team. He then brought me one dozen pale ale. After each over, I drank one, so by the time Andy and Deryck saw us safely home on the fourth ball of the last over, I was feeling no pain. However that was more than just a win, it was a defining moment, as a West Indies team that was to be one of the most dominant in cricket history had begun to come together as a unit.

The Cup Final at Lord's against Ian Chappell and the gritty Australians – which, with the massive West Indian crowd support, seemed like more of a home game for us – was a landmark victory for the West Indies and a personal triumph for me. I will long remember that 102 off 82 balls against the unrelenting Lillee and Thomson, Gilmour and Walker, gathered with none of the fielding and bowling restrictions of today. But it was truly a team effort, with the great Rohan Kanhai, at 39 years old, grafting an invaluable half-century, and Viv Richards and Alvin Kallicharan putting on a fielding clinic as they garnered no fewer than five runouts. Oh, by the way, I sent down 12 overs for 38 runs, and claimed the wicket of Doug Walters.

There was no more exhilarating experience than holding the Prudential Trophy aloft, with my teammates round me on the balcony, about nine o'clock that night.

To have captained the West Indies team was a signal honour. To have gained the confidence and commitment of my teammates, and won the World Cup for the people of the Caribbean, within the first year of attaining the captaincy, made me extremely proud.

Winning the World Cup for the second time in 1979, the only captain to have done so up to now, remains one of my greatest achievements; but again it was a tribute to a remarkable team. How could one forget the enthralling exhibition of batsmanship by Richards and Collis King in the final against England, or the awesome spectacle of Garner, Marshall, Holding and Roberts in full flight.

Equally unforgettable are the only two losses we suffered in my three World Cup campaign, both against India. But my Saturday afternoons at Lord's have been mostly pleasant memories, and I look forward to reliving them through these pages. It will be fascinating to compare my recollections of the first two Finals with those of Ian Chappell and Mike Brearley. Along with all the other fine players who have contributed to Peter Baxter's book, I am proud to have been a part of cricket's Clash of the Titans.

Left: Clive Lloyd in action during the 1975 World Cup

FROM CRAZY PIPE DREAM TO WORLD CUP REALITY

BY
PETER BAXTER

I t had long been a bit of a pipe dream. A World Cup of cricket. How could it be achieved? Surely it would all take too long. How many matches would be needed to make it a fair test? No one, for nearly the first hundred years of international cricket, could imagine any such championship consisting of anything less than full-scale Test matches.

There *had* been a kind of World Cup in 1912. A Triangular Tournament between England, Australia and South Africa – the existing cricket powers of the time – had been staged in England. A preview of it can be read on a newspaper recovered from the wreck of the *Titanic*, where it had somehow survived at the bottom of the Atlantic. That article suggests that the enterprise would be a success if only the weather were kind. In England? Such kindness was not forthcoming.

Those matches were, as was normal at the time, three-day Test matches. Each side played the others three times with, of course, two innings a side. Australia and South Africa opened the tournament at Old Trafford at the end of May in a match made notable by the unique performance of T. J. Matthews of Australia, who took two hat-tricks – one in each innings. Even more remarkably, he got them both on the same day – the second – on which South Africa lost 19 wickets, to lose by an innings and 88 runs.

England beat South Africa three times by large margins, with the great S. F. Barnes taking no fewer than 34 wickets. South Africa were the whipping boys for Australia, too, who beat them twice with one match rained off. The first two England-Australia games were also rained off.

Therefore the final match between those two teams at The Oval in mid-August would decide the tournament and, amazingly, the Ashes. So this game, for the first time in England, was declared a 'timeless Test'. In fact it took four days and was won by England by 244 runs, with Frank Woolley taking ten wickets in the match.

After the First World War, more countries emerged to play Test cricket. The logistics became more insurmountable, even had there been a will. The Triangular Tournament remained a cricketing curiosity.

In 1963 English cricket started a County Knockout Cup, later known as the Gillette Cup (and from 1981 the NatWest Trophy). It was played over 65 overs, later reduced to 60. Public appetite for this new form of the game was soon evident. By the late Sixties the International Cavaliers, featuring stars such as Gary Sobers and Graeme Pollock, were entertaining large Sunday crowds and television audiences – so much so that a county Sunday league was started in 1969 under the patronage of John Player.

On January 5 1971, what is now considered to be the first one-day international was played in Melbourne. It was arranged to salvage something from a washed-out Test match between Australia and England, and played over 40 eight-ball overs a side. It proved a great success with the crowd of 46,000, as Bill Lawry's Australia, with no limited-overs experience, beat Ray Illingworth's England by five wickets.

The following year in England, at the end of a drawn Ashes series, a series of three internationals was staged between the same two sides for the first Prudential Trophy. England won 2-1 and Dennis Amiss scored

Hey guys, look who got there first

BY

RACHAEL HEYHOE FLINT

The former England women's captain – seen above celebrating with Jack Hayward – recalls how the first World Cup was launched

Women are not always second-best in cricket. It was women, after all, who staged the first ever World Cup – an idea born out of a few after-dinner brandies in 1971. Jack Hayward had already sponsored two England tours to the Caribbean. Now, glass in hand, the Wolverhampton-born businessman was trying to dream up some new method of helping the women's game.

"Why," he asked me, "couldn't we bring every national women's team to England for a World Cup competition?" The very next day, work began on organising the tournament, which was funded by Jack Hayward at a cost of £40,000.

Seven teams assembled in London in June 1973 – England, Young England, Australia, New Zealand, Jamaica, Trinidad & Tobago, and an International XI. There was a chance for the teams to get together when Prime Minister Edward Heath gave a most splendid champagne reception at Number 10. You can imagine the effect on the snap-happy tourists who used to linger in Downing Street when they saw more than 100 women invading the residence of the bachelor PM.

Then we all dispersed to venues as far afield as Bradford, Exmouth and Liverpool for a series of 21 sixty-over matches. The tournament got off to a damp start when the first game, between Jamaica and New Zealand, was washed out without a ball being bowled. As I studied the sodden scene at Kew Green, I felt sorry for the West Indian girls who were bravely trying to keep warm on this 'flaming' June day in Ascot week!

The entire competition was run on a league basis – which, in retrospect, could have been a mistake. It only worked out because England and Australia met in the last game at Edgbaston on July 28 with the Cup still undecided – so that match in effect turned out to be 'the Final'.

England won the toss and virtually put Australia out of the running with a 60-over total of 279 for three, the highest in the competition. Opener Enid Bakewell, a PE teacher from Nottinghamshire, scored 118 – her second century of the tournament – while Lynne Thomas and I both reached half-centuries.

The Aussies eventually fell 92 short; too many to make the closing overs at all exciting for the spectators. As I bowled the last over, even I felt certain that Australia could not score 90-odd off my six deliveries.

Among the audience in the packed grandstand was Princess Anne, who had kindly agreed to present the Cup. She was thrilled by England's success – a feat repeated in 1994 when England beat New Zealand at Lord's to lift the World Cup again. Now let's see England's men do it!

• *Rachael Heyhoe Flint is now a sports marketing consultant. She is also on the main board of Wolverhampton Wanderers FC*

the first one-day international century – a feat the Warwickshire opener would repeat in his first World Cup match.

One-day internationals have been a part of every English season since, and the rest of the world was not slow to take to the new format. Now surely a World Cup was a possibility, and 1975 was named as the date. The International Cricket Conference, known more for setting up working parties to look at possible changes to the accepted order, had moved with unaccustomed speed. Prudential Assurance would put their name to the trophy. Matches would be 60 overs a side, on the basis that the truest test was over the longest distance possible in the day.

There was still the caveat that it was all a bit experimental, and no guarantee that it would be repeated was given. But few doubted that, once started, the World Cup would have a momentum all of its own...

1975

THE PRUDENTIAL CUP

In England

ONE-DAY INTERNATIONALS WERE
STILL RELATIVELY NEW WHEN
CRICKET TOOK THE PLUNGE INTO
A FULL-SCALE WORLD CUP.
THE GRAND EXPERIMENT WAS
SUCH A STUNNING SUCCESS, IT
LEFT EVERYONE WONDERING:
WHY DIDN'T WE DO THIS BEFORE?

**Right: Alvin Kallicharran of the West Indies makes his mark on the
first World Cup with a dramatic innings against Australia at The Oval**

CRICKET EMBARKS ON A BIG ADVENTURE

On June 6 1975, 112 cricketers from eight countries assembled at Buckingham Palace to launch cricket's first World Cup. Clustered round HM the Queen in their blazers and flares, there was one question on all their minds: Who would wear the crown on June 21?

T he crucial factor for the success of the first World Cup would be the weather. And the signs were not good. Thick snow prevented any play at one English county ground on June 2. There were even suggestions that the odd snowflake had been seen at Lord's. But the competition – known simply as the Prudential Cup – evidently had Divine approval. The sun shone brightly for the start of the tournament on June 7 and for the fortnight that followed.

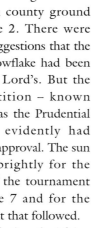
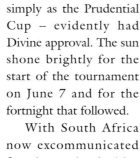

'The first World Cup – known simply as the Prudential Cup – evidently had Divine approval'

With South Africa now excommunicated from international cricket over its government's policy of apartheid, there were six full members of the International Cricket Conference – the Test-playing countries. To this number were added Sri Lanka, not yet enjoying full Test status, and East Africa, to make up two leagues of four which could be resolved into semi-finalists.

The groups were: A – England, India, New Zealand and East Africa; and B – Australia, Pakistan, West Indies

and Sri Lanka. There was little doubt in most people's minds that England, by avoiding the West Indies and Australia, who had given them such a torrid time in the recent Ashes series, had found themselves in the easier group. On the eve of the tournament, a rash of complaints appeared in the Australian press about the draw being loaded. In fact, there hadn't been a draw. The groups had been decided in 1973 and Australia had not demurred.

On Saturday June 7, at Lord's, Edgbaston, Headingley and Old Trafford, the World Cup pipe-dream became reality. Twenty thousand were at Lord's to see England take on India – though one Englishman was notable by his absence. Geoff Boycott had declined to tour Australia in the winter and now, on the eve of the Cup, had decided he would not play for England this summer either. His announcement had coincided with the reappointment of Mike Denness as captain.

But England's hopes rested on a different opening

batsman. Dennis Amiss had scored 1,379 Test runs the previous year, a year that had ended for all the England batsmen fending off the ferocious pace attack of Messrs Lillee and Thomson. Now the Warwickshire opener plundered the Indian medium pace bowlers, none more than Karsan Ghavri, whose 11 overs cost 83. Amiss' 137 was the foundation of England's score, with Chris Old taking only 28 balls to add 51 of his own at the end. A daunting 334 for four was the highest total to date for a 60-over match in England.

There then followed one of the strangest performances ever seen in a World Cup. To the astonishment of the crowd, India – or at least Sunil Gavaskar – made no attempt on the target. By the end of the 60 overs, the opener had made just 36 not out. India finished on 132 for three and lost by 202 runs. It was the beginning of a

Above: The players meet the Queen, Prince Philip and Prince Charles at Buckingham Palace on June 6 1975. Far left: The Oval. Hands up if you think the World Cup's a winner

'I HAD A COMPLETE MENTAL BLOCK'

• Sunil Gavaskar on his bizarre innings of 36 not out •

Sunil Gavaskar's innings against England in the first World Cup match at Lord's will go down in history as one of the most baffling incidents in cricket. Facing an England total of 334 for four, the great Indian opener batted throughout the 60 overs for an undefeated score of just 36 runs. As John Woodcock put it in The Times: "To many among a good-sized crowd, it must have seemed as though no one had told Venkataraghavan and his team that this was a one-day competition."

England captain Mike Denness realised that all was not right in the Indian camp. "The strangest thing was the way Gavaskar played, which was very unusual for him. Something, I believe, happened in the dressing room. It detracted a little bit from our success, because Sunil obviously didn't play to his potential."

In truth, Venkat was tearing his hair out during Gavaskar's display. "Our place in the semi-final could depend on our scoring rate," he said miserably. "That's where we are going to be left out."

India's manager, G. S. Ramchand, added: "I was personally more than disappointed. I made my views felt to Gavaskar, and he was told during the innings. I am sure he is upset. He thought the wicket was too slow." Dissatisfied with this explanation, Ramchand later accused Gavaskar of playing "contrary to the interests of the team", and the little man was hauled up before the Indian Cricket Board.

Years later, Gavaskar finally 'explained' his bizarre innings in his autobiography, Sunny Days, quoted in Ayaz Memon's book One-Day Cricket:

"As I waited for the bowler to run up and bowl, my mind used to be made up to have a shy at the ball, but as soon as the ball was delivered, my feet would move to a position for a defensive shot. The awful noise made by the crowd didn't help my thinking, but only confused me as hell. Right from the start we knew that the chase was out of the question. Even my attempts to take a single and give the strike to the other batsmen failed. There was a complete mental block, as far as I was concerned."

Right: Keith Fletcher takes the aerial route during his audacious 131 at Trent Bridge against New Zealand. But the Englishman was not the scorer of the first World Cup century – that distinction went to Glenn Turner

dismal tournament for India that would confirm they hadn't quite got the hang of this one-day cricket yet.

In the same group, New Zealand, too, topped 300, with Glenn Turner making 171 not out against East Africa, who finished 181 runs short of their target. Some of the East Africans generously applauded Turner's first boundary; they must have had sore hands by the end of his innings.

Australia were many people's favourites for the Cup and on that opening day their game against Pakistan caused the gates to be closed on a full house of 22,000 and a sea of green-and-white Pakistani flags at Headingley. Ian Chappell's team had some late heroics from Ross Edwards, with 80 not out, to thank for a total of 278 for seven. Despite a rash of no-balls from Jeff Thomson, and the panache of Pakistan captain Asif Iqbal and vice-captain Majid Khan, it proved

'When the West Indies' number seven batsman Bernard Julien was out, he rang the hospital where his Kent county colleague Asif Iqbal was languishing, to congratulate him on Pakistan's victory. It cannot have aided Asif's recovery that his wife appeared soon afterwards to tell him that it had in fact been a defeat for Pakistan. Deryck Murray and Andy Roberts had added 64 together to sneak a one-wicket win with two balls to spare.'

too much as Dennis Lillee took the Man of the Match award with five for 34. Asif was to take no further part in the World Cup, taken ill and confined to a hospital bed.

The other Group B match was at Old Trafford, where the bookies' favourites, the West Indies, disposed of Sri Lanka by half past three. Sri Lanka could not cope with the pace of Andy Roberts, Keith Boyce and Bernard Julien, and were bowled out for 86 – which represented a recovery from 58 for nine. The West Indies won by nine wickets, and the teams then staged an exhibition match to entertain the crowd.

The following Wednesday found England at Trent Bridge playing New Zealand. Dick Collinge removed both England openers cheaply, but then Keith Fletcher took over, making 131, run out off the last ball of the innings of 266 for six. There was never any real threat to that total and, with

Tony Greig taking four for 45, England won by 80 runs.

East Africa, meanwhile, found it impossible to force the pace against India's bowlers and were dismissed in the 56th over at Headingley for 120, Madan Lal taking three for 15. Gavaskar, showing the strokes he had hidden at Lord's on Saturday, and Farokh Engineer saw India home by ten wickets before the halfway point in their innings.

One of the most tense matches of the competition, and one which was to have a bearing on the destination of the Cup, was being played at Edgbaston. Led by Majid Khan, with 60, Pakistan made 266 for seven – then had the West Indies staring down the barrel at 203 for nine, with Sarfraz Nawaz having taken four wickets. When the West Indies' number seven batsman Bernard Julien was out, he rang the hospital where his Kent county colleague Asif Iqbal was

Left: The cavalier Asif Iqbal can only laugh as his off stump is sent cartwheeeling by Dennis Lillee. Ian Chappell and Rod Marsh know the game's up for Pakistan

languishing, to congratulate him on Pakistan's victory. It cannot have aided Asif's recovery that his wife appeared soon afterwards to tell him that it had in fact been a defeat for Pakistan. Deryck Murray and Andy Roberts had added 64 together to sneak a one-wicket win with two balls to spare.

At The Oval the might of Australia was pitted against Sri Lanka, still new boys on the world stage. Alan Turner made 101 and Australia 328 for five. The BBC's Brian Johnston witnessed the reply by the small but talented Sri Lankans. "It was a rather unpleasant match," he recalled, "like the Masters playing against the Boys, but with the Masters trying. Sri Lanka did look rather minute as they went out to face this withering attack of Lillee and Thomson, and I'm afraid they did bowl a little bit short at them. It wasn't much fun watching.

"Sidath Wettimuny was hit on the body. He got a runner but was hit again next ball, on the ankle, and went off to hospital having made 53 retired hurt.

"Then Duleep Mendis was hit on the head and he was carried off to hospital too. He made 32 retired hurt. So it was up to the captain, a marvellous chap, Tennekoon, who made a very good 48. And the interesting thing is that with two men sent to hospital, and facing this very fast attack, they still put up 276 for four in 60 overs."

After two rounds of matches, three semi-finalists had been established: England, Australia, West Indies. The remaining place went to the winners of India versus New Zealand at Old Trafford on the second Saturday. India never broke the shackles of tight New Zealand bowling and needed a late innings of 70 from Abid Ali to get them to 230. Glenn Turner's second century of the competition ensured a New Zealand win by four wickets, with seven balls to spare.

England's last group match was against East Africa at Edgbaston. As they amassed 290 for five, could they have

> 'What will Lillee do? He bowls to Kallicharran, a short ball – and he hooks away to midwicket! Another four! A magnificent stroke. And it's almost like a carnival on the far side as the flags are waving and the colourful shirts come off and are waved as well. The West Indians enjoying this onslaught. It's murder from Kallicharran.'
>
> JEFF CHARLES

Plunder at The Oval: Alvin Kallicharran hooks Dennis Lillee for six

known that one of the opposition's opening bowlers had a son who would be part of two future England World Cup squads? Don Pringle bowled his 12 overs for 41 runs, not receiving too bad a mauling at the hands of the team that young Derek would one day represent.

Since the fixtures had been published there had been much anticipation of the clash between Australia and the West Indies at The Oval. It was seen as the fearsome Australian fast bowling coming up against the cavalier Caribbean batting. A newspaper cartoon that day had a nervous West Indian batsman at the crease, flanked by stretcher-bearers, a nurse, surgeons, operating table and priest. The Aussie wicketkeeper says, with a smile: "They say you never see the one that gets you."

But Roberts, Boyce, Julien and Holder were not a bad quartet of bowlers themselves, and without half-centuries from Edwards and Marsh, Australia would have got nowhere near their eventual 192 all out in the 54th over. Could Dennis Lillee bowl Australia back into the match? Not with Alvin Kallicharran taking him on, as an excited Jeff Charles revealed to Caribbean listeners:

"Lillee then to bowl to Kallicharran – and he hooks it beautifully! Is it a six? The umpires are conferring. No, it's just bounced inside of the boundary for four. Oh, what a magnificent stroke from the little man! And that's his 50.

"Lillee bowls to Kallicharran. He has gone for the square cut – and it goes over the slips for four! That went high and wide over the slips down to the third man boundary for four. 123 it is for one, Kallicharran 55. We're in the 31st over.

"What will Lillee do? He bowls to Kallicharran, a short ball – and he hooks away to

> 'It was a rather unpleasant match, like the Masters playing against the Boys, but with the Masters trying.'
>
> BRIAN JOHNSTON
> on Australia v Sri Lanka

midwicket! Another four! A magnificent stroke. And it's almost like a carnival on the far side as the flags are waving and the colourful shirts come off and are waved as well. The West Indians enjoying this onslaught. It's murder from Kallicharran.

"Lillee bowls – and Kallicharran hooks him again! It's away for four – yes, it is into the boundary fence for yet another four. Four bouncers and four fours. And it's plunder at The Oval."

Lillee eventually got his man, but not before Kallicharran had made 78 and, off the previous ten balls from Lillee, hit seven fours and a six. The West Indies won by seven wickets, with no fewer than 14 overs to spare.

In the final match in Group B, Sri Lanka, made the mistake of putting Pakistan in at Trent Bridge and then saw Sadiq Mohammad, Majid and Zaheer Abbas run riot in a total of 330. In reply they were all out in the 51st over for 138.

GROUP A FINAL TABLE

	P	W	L	Pts
England	3	3	0	12
New Zealand	3	2	1	8
India	3	1	2	4
East Africa	3	0	3	0

GROUP B FINAL TABLE

	P	W	L	Pts
West Indies	3	3	0	12
Australia	3	2	1	8
Pakistan	3	1	2	4
Sri Lanka	3	0	3	0

· GROUP A ·

JUNE 7 AT LORD'S
England 334 for 4 (D L Amiss 137, K W R Fletcher 68, C M Old 51*) **beat India 132 for 3 by 202 runs.**

JUNE 7 AT EDGBASTON
New Zealand 309 for 5 (G M Turner 171*, J M Parker 66) **beat East Africa 128 for 8** (H J Howarth 3-29, D R Hadlee 3-21) **by 181 runs.**

JUNE 11 AT TRENT BRIDGE
England 266 for 6 (K W R Fletcher 131) **beat New Zealand 186** (J Morrison 55; Greig 4-45) **by 80 runs.**

JUNE 11 AT HEADINGLEY
India 123 for 0 (S M Gavaskar 65*, F M Engineer 54*) **beat East Africa 120** (Madan Lal 3-15) **by ten wickets.**

JUNE 14 AT EDGBASTON
England 290 for 5 (D L Amiss 88, B Wood 77, F C Hayes 52; Zulfiqar 3-63) **beat East Africa 94** (Snow 4-11, Lever 3-32) **by 196 runs.**

JUNE 14 AT OLD TRAFFORD
New Zealand 233 for 6 (G M Turner 114*) **beat India 230** (S Abid Ali 70, McKechnie 3-49) **by four wickets.**

· GROUP B ·

JUNE 7 AT HEADINGLEY
Australia 278 for 7 (R Edwards 80) **beat Pakistan 205** (Majid Khan 65, Asif Iqbal 53, D K Lillee 5-34) **by 73 runs.**

JUNE 7 AT OLD TRAFFORD
West Indies 87-1 beat Sri Lanka 86 (B D Julien 4-20, K D Boyce 3-22) **by nine wickets.**

JUNE 11 AT EDGBASTON
West Indies 267 for 9 (D L Murray 61*, C H Lloyd 53) **beat Pakistan 266 for 7** (Majid Khan 60, Wasim Raja 58, Mushtaq Mohammad 55) **by one wicket.**

JUNE 11 AT THE OVAL
Australia 328 for 5 (A Turner 101, R B McCosker 73, K D Walters 59, G S Chappell 50) **beat Sri Lanka 276 for 4** (S Wettimuny 53 ret ht, M Tissera 52) **by 52 runs.**

JUNE 14 AT THE OVAL
West Indies 195 for 3 (A I Kallicharran 78, R C Fredericks 58) **beat Australia 192** (R Edwards 58, R W Marsh 52, Roberts 3-39) **by seven wickets.**

JUNE 14 AT TRENT BRIDGE
Pakistan 330 for 6 (Zaheer Abbas 97, Majid Khan 84, Sadiq Mohammad 74, Warnapura 3-42) **beat Sri Lanka 138** (Imran 3-15) **by 192 runs.**

1975

THE
· SEMI-FINALS ·

Australia's defeat by the West Indies had meant that, as group runners-up, they would meet the winners of Group A in the semi-final at Headingley. It would be England v Australia for a place in the first World Cup Final. And what a match it turned out to be…

Finding a green-looking pitch, Ian Chappell inevitably put England in – and Australia found a new hero. The 23-year-old Gary Gilmour opened the bowling with Dennis Lillee and bowled his 12 overs straight through, destroying England with movement in the air and off the pitch as he went. The New South Wales left-armer took six wickets for just 14 runs, with five Englishmen bowled or lbw to his inswinger. Burly Max Walker also enjoyed the conditions he found, taking three for 22 and finishing off the innings in the 37th over. At one point England were down and out at 37 for seven, but captain Mike Denness and Geoff Arnold managed to scrape together a total of 93. With the skies still overcast, could England yet pull off a miraculous escape?

It was the eighth over of the Australian reply before Arnold had Turner lbw for seven, but then John Snow and Chris Old started to wreak havoc. Snow had both Chappells lbw with full-length balls and Old bowled Rick McCosker, Ross Edwards and Rod Marsh. Five more wickets had gone down for the addition of only 15 runs and Australia were reeling at 39 for six.

Denness recalls: "John Snow played quite brilliantly.

'Australia found a new hero. The 23-year-old Gary Gilmour opened the bowling with Dennis Lillee and bowled his 12 overs straight through, destroying England with movement in the air and off the pitch as he went. The New South Wales left-armer took six wickets for just 14 runs, with five Englishmen bowled or lbw to his inswinger.'

**Gary Gilmour appeals,
Dennis Amiss is lbw
and the slide is on**

Outgunned by the king of swing

THE 1975 WORLD CUP SEMI-FINAL • ENGLAND v AUSTRALIA

*Gary Gilmour had taken six for 14 in a sensational spell of swing bowling.
But anything Gilmour could do, surely Snow, Old and Arnold could match …*

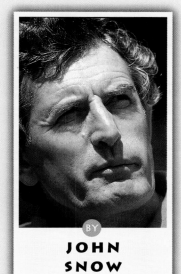

BY

JOHN SNOW

'With Chris Old snapping up three wickets, we had them at 39 for six and were basically one wicket away from winning the game. But then Gus Gilmour came in …'

After the previous winter's experiences in Australia – when the new partnership of Dennis Lillee and Jeff Thomson had crushed England 4-1 – we probably considered ourselves the underdogs on form. But these were English conditions.

In fact, I thought it was a typical Leeds pitch. It was slightly damp and, in overcast conditions, the ball would probably swing around a bit. It was certainly a good pitch to bowl on, though I am not so sure that it was such an advantage to win the toss, because in a one-day game both sides are going to get a bite of the same cherry. But we probably would have put them in, as they did to us, if Mike Denness had won the toss. We knew it was going to be a bowler's game. It was the sort of situation where it could have gone either way.

'Gus' Gilmour could always swing it a lot and on a heavy, overcast Headingley day he was in his element – and started to do just that. He seamed it a bit as well, and he bowled just the right line and length. He really bowled very well, taking six for 14 in 12 overs as England slumped to 93 all out.

Yet, despite our low score, we knew that we also had the ideal bowling attack for those sort of very English conditions. It was difficult to score runs on that pitch, because it didn't come on to the bat, and in Geoff Arnold, myself and Chris Old we had the bowling resources to do the job. We thought we could still win.

I got both the Chappell brothers lbw cheaply: I still have a photograph of Ian Chappell right back on his stumps – absolutely plumb lbw. With Chris Old snapping up three wickets, we had them at 39 for six and were basically one wicket away from winning the game. But then Gus Gilmour came in.

Early on he played forward to me and edged one past third slip at catchable height. I seem to remember that, to add insult to injury, he even got a four for it, because we had all the fielders up in catching positions.

I think that missed chance was the turning point. By then I had almost blown my allotment of 12 overs in the attempt to get wickets. After that Gus, batting with Doug Walters, managed to smash a few. He finished with 28 not out, while Walters was still there on 20. In the event we just didn't have enough runs to bowl at.

It was better for the Final that Australia beat us at Headingley. On a good pitch and a good day you would have to have said that they were a better team than we were. Their win over us made for a cracking first World Cup Final. You couldn't have asked for anything better at that time than Australia v West Indies. But I just watched it on television.

• *John Snow is now a travel agent, handling tours for England cricket supporters and the travelling press contingent*

· SEMI-FINAL ·

HEADINGLEY • JUNE 18

ENGLAND

D L Amiss lbw b Gilmour	2
B Wood b Gilmour	6
K W R Fletcher lbw b Gilmour	8
A W Greig c Marsh b Gilmour	7
F C Hayes lbw b Gilmour	4
*M H Denness b Walker	27
†A P E Knott lbw b Gilmour	0
C M Old c G S Chappell b Walker	0
J A Snow c Marsh b Lillee	2
G G Arnold not out	18
P Lever lbw b Walker	5
Extras (L-b 5, w 7, n-b 2)	14
Total (36.2 Overs)	**93**

Fall of wickets: 1/2 2/11 3/26 4/33 5/35 6/36 7/37 8/52 9/73

Bowling: Lillee 9-3-26-1; Gilmour 12-6-14-6; Walker 9.2-3-22-3; Thomson 6-0-17-0.

AUSTRALIA

won the toss

A Turner lbw b Arnold	7
R B McCosker b Old	15
*I M Chappell lbw b Snow	2
G S Chappell lbw b Snow	4
K D Walters not out	20
R Edwards b Old	0
†R W Marsh b Old	5
G J Gilmour not out	28
Extras (B 1, l-b 6, n-b 6)	13
Total (28.4 overs, for 6 wkts)	**94**

Did not bat: M H N Walker, D K Lillee, and J R Thomson

Fall of wickets: 1/17 2/24 3/32 4/32 5/32 6/39

Bowling: Arnold 7.4-2-15-1; Snow 12-0-30-2; Old 7-2-29-3; Lever 2-0-7-0.

Umpires: W E Alley and D J Constant

Man of the Match: Gary Gilmour

AUSTRALIA

won by four wickets

He got both the Chappells lbw, yorking them both. And, as history will show, one dropped catch when the Australians had 39 on the board for six, if we had got that one catch, who knows how the game would have finished?

"I did in fact bowl John Snow right through his overs because I was looking to him to make sure that we kept in the game. And if we had just got that one wicket more, I think the chances were that we would have gone through. But Gary Gilmour

> 'John Snow played brilliantly. He got both the Chappells lbw, yorking them both. And, as history will show, one dropped catch when the Australians had 39 on the board for six, if we had got that one catch, who knows how the game would have finished?'
>
> MIKE DENNESS

and Dougie Walters saw them through at the end of the day. Disappointment for us because we actually fancied our chances against them."

Now, indeed, it was Gilmour the batsman, coming in at number eight. He survived a chance off Snow through the slips, which was crucial, and ended up as the top scorer for the match with 28 not out, adding 55 undefeated with Doug Walters, who was 20 at the end – though there was much tension among the onlookers in

Below: Snow has Greg Chappell lbw

GILMOUR'S SECRET WEAPON

• How one Aussie knocked England for six •

There was great controversy in the semi-final at Headingley when Australia's fast-medium left-arm bowler Gary Gilmour took six wickets for 14 runs to shoot England out for 93. Wisden noted: "In recent years the Headingley pitch has often been criticised as unsuitable for the big match occasion. This surface was strongly criticised by both captains – and in that a game supposedly between some of the finest batsmen in the world could be finished in 65 overs, there was much to be said for that opinion.

"Yet there was great excitement, especially when Australia, in search of 94 runs needed to win, lost six wickets for 39 runs. Gasps, groans or cheers followed every ball."

After the match, England captain Mike Denness said: "It was certainly strange to play again on the wicket used ten days earlier for the opening match of the competition between Australia and Pakistan. It had not been watered and the grass had been allowed to grow.

"I'm not complaining, but I think a better wicket should have been prepared. In one-day cricket we want a pitch with bounce on which batsmen can play their strokes. Certainly the atmosphere helped the bowlers early on but Gilmour, left arm and bowling over the wicket, had the ball hitting on the seam and coming back from the off. That was the cause of so many early batsmen being out leg before."

Yorkshire groundsman George Cawthray agreed that it would have been preferable to play on a new pitch, but said he had no option. "The atmosphere was responsible for the way the pitch behaved. I have only a width of about 18 yards on the square. I have already had five first-class matches this season and have five more including a Test, the Roses match and one-day games. You tell me where I'm going to fit in all those pitches."

Australia captain Ian Chappell said: "It seamed all day and the bounce was uneven, more balls staying low than coming through high. Hence the number of lbw's. I decided on Tuesday night that Gilmour would be in my team for this game and that he would open. Jeff Thomson gets more wickets at home when he comes back for later spells, and he was not upset about being deprived of the new ball.

"I intended bowling Lillee and Thomson from one end and Gilmour and Walker from the other, but Lillee preferred to bowl downhill so I changed my plans. That gave Gilmour the wind coming over his left shoulder and it suited him fine. It was a magnificent piece of bowling."

the Australian dressing room until the winning runs were scored.

Australia were in the Final, while their opponents were still being decided at The Oval. There New Zealand were shot out in the 53rd over by Julien, Holder and Roberts for 158, a total that was never likely to challenge such a powerful batting side. The West Indies won with five wickets and nearly ten overs to spare, with Kallicharran making 72 and Gordon Greenidge 55.

The Final would be the second meeting of probably the best two teams in the world at the time. It turned out to be a match worthy of such a great occasion and one to live long in the memory of all who were there.

• SEMI-FINAL •

THE OVAL • JUNE 18

NEW ZEALAND

*G M Turner c Kanhai b Roberts	36
J F M Morrison lbw b Julien	5
G P Howarth c Murray b Roberts	51
J M Parker b Lloyd	3
B F Hastings not out	24
†K J Wadsworth c Lloyd b Julien	11
B J McKechnie lbw b Julien	1
D R Hadlee c Holder b Julien	0
B L Cairns b Holder	10
H J Howarth b Holder	0
R O Collinge b Holder	2
Extras (B 1, l-b 5, w 2, n-b 7)	15
Total (52.2 Overs)	**158**

Fall of wickets: 1/8 2/98 3/106 4/106 5/125 6/133 7/139 8/155 9/155

Bowling: Julien 12-5-27-4; Roberts 11-3-18-2; Holder 8.2-0-30-3; Boyce 9-0-31-0; Lloyd 12-1-37-1.

WEST INDIES

won the toss

R C Fredericks c Hastings b Hadlee	6
C G Greenidge lbw b Collinge	55
A I Kallicharran c and b Collinge	72
I V A Richards lbw b Collinge	5
R B Kanhai not out	12
*C H Lloyd c Hastings b McKechnie	3
B D Julien not out	4
Extras (L-b 1, n-b 1)	2
Total (40.1 overs, for 5 wkts)	**159**

Did not bat: †D L Murray, K D Boyce, V A Holder and A M E Roberts

Fall of wickets: 1/8 2/133 3/139 4/142 5/151

Bowling: Collinge 12-4-28-3; Hadlee 10-0-54-1; Cairns 6.1-2-23-0; McKechnie 8-0-37-1; H J Howarth 4-0-15-0.

Umpires: W L Budd and A E Fagg

Man of the Match: Alvin Kallicharran

WEST INDIES

won by five wickets

1975

LORD'S
·THE FINAL·

Following the previous Saturday's match at The Oval, Australia had relinquished any 'favourite' status. But in the Final at Lord's, it was Ian Chappell's team who took the early advantage after he won the toss and put the West Indies in to bat. John Arlott commented on the early overs:

"The shadow of cloud just slides across the ground and then it's all in bright sunshine again as Lillee prepares to bowl. He comes up now from the nursery end, body thrown well forward. Bowls. And Fredericks hooks this bouncer – and knocks a bail off. He's out! He's out. He hooked that bouncer, swung completely round and knocked the bail off as he went."

Trevor Bailey: *"Very unfortunate, because he fell on his wicket and the ball actually went over the boundary for a six."*

Now, at 12 for one, came Alvin Kallicharran, the man who had inflicted such havoc on the Australian bowling attack a week before. In the BBC radio commentary box, Brian Johnston had taken over from John Arlott:

Roy Fredericks was one of the greatest exponents of the hook shot. Early in the Final he hooked Lilllee for six – but fell over and knocked the bails off

"Gilmour running away from us now, approaching umpire Spencer. Bowls to Kallicharran outside the off stump. He goes for a cut … and he's caught – caught behind! – and Marsh flings the ball up. And West Indies, put in to bat, are now 27 for two in this tenth over. Kallicharran caught Marsh bowled Gilmour. And the crowd very sad."

To make matters worse for the West Indies, it seemed that Gordon Greenidge was having one of his introspective days. He took 13 overs in scoring 19. His demise – caught behind off Jeff Thomson – brought in Clive Lloyd at 50 for three to join Rohan Kanhai. Early on he hooked Lillee for six and cover-drove Walker off the back foot for four and, despite giving a chance, he was on his way.

Twenty-six thousand people were crammed into Lord's, all of them conscious of the great feeling of occasion. The innings to grace the moment was forming and high in the Pavilion commentary box, John Arlott was in his element as he brought it to a radio audience round the world:

"And they've scored off the last 15 balls. It's now difficult not only to bowl a maiden over but apparently to bowl a maiden ball. One hundred and eighty-five for three and Gilmour, my word, how life can change between Wednesday and Saturday…

"He comes in. Bowls – and Lloyd hits him high away over midwicket for four! The stroke of a man knocking a thistle top off with a walking stick. No trouble at all. And it takes Lloyd to 99. Lloyd 99 and 189 for three.

"And umpire Bird having a wonderful time. Signalling everything in the world, including stop to traffic coming on from behind. But he lets Gilmour in now and he comes in. Bowls – and Lloyd hits him into the covers. There's his hundred. Only half-fielded out there on the cover boundary. And the century's up and the whole ground seething with leaping West Indian delight.

"I can only say it was worth this. It was worth the treatment it's getting. I thought I saw a policeman applauding. Hah! What an innings. One hundred off 82 balls in 100 minutes, with two sixes, 12 fours and even Kanhai outshone."

After suffering at Lloyd's hand, Gilmour

'The Australians bowled rather quick I must say,' said Clive Lloyd. But the quicker they bowled, the quicker they left the bat. Lloyd hit 14 boundaries as he became the first man to score a century in a World Cup Final

did at last get his wicket – caught behind by the lonely Rod Marsh, with the defensive field spread wide, after a debate between the umpires about whether it had carried. With Kanhai, Clive Lloyd had put on 149 for the fourth wicket and himself had contributed 102 of them.

Gilmour struck back now for Australia. He bowled Rohan Kanhai for 55 and Vivian Richards for five, but Bernard Julien and Keith Boyce, two who were well capable of maintaining the momentum, added 52 for the seventh wicket.

As the total continued to build well past 250, there were many onlookers who felt that it was already too much for Australia. John Arlott, for once mixing his metaphors,

> 'Lloyd hits him high away over midwicket for four. The stroke of a man knocking a thistle top off with a walking stick.'
>
> JOHN ARLOTT
> on Clive LLoyd

described the West Indies innings "sailing out ahead of Australia like an express train leaving a station". Certainly the eventual total of 291 for eight did look an impossibility, particularly in these days before the introduction of fielding restrictions in one-day cricket.

It was made to look no easier by the early loss of Rick McCosker. Ian Chappell, the captain, came in and, with Alan Turner, started to accelerate the scoring rate. There was one potential problem for the West Indies in the form of finding 12 overs from a fifth bowler. Lloyd himself was carrying that duty, as Tony Cozier took over in the radio box.

"Here's Lloyd. With his first ball he comes in to Ian Chappell, captain to captain, and Chappell is on the front foot.

THE BUSINESS

The first World Cup was sponsored by Prudential Assurance, who put in £100,000. A total of 160,000 spectators watched the games, paying £188,598. The Final was watched by 26,000 people who paid record one-day takings of £66,000. The winning team received £4,000, the losing finalists £2,000, and the losing semi-finalists £1,000 each.

'ONE OF THOSE SITUATIONS THAT YOU ONLY DREAM OF'

• **West Indies captain Clive Lloyd on the 1975 World Cup Final** •

'We had got to the first Final. Some of the boys were very nervous, because it was a very big occasion for all of us. We had beaten the Australians earlier in the tournament, so at least that gave us a bit of an edge. But we knew that they had some very good cricketers.

"Lord's had always been a ground where I made quite a few runs and, from the first ball, I felt pretty good. We had a lot of supporters there. The atmosphere was electric and it gave you that little extra.

"I remember batting with Rohan – we kept talking to one another and he, for the first time in his life, would be playing second fiddle to me. It was one of the best innings I've played in a one-day game because of the quality of the bowling: Jeff Thomson, Dennis Lillee, Max Walter, Gary Gilmour and Greg Chappell – that was Australia's Test line-up. They were young, strong, vigorous and very keen. They bowled rather quick, I must say.

"We had a few scares. I was dropped at midwicket by Ross Edwards, who was one of their best fielders. That was a very costly slip for them."

Another turning point came when Viv Richards

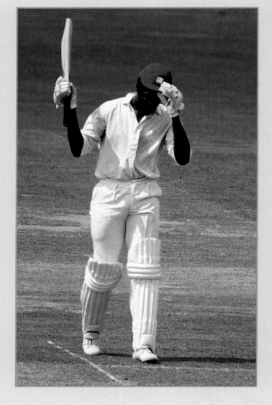

ran out three of Australia's top batsmen. "The Australians never ran very well between the wickets," says Lloyd, "and I think that cost them the game."

Then, when the West Indies had almost wrapped it up, Lillee and Thomson staged a brave fightback with the bat. "I think we were getting a bit complacent. We said, well, it's all over, it's only a matter of time. But then they started to get perilously close to our target. The chaps were looking a little bit worried. I was too, but I didn't show it.

"When it was all over I was quite relieved – but then it sank in that we had won the first World Cup ever. It was one of those situations that you only dream of. You play in your first World Cup, you make a century, you are Man of the Match and it's all come together on the day.

"Those are moments you can look back on and say it was all worthwhile. It was a marvellous day and I think it did a lot for cricket. A wonderful occasion.

"They were dancing in the street. St John's Wood was alight with West Indians, and I presume drunken ones too … but happy."

INTERVIEW COURTESY OF BBC RADIO

There is hesitation in running between the wickets – and he's out! A brilliant bit of fielding by Richards. A brilliant bit of fielding by Richards runs Turner out. There was hesitation in the run as it was played on the on side by Chappell, and just enough hesitation to allow Richards to come in from midwicket and throw the stumps down at the striker's end, to which Turner was trying to get home, and Turner is run out. And that's an appreciable setback for Australia. Really a fine bit of throwing, picking up on the run and throwing by Richards. Eighty-one for two. Turner run out 40.'

Viv Richards might not have made many with the bat, but the 23-year-old's lightning speed in the field was beginning to have a big impact on the game.

Brian Johnston: 'And there's Ian Chappell waiting as Roberts comes in. Bowls to him, and he shuffles across outside the off stump, plays it square on the off side. A misunderstanding between batsmen and fielders – and he's run out! Greg Chappell is run out. Richards threw the ball there, hit the stump, the off bail came off. There was a misunderstanding with the fielders – they couldn't decide who to take it, but Richards did in the end and the two batsmen were in a muddle as well. Now Ian Chappell has seen two batsmen at the non-striker's end coming up and answering his call and being run out. Whether Ian was to blame or not I don't know. Just very good throwing.'

It was 115 for three with Greg Chappell run out for 15.

The Australian Broadcasting Commission had not sent a commentator for this tournament, because the great broadcaster Alan McGilvray was not over-keen on this new form of the game he revered. However, Graham Dawson, an ABC commentator from Melbourne, was on holiday in England and had been invited by the BBC to join the commentary team for this great day. He now joined Fred Trueman at the microphone.

Graham Dawson: *"Here's Lloyd to Chappell, who turns it nicely towards midwicket. But a good stop by Richards. The ball comes in – and that's the third runout! Ian Chappell run out for 62. Richards doing the fielding, stopping the ball with his left hand and ripping the return in to Clive Lloyd at the bowler's wicket and Chappell beaten by a good yard. That is the third runout in the Australian innings and they're 132 for six – and a tragic blow for Australia."*

Fred Trueman: *"Each time Australia have got themselves into a position where it looks like they are counterattacking with success, a runout has happened. That was the third runout and Ian Chappell, who has been involved in all three of them, found himself now at the receiving end. Once again it was Richards who threw that ball in and he never looked like making his ground. It's really only a little bit of panic, trying to keep the score moving along."*

But Doug Walters could hit a ball, and he made 35 before Clive Lloyd bowled him in the 41st over. It was 170 for five – 122 still needed in 19 overs. Ross Edwards helped Marsh add 25 and then, with Gilmour, put on 26 for the seventh wicket. But all three fell victim to Keith Boyce, and Max Walker became the fourth runout. It was 233 for nine and the crowd were already in their starting blocks to run on and salute the West Indies as the first World Cup winners.

But Australia's last-wicket pair were two men of resilience and character – Lillee and Thomson. They needed a daunting 59 from the last seven overs. Yet the runs were coming and Jeff Thomson, for one, was confident: *"Always, you go out there to win. We were hitting the ball well and I just thought, we'll get these runs away. But it was getting a bit dark, that was the trouble. Vanburn Holder was bowling from the members' end and he's a pretty big guy, and it was pretty hard to pick him out of that building."*

It was now past eight o'clock, albeit on the summer's longest day. One no-ball from Holder to Thomson was caught by Fredericks – but the crowd, not having heard the call by umpire Tom Spencer in the general hubbub, stormed on, thinking the match was over. Kallicharran threw at the stumps and missed, and the ball disappeared

'There is hesitation in running between the wickets – and he's out! A brilliant bit of fielding by Richards runs Turner out.'
TONY COZIER

Alan Turner was the first of Viv Richards' runouts in the Final. The Chappell brothers would soon follow

A great day, even for the losers

THE 1975 WORLD CUP FINAL • AUSTRALIA v WEST INDIES

*The Australian captain had a formidable armoury of fast bowlers at his disposal – but after
Clive Lloyd's majestic century, it was Lillee and Thomson's batting that turned it into a thriller*

BY

IAN CHAPPELL

*'I was packing my bag when
I heard all this racket from
the balcony – and there were
these two dopey fast bowlers
trying to win the game'*

It was a great occasion, but it has grown in significance in my memory as the years have gone by since. I don't think we really appreciated what it meant to be in the World Cup Final then. When we had met the West Indies at The Oval in the group match a week earlier, we had both already qualified for the semi-finals and I think our team was rather saving its best for when it really mattered.

On that day, Australia being the first named team, I was the 'home' captain, so I had to spin the coin when we went out to toss. If there were 19,000 in The Oval, 18,000 of them must have been West Indians. I said to Clive Lloyd: "I don't know why I'm the home captain here, I think you ought to be."

Everyone seemed to be at the ground very early on the day of the Final. In fact, at the end of the day, when I was having a drink in the Tavern pub with Clive Lloyd and Mike Procter, I realised I had been wearing creams for 14 hours.

Clive came in to bat when we had them in a bit of trouble at 50 for three, but he didn't play just to shore up the innings, he simply went for his shots. Rod Marsh has said he's not sure who was the better one-day batsman, Viv Richards or Clive Lloyd, but he thinks it might be Lloydy. And it was his ground. He played some great innings in county cup finals at Lord's and that World Cup Final knock of 102 was fantastic.

It had snowed in Derbyshire on the day we arrived from playing a few matches in Canada, but since then there had been a heatwave, so the ground was really fast and we fancied our chances of reaching the target of 292 to win. But then we had those runouts.

I remember when Greg Chappell was out, I played it well to Viv Richards' left and I thought, "He's got to move all that way and then it's still on his left hand so he's got to pick it up left-handed and throw." But he did. And it hit the stumps. I was always very grateful to Warwickshire that their seven runouts in a Lord's final beat our five.

I thought we still had a chance while Gus Gilmour was batting, but when he was out I went inside to start packing my kit. And then I heard all this racket from the dressing room balcony and there were these two dopey fast bowlers trying to win the game. When Jeff Thomson was caught off a no-ball and people were swarming everywhere, it shows the difference between the two characters that Dennis said, "Come on, run!" while Thommo said, "No, I don't know who's going to turn up with the ball."

So there we were, drinking in the Tavern after the game with all those West Indian supporters around and I remember one coming up and shaking Lloydy and me by the hand and then asking Mike Procter who he was. I wasn't sure what the reaction would be to a South African then. Mike said: "I'm Mike Procter."

The man shook his hand and said: "You're a great player. It's a pleasure to meet you." It was that sort of day.

• *Ian Chappell is now a commentator and presenter with Australia's
Channel Nine televison*

into a crowd of spectators. Thomson recalls: "Because they were making so much noise, no one heard the no-ball call, and everyone thought I was out. I said to Dennis: 'Come on, run!' So we started running.

"Meanwhile all the crowd ran on to the field. We kept on running and I think we ran three or four. And when it was all stopped and they cleared the ground, Dennis said: 'Come on, run,' and I said: 'No, I'm not sure which one of these blokes has got the ball now because of all the people on the ground.'

"When it was all settled, I said to the umpire: 'How many's that?' He said: 'Er, one.' I said: 'Wait a minute, we've been running up and down here all bloody day, I've got to have more for it than that!' "

They were awarded three runs. Forty-one runs came in six overs. Incredibly, the target was still just about attainable.

Brian Johnston: *"And Lillee goes up to 16, Thomson is 21, 274 for nine and they need 18 off nine balls. Holder walks back. 274 for nine.*

"The crowd stand round, ready to surge on. The policemen already standing there too. Here's Holder coming up to bowl to Thomson, and bowls. Thomson has a wild hit at that one – and Murray throws it and he's out, stumped! He is out. Murray threw the ball and Australia have been beaten.

"West Indies have won by 17 runs and they are the world champions."

It was almost dark by the time the Duke of Edinburgh, president of the MCC, presented Clive Lloyd with the Prudential Cup and the Man of the Match award at the end of a dramatic and unforgettable day's cricket.

'I was sitting on the boundary when Jeff Thomson was "caught" off a no-ball, and we all spilled on to the outfield thinking the game was over. Meanwhile the two batsmen were running up and down. There was something touchingly unpredictable about it. It could have happened on the village green – the blacksmith Lillee and the dashing fast bowler Thommo haring up and down. The ball lost down a rabbit hole. Some lady who doesn't know the rules walking on and picking up the ball. The umpire not knowing what to do. It was very delightful.'
MIKE BREARLEY

Right: Clive Lloyd receives the Prudential Cup from Prince Philip

· THE FINAL ·
LORD'S • JUNE 21

WEST INDIES

R C Fredericks hit wkt. b Lillee	7
C G Greenidge c Marsh b Thomson	13
A I Kallicharran c Marsh b Gilmour	12
R B Kanhai b Gilmour	55
*C H Lloyd c Marsh b Gilmour	102
I V A Richards b Gilmour	5
K D Boyce c G S Chappell b Thomson	34
B D Julien not out	26
†D L Murray c and b Gilmour	14
V A Holder not out	6
Extras (L-b 6, n-b 11)	17
Total (60 Overs, for 8 wickets)	**291**

Did not bat: A M E Roberts

Fall of wickets: 1/12 2/27 3/50 4/199 5/206 6/209 7/261 8/285

Bowling: Lillee 12-1-55-1; Gilmour 12-2-48-5; Thomson 12-1-44-2; Walker 12-1-71-0; G S Chappell 7-0-33-0; Walters 5-0-23-0.

AUSTRALIA
won the toss

A Turner run out	40
R B McCosker c Kallicharran b Boyce	7
*I M Chappell run out	62
G S Chappell run out	15
K D Walters b Lloyd	35
†R W Marsh b Boyce	11
R Edwards c Fredericks b Boyce	28
G J Gilmour c Kanhai b Boyce	14
M H N Walker run out	7
J R Thomson run out	21
D K Lillee not out	16
Extras (B 2, l-b 9, n-b 7)	18
Total (58.4 Overs)	**274**

Fall of wickets: 1/25 2/81 3/115 4/162 5/170 6/195 7/221 8/231 9/233

Bowling: Julien 12-0-58-0; Roberts 11-1-45-0; Boyce 12-0-50-4; Holder 11.4-1-65-0; Lloyd 12-1-38-1

Umpires: H D Bird and T W Spencer

Man of the Match: Clive Lloyd

AUSTRALIA
won by five wickets

· 1975 STATISTICS ·

Highest totals

334 for 4   England against India
330 for 6   Pakistan against Sri Lanka
328 for 5   Australia against Sri Lanka
309 for 5   New Zealand against East Africa
290 for 5   England against East Africa

Lowest totals (completed innings)

86   Sri Lanka against West Indies
93   England against Australia
94   East Africa against England
120   East Africa against India
128   East Africa against New Zeland

Highest winning margins

10 wickets India against East Africa
9 wickets   West Indies against Sri Lanka
202 runs   England against India
196 runs   England against East Africa
192 runs   Pakistan against Sri Lanka

Closest winning margins

1 wicket   West Indies against Pakistan
17 runs   West Indies against Australia

Highest match aggregates

604 for 9   Australia v Sri Lanka
565 for 18   Australia v West Indies (Final)
533 for 16   West Indies v Pakistan
483 for 17   Australia v Pakistan
468 for 16   Pakistan v Sri Lanka

Wins by non-Test nations   0

Centuries

171   G M Turner, New Zealand v East Africa
137   D L Amiss, England v India
131   K W R Fletcher, England v New Zealand
114   G M Turner, New Zealand v India
102   C H Lloyd, West Indies v Australia (Final)
101   A Turner, Australia v Sri Lanka

Highest scores for each position

1   G M Turner 171, New Zealand v East Africa
2   D L Amiss 137, England v India
3   K W R Fletcher 131, England v New Zealand
4   J M Parker 66, New Zealand v East Africa
5   C H Lloyd 102, West Indies v Australia
6   R Edwards 80 n.o., Australia v Pakistan
7   C M Old 20 n.o., England v New Zealand
8   D L Murray 61 n.o., West Indies v Pakistan
9   J R Thomson 20 n.o., Australia v Pakistan
10   S Vekataraghavan 26 n.o., India v NZ
11   D K Lillee 16 n.o., Australia v W Indies (Final)

Leading scorers

G M Turner, New Zealand	333	Ave: 166.50
D L Amiss, England	243	Ave: 60.75
K W R Fletcher, England	207	Ave: 69.00
A Turner, Australia	201	Ave: 40.20
A I Kallicharran, West Indies	197	Ave: 49.25

Most wickets in tournament

11 at 5.63   G J Gilmour, Australia
10 at 17.70   B D Julien, West Indies
10 at 18.50   K D Boyce, West Indies
8 at 20.25   D R Hadlee, New Zealand
8 at 27.87   D K Lillee, Australia

Most wickets in a match

6-14   G J Gilmour, Australia v England
5-34   D K Lillee, Australia v Pakistan
5-48   G J Gilmour, Australia v West Indies
4-11   J A Snow, England v East Africa
4-44   Sarfraz Nawaz, Pakistan v West Indies
4-45   A W Greig, England v New Zealand

Most dismissals by a wicketkeeper

10 (9ct, 1st)   R W Marsh, Australia
9   (9ct)   D L Murray, West Indies
6   (6ct)   Wasim Bari, Pakistan
4   (3ct, 1st)   K J Wadsworth, New Zealand
2   (2ct)   F M Engineer, India

Most catches by an outfielder

4   C H Lloyd, West Indies
3   R B Kanhai, West Indies
3   B F Hastings, New Zealand
3   A Turner, Australia
3   G S Chappell, Australia

Australia *batting*

	M	I	NO	Runs	HS	Avge	100	50	Ct	St
R.Edwards	5	4	1	166	80*	55.33	-	2	-	-
G.J.Gilmour	2	2	1	42	28*	42.00	-	-	1	-
A.Turner	5	5	0	201	101	40.20	1	-	3	-
K.D.Walters	5	5	1	123	59	30.75	-	1	-	-
R.W.Marsh	5	5	2	78	52*	26.00	-	1	9	1
G.S.Chappell	5	5	0	129	50	25.80	-	1	3	-
J.R.Thomson	5	4	2	51	21	25.50	-	-	1	-
I.M.Chappell	5	5	0	121	62	24.20	-	1	-	-
R.B.McCosker	5	5	0	120	73	24.00	-	1	-	-
D.K.Lillee	5	2	1	19	16*	19.00	-	-	-	-
M.H.N.Walker	5	3	0	33	18	11.00	-	-	1	-
A.A.Mallett	3	1	0	0	0	0.00	-	-	1	-

Australia *bowling*

	O	M	R	W	Avge	Best	5w	Econ
G.J.Gilmour	24	8	62	11	5.63	6-14	2	2.58
J.R.Thomson	44	9	129	4	32.25	2-44	-	2.93
I.M.Chappell	7	1	23	2	11.50	2-14	-	3.28
M.H.N.Walker	57.2	10	210	6	35.00	3-22	-	3.66
D.K.Lillee	53	6	223	8	27.87	5-34	1	4.20
A.A.Mallett	35	3	156	3	52.00	1-35	-	4.45
G.S.Chappell	18	0	88	0	-	-	-	4.88
K.D.Walters	17	1	85	1	85.00	1-29	-	5.00

East Africa *batting*

	M	I	NO	Runs	HS	Avge	100	50	Ct	St
Mehmood Quraishy	3	3	1	41	19	20.50	-	-	-	-
Zulfiqar Ali	3	3	1	39	30	19.50	-	-	1	-
Frasat Ali	3	3	0	57	45	19.00	-	-	-	-
Ramesh Sethi	3	3	0	54	30	18.00	-	-	1	-
Jawahir Shah	3	3	0	46	37	15.33	-	-	-	-
S.Walusimba	3	3	0	38	16	12.66	-	-	-	-
Praful Mehta	1	1	0	12	12	12.00	-	-	-	-
P.G.Nana	3	3	2	9	8*	9.00	-	-	2	-
Shiraz Sumar	1	1	0	4	4	4.00	-	-	-	-
H.McLeod	2	2	0	5	5	2.50	-	-	-	-
D.Pringle	2	2	0	5	3	2.50	-	-	-	-
Harilal Shah	3	3	0	6	6	2.00	-	-	-	-
Yunus Badat	2	2	0	1	1	0.50	-	-	-	-
J.Nagenda	1	0	0	0	0	-	-	-	-	-

East Africa *bowling*

	O	M	R	W	Avge	Best	5w	Econ
D.Pringle	15	0	55	0	-	-	-	3.66
P.G.Nana	28.5	4	116	1	116.00	1-34	-	4.02
Frasat Ali	24	1	107	0	-	-	-	4.45
Zulfiqar Ali	35	3	166	4	41.50	3-63	-	4.74
Ramesh Sethi	20	1	100	1	100.00	1-51	-	5.00
Mehmood Quraishy	18	0	94	3	31.33	2-55	-	5.22
J.Nagenda	9	1	50	1	50.00	1-50	-	5.55

Left: Ross Edwards topped the Australian batting averages

England *batting*

	M	I	NO	Runs	HS	Avge	100	50	Ct	St
K.W.R.Fletcher	4	3	0	207	131	69.00	1	1	1	-
D.L.Amiss	4	4	0	243	137	60.75	1	1	1	-
M.H.Denness	4	4	2	113	37*	56.50	-	-	-	-
C.M.Old	4	4	2	89	51*	44.50	-	1	1	-
B.Wood	3	2	0	83	77	41.50	-	1	-	-
F.C.Hayes	3	3	0	90	52	30.00	-	1	-	-
A.P.E.Knott	4	2	1	18	18*	18.00	-	-	1	-
J.A.Jameson	2	2	0	32	21	16.00	-	-	-	-
A.W.Greig	4	4	0	29	9	7.25	-	-	-	-
P.Lever	4	1	0	5	5	5.00	-	-	1	-
J.A.Snow	3	1	0	2	2	2.00	-	-	-	-
G.G.Arnold	3	1	1	18	18*	-	-	-	1	-
D.L.Underwood	2	0	0	0	0	-	-	-	2	-

England *bowling*

	O	M	R	W	Avge	Best	5w	Econ
B.Wood	12	5	14	0	-	-	-	1.16
J.A.Jameson	2	1	3	0	-	-	-	1.50
J.A.Snow	36	8	65	6	10.83	4-11	-	1.80
D.L.Underwood	22	7	41	2	20.50	2-30	-	1.86
G.G.Arnold	29.4	7	70	3	23.33	1-15	-	2.35
P.Lever	36	3	92	5	18.40	3-32	-	2.55
C.M.Old	32.3	8	86	7	12.28	3-29	-	2.64
A.W.Greig	31	2	89	6	14.83	4-45	-	2.87

India *batting*

	M	I	NO	Runs	HS	Avge	100	50	Ct	St
S.M.Gavaskar	3	3	2	113	65*	113.00	-	1	-	-
F.M.Engineer	3	2	1	78	54*	78.00	-	1	2	-
S.Abid Ali	3	1	0	70	70	70.00	-	1	-	-
A.D.Gaekwad	3	2	0	59	37	29.50	-	-	1	-
B.P.Patel	3	2	1	25	16*	25.00	-	-	-	-
Madan Lal	3	1	0	20	20	20.00	-	-	-	-
G.R.Viswanath	3	2	0	39	37	19.50	-	-	-	-
E.D.Solkar	3	2	0	21	13	10.50	-	-	1	-
B.S.Bedi	2	1	0	6	6	6.00	-	-	-	-
M.Amarnath	3	1	0	1	1	1.00	-	-	-	-
S.Venkataraghavan	3	1	1	26	26*	-	-	-	1	-
K.D.Ghavri	1	0	0	0	0	-	-	-	-	-

India *bowling*

	O	M	R	W	Avge	Best	5w	Econ
B.S.Bedi	24	14	34	2	17.00	1-6	-	1.41
S.Venkataraghavan	36	4	109	0	-	-	-	3.02
S.Abid Ali	36	7	115	6	19.16	2-22	-	3.19
Madan Lal	33.2	4	141	5	28.20	3-15	-	4.23
M.Amarnath	30	3	139	4	34.75	2-39	-	4.63
E.D.Solkar	4	0	28	0	-	-	-	7.00
K.D.Ghavri	11	1	83	0	-	-	-	7.54

New Zealand *batting*

	M	I	NO	Runs	HS	Avge	100	50	Ct	St
G.M.Turner	4	4	2	333	171*	166.50	2	-	-	-
G.P.Howarth	3	3	0	80	51	26.66	-	1	-	-
B.F.Hastings	4	4	1	76	34	25.33	-	-	3	-
J.F.M.Morrison	4	4	0	91	55	22.75	-	1	2	-
B.G.Hadlee	1	1	0	19	19	19.00	-	-	-	-
J.M.Parker	4	4	0	71	66	17.75	-	1	-	-
K.J.Wadsworth	4	4	0	68	25	17.00	-	-	3	1
D.R.Hadlee	4	3	1	28	20	14.00	-	-	-	-
B.J.McKechnie	4	2	0	28	27	14.00	-	-	1	-
R.J.Hadlee	3	3	1	21	15	10.50	-	-	1	-
B.L.Cairns	1	1	0	10	10	10.00	-	-	-	-
R.O.Collinge	4	2	0	8	6	4.00	-	-	1	-
H.J.Howarth	4	2	1	1	1*	1.00	-	-	2	-

New Zealand *bowling*

	O	M	R	W	Avge	Best	5w	Econ
R.O.Collinge	48	13	137	6	22.83	3-28	-	2.85
R.J.Hadlee	36	10	124	3	41.33	2-48	-	3.44
D.R.Hadlee	46	5	162	8	20.25	3-21	-	3.52
H.J.Howarth	40	5	148	5	29.60	3-29	-	3.70
B.J.McKechnie	44	5	163	4	40.75	3-49	-	3.70
B.L.Cairns	6.1	2	23	0	-	-	-	3.72

Pakistan *batting*

	M	I	NO	Runs	HS	Avge	100	50	Ct	St
Majid Khan	3	3	0	209	84	69.66	-	3	-	-
Asif Iqbal	1	1	0	53	53	53.00	-	1	1	-
Javed Miandad	2	2	1	52	28*	52.00	-	-	2	-
Zaheer Abbas	3	3	0	136	97	45.33	-	1	3	-
Wasim Raja	3	3	0	91	58	30.33	-	1	2	-
M/taq Mohammad	3	3	0	89	55	29.66	-	1	1	-
Sadiq Mohammad	3	3	0	85	74	28.33	-	1	-	-
Parvez Mir	2	2	1	8	4*	8.00	-	-	1	-
Asif Masood	3	1	0	6	6	6.00	-	-	-	-
Imran Khan	2	2	0	9	9	4.50	-	-	-	-
Wasim Bari	3	2	1	3	2	3.00	-	-	6	-
Sarfraz Nawaz	2	2	1	0	0*	0.00	-	-	1	-
Naseer Malik	3	1	1	0	0*	-	-	-	-	-

Pakistan *bowling*

	O	M	R	W	Avge	Best	5w	Econ
Wasim Raja	9.4	4	23	1	23.00	1-7	-	2.37
Naseer Malik	30	5	98	5	19.60	2-37	-	3.26
Mushtaq Mohammad	7	0	23	0	-	-	-	3.28
Sadiq Mohammad	6	1	20	2	10.00	2-20	-	3.33
Imran Khan	17.1	3	59	5	11.80	3-15	-	3.43
Javed Miandad	19	2	68	3	22.66	2-22	-	3.57
Parvez Mir	15	2	59	2	29.50	1-17	-	3.93
Asif Masood	30	3	128	2	64.00	1-50	-	4.26
Sarfraz Nawaz	24	1	107	5	21.40	4-44	-	4.45
Asif Iqbal	12	0	58	1	58.00	1-58	-	4.83

Sri Lanka *batting*

	M	I	NO	Runs	HS	Avge	100	50	Ct	St
L.R.D.Mendis	2	2	1	40	32*	40.00	-	-	1	-
A.P.B.Tennekoon	3	3	0	78	48	26.00	-	-	2	-
M.Tissera	3	3	0	78	52	26.00	-	1	-	-
D.S.de Silva	3	2	0	47	26	23.50	-	-	-	-
E.R.Fernando	3	3	0	47	22	15.66	-	-	-	-
B.Warnapura	3	3	0	41	31	13.66	-	-	1	-
A.Ranasinghe	3	3	1	23	14*	11.50	-	-	-	-
H.S.M.Pieris	3	3	1	19	16	9.50	-	-	-	-
A.R.M.Opatha	3	2	0	11	11	5.50	-	-	3	-
P.D.Heyn	2	2	0	3	2	1.50	-	-	1	-
G.R.A.de Silva	1	1	0	0	0	0.00	-	-	-	-
S.Wettimuny	1	1	1	53	53*	-	-	-	1	-
L.Kaluperuma	3	2	2	19	13*	-	-	-	-	-

Sri Lanka *bowling*

	O	M	R	W	Avge	Best	5w	Econ
L.Kaluperuma	27.4	2	102	1	102.00	1-50	-	3.68
A.R.M.Opatha	25	0	118	2	59.00	2-67	-	4.72
D.S.de Silva	32	5	154	4	38.50	2-60	-	4.81
B.Warnapura	17	0	82	3	27.33	3-42	-	4.82
H.S.M.Pieris	22	0	135	2	67.50	2-68	-	6.13
A.Ranasinghe	10	0	65	0	-	-	-	6.50
G.R.A.de Silva	7	1	46	0	-	-	-	6.57

West Indies *batting*

	M	I	NO	Runs	HS	Avge	100	50	Ct	St
D.L.Murray	5	3	2	105	61*	105.00	-	1	9	-
R.B.Kanhai	5	4	2	109	55	54.50	-	1	3	-
C.H.Lloyd	5	3	0	158	102	52.66	1	1	4	-
A.I.Kallicharran	5	5	1	197	78	49.25	-	2	2	-
B.D.Julien	5	3	2	48	26*	48.00	-	-	-	-
R.C.Fredericks	5	5	0	116	58	23.20	-	1	2	-
V.A.Holder	5	2	1	22	16	22.00	-	-	2	-
C.G.Greenidge	4	4	0	88	55	22.00	-	1	-	-
K.D.Boyce	5	2	0	41	34	20.50	-	-	-	-
I.V.A.Richards	5	4	1	38	15*	12.66	-	-	-	-
A.M.E.Roberts	5	1	1	24	24*	-	-	-	-	-
L.R.Gibbs	1	0	0	0	0	-	-	-	-	-

West Indies *bowling*

	O	M	R	W	Avge	Best	5w	Econ
A.M.E.Roberts	56.4	11	165	8	20.62	3-39	-	2.91
B.D.Julien	60	11	177	10	17.70	4-20	-	2.95
C.H.Lloyd	36	4	125	3	41.66	1-31	-	3.47
K.D.Boyce	52	3	185	10	18.50	4-50	-	3.55
I.V.A.Richards	10	0	39	3	13.00	2-18	-	3.90
V.A.Holder	43.2	4	184	5	36.80	3-30	-	4.24
L.R.Gibbs	4	0	17	0	-	-	-	4.25

1979

THE PRUDENTIAL CUP

In England

FOUR YEARS ON, THE CRICKET WORLD HAD UNDERGONE A REVOLUTION. BUT WHETHER ANYONE COULD OVERTHROW CLIVE LLOYD'S ONE-DAY KINGS – THAT WAS ANOTHER MATTER

Right: Enter Derek Randall, stage right, to run out Gordon Greenidge in the 1979 World Cup Final

THE CARIBBEAN CARNIVAL ROLLS ON

Not satisfied with one World Cup, the West Indies were now even stronger. Australia were under strength but Pakistan looked powerful, and Mike Brearley commanded an exciting England team: Botham, Gower, Gooch, Randall... It was going to be another hot summer

'Much had happened in world cricket since the 1975 World Cup. Kerry Packer's rebel World Series Cricket had riven the sport. After two years of discord, that had been settled, but it was too early for Australia or England to select their Packer players. The West Indies, on the other hand, having supplied a complete team to the Packer circus, now had them all back...'

There had been little doubt that, when the member countries of the ICC met in London at the end of June 1975 after the dramatic and successful conclusion of the first World Cup, they would endorse the staging of another.

India had said then that they were keen to host the tournament, but the convenience of England logistically appealed to the majority. June was out of season for every other member and there was a keenness to preserve the 60-over format, which made the length of daylight hours in an English summer an important factor.

So, England it was, four years on. Much had happened in world cricket in the interim. The name Kerry Packer had featured large: the Australian media mogul's rebel World Series Cricket had riven the sport. After two years of discord, that had been settled, but it was too early for Australia or – less seriously – England to select their Packer players. The West Indies, on the other hand, having supplied a complete team to the Packer circus, now had them all back, just to endorse the holders as overwhelming favourites.

Mike Brearley's secret weapon: Boycott suddenly turned into an all-rounder

To make the numbers for the tournament up to eight, a new competition, the International Cricket Conference Trophy, had thrown up Sri Lanka and Canada only three days before the start of the World Cup. The draw had settled the two groups as: Group A – Australia, England, Pakistan and Canada; and Group B – India, New Zealand, West Indies and Sri Lanka.

As four years before, the early-season weather gave cause for concern but, again, with the timing of an old theatrical trouper, it was perfect when the curtain went up. And what better start could there be than England playing Australia before 25,000 people at Lord's on a perfect Saturday in early June?

Mike Brearley had led England to victory in Australia just a few months before and now he put Kim Hughes' team in, but before lunch he had only managed to capture one wicket and Australia were building the platform for a later assault. Then Brearley called up his secret weapon – Geoff Boycott. As Boycott himself put it: "Mike Brearley had this brainwave to get me bowling, which didn't thrill me

too much at the start. But it worked." John Arlott watched from the radio commentary box as Boycott, still wearing his cap, ambled up to bowl to opener Andrew Hilditch:

"Boycott, who bowls medium-pace inswing, comes up again. And he's bowled him! Hah! Boycott is delighted."

But the demon bowler wasn't finished.

"Boycott comes in. Bowls to him. And Hughes hits that boldly out on the leg side – and it's caught magnificently by Hendrick! On the run from midwicket, and he took the catch as his legs went and his feet slid from under him. He ran 14 yards in, but he held on as he fell, and Australia are 111 for three."

Boycott remembers it all well: "I think Hilditch played an inside edge on. Bowling from the Pavilion end, I bowl, he got an inside edge on to the stumps and that's bowled. Every time I see him in Australia he walks past me with his head in his hands. And Kim Hughes, he thought I couldn't bowl, so he tried to whack me over the pavilion!"

The Australian momentum had been slowed. With David Gower and Derek Randall prowling either side of the wicket, they fell victim to four runouts and their 60 overs produced a rather disappointing 159 for nine. Boycott's medium-pace in-duckers had taken two for 15 in

West Indies supporters enjoy another day out at Lord's, which was becoming their team's home from home

THE BUSINESS

The second World Cup was again sponsored by Prudential Assurance, which increased its input to £250,000. A total of 132,000 spectators watched the games, down 38,000 due to bad weather, and paid £359,700. The Final was watched by 25,000 people. The winning team received £10,000, the losing finalists £4,000, the losing semi-finalists £2,000 each, and group match-winning teams £500. Players winning the Man of the Match award received £300 in the Final, £200 in the semi-finals, and £100 in group matches. A surplus of £350,000 was distributed between the full and associate members of the ICC.

six overs. Australia must have been encouraged, though, by their start in the field, when Rodney Hogg and Geoff Hurst reduced them to five for two and provided a possibly unique instance of Geoff Boycott having fewer runs than wickets to his name in a match. The crisis was averted by Brearley and Graham Gooch in a third-wicket stand of 108, and then David Gower and Ian Botham turned on the style as England won by six wickets with 13 overs to spare.

Canada made their entry to big-time cricket at Headingley, meeting Pakistan. Seven Canadian players had been born in the West Indies but as their captain, Garnett Brisbane, pointed out: "Most of us have lived in Canada for years. We're Canadians. We pay taxes and go to the ice hockey!" Pakistan froze them out, passing their 139 for nine with eight wickets and nearly 20 overs in hand.

Clive Lloyd's champions had spent the intervening four years honing a battery of fast bowlers which had swept – or rather bounced – all before them. A daunting prospect for India, put in at Edgbaston. Roberts, Holding, Garner, Croft and King found resistance only from Gundappa Viswanath as they dismissed India in the 54th over for 190.

Gordon Greenidge had limped off the field earlier in the week while playing for Hampshire against Somerset – always a danger sign for the opposition. Now, nursing a knee injury, he hammered an undefeated 106 to give the West Indies a nine-wicket win with eight-and-a-half overs to spare.

At Trent Bridge, Sri Lanka's batsmen went for their shots against New Zealand's medium-pacers and were bowled out for 189 three overs inside the distance. Glenn Turner and Geoff Howarth had no trouble overhauling that target with one wicket down and 12 overs to spare.

For the first time in a World Cup, the weather took a hand in the next round of matches. At The Oval, the West Indies and Sri Lanka could not make a start in the three days allocated and had to share the points. At Old Trafford there was no play on Wednesday June 13 thanks to a heavy Manchester downpour, but England and Canada managed to take the field the following day between the showers.

> 'Seven of the Canadian players had been born in the West Indies but as their captain, Garnett Brisbane, pointed out: "Most of us have lived in Canada for years. We're Canadians. We pay taxes and go to the ice hockey!"'

The late start did Canada little good. They were shot out for 45, which took them 41 overs to amass. It produced some remarkable bowling figures: Bob Willis 4-11 in 10.3 overs, Chris Old 4-8 in 10 overs, and Mike Hendrick eight overs, five maidens, 1-5.

England did lose two wickets in the 14 overs it took them to score the 46 they needed. That brief period also caused some consternation in the radio commentary box, where Brian Johnston was in action when a Canadian substitute fielder called Shokat Baksh made an appearance. Unfortunately Brian could not get the unfamiliar name out without dissolving in helpless mirth and for a time the radio audience was none the wiser about the fielder's name – or, indeed, anything else.

Further south and east, at Trent Bridge, Pakistan had made 286 against an Australian attack deprived of its main cutting edge in the form of Rodney Hogg, who was suffering from bronchitis. Pakistan, too, were depleted, with Sarfraz Nawaz injured, but a somewhat makeshift attack, opened by Asif Iqbal and Majid Khan, dismissed Australia for 192 inside the distance, despite Andrew Hiltitch's 72. The result, with England's two victories so far, meant that England and Pakistan would be the two semi-finalists from Group A and 1975 finalists Australia would be out.

At Headingley, New Zealand's medium-pace bowlers used a damp Leeds morning to dismiss India for 182 and the left-handed opener Bruce Edgar, with 84 not out, made sure of their place in the semi-finals.

The West Indies had to beat New Zealand at Nottingham on the Saturday to join them in the semis, which they duly did – but not without some alarm. Gordon Greenidge guided the first half of the West Indies innings with his 65, and Clive Lloyd dominated the rest with 73 not out, but for a time the New Zealanders threatened the West Indies score of 244 for seven. In the end they just lost too many wickets to the fast bowlers to mount a serious challenge.

In Manchester, meanwhile, the match between Sri Lanka and India was delayed for two days – and then the Sri Lankan batsmen, who had already given an indication

Left: Oops! Graham Yallop of Australia swings round to see his bails in the air as he is bowled out for 37 by Majid Khan, who opened both the batting and the bowling for Pakistan

of what they were capable of, took the Indian bowling by surprise. Sidath Wettimuny, Roy Dias and Duleep Mendis ensured a score of 238 for five.

Despite knowing that their unlikely chance of a semi-final place had already gone, Sri Lanka's bowlers, led by the leg-spinner Somachandra de Silva with three for 29 from 11 overs, inflicted an embarrassing 47-run defeat on India, who were evidently still having trouble getting the hang of this one-day cricket. It was the first World Cup win for one of the associate members. Sri Lanka had made history, and by the time the next World Cup was played, they would be a fully-fledged Test nation.

The under-strength Australia team ended a miserable World Cup for them by securing their only points in the defeat of Canada at Edgbaston, where Hurst bowled out the junior side for 105 and the target was reached in the 26th over by seven wickets.

Possibly the most thrilling match of the tournament was being staged that weekend at Headingley, where England and Pakistan, having both qualified, were meeting effectively to try to avoid the West Indies in the semi-final.

On a cloudy Leeds morning, Asif Iqbal put England in to bat with immediate success. Mike Brearley and Derek Randall were back in the dressing room with only four runs on the board. Coming in at four, Graham Gooch got things moving, hitting five fours in his 33 and sharing a stand of 47 with Geoff Boycott. But that stand was followed by a slide caused largely by the off breaks of Majid Khan, who took three for 27 in 12 overs. At 118 for eight it looked very much as if England were beyond help.

A respectable score was only reached through the unlikely agency of Bob Taylor and Bob Willis, who put on 43 for the ninth wicket. Still, a glance at the Pakistani batting line-up would not have given England confidence that they could defend 165 for nine.

It was a calm enough start, but remarkable things

'Sri Lanka's bowlers, led by the leg-spinner Somachandra de Silva, inflicted an embarrassing 47-run defeat on India, who were evidently still having trouble getting the hang of this one-day cricket. It was the first World Cup win for one of the associate members. Sri Lanka had made history'

Right: Wasim Raja, watched by his captain Asif Iqbal, drives a delivery from Ian Botham as Pakistan stage a stirring fightback against England at Headingley

'England-Pakistan at Headingley was one of the best World Cup matches I have participated in. Both the teams had already qualified for the semi-finals. It was a matter of playing not to meet the West Indies, because the other semi-finalists were New Zealand. We won the toss, we fielded first, everybody chipped in with wickets and we got England out quite cheaply. We had only 160-something to get. We had a tremendous start, 27 for no loss in no time. And then suddenly we were 33 for six...'

ASIF IQBAL

started to happen in the eighth over, with Christopher Martin-Jenkins the radio commentator:

"Hendrick coming back, a frown on his face. Grimly intent on getting this breakthrough that England now desperately need. Away he goes from this grandstand end. Bowls to Majid Khan, on a line. And he's caught by Botham at second slip! A very good catch, moving to his left, and well bowled, Hendrick. A thoroughly deserved wicket if ever there was one."

In came Mudassar Nazar. *"Hendrick right bang on the spot now and bowling formidably well. He turns, goes away, with long pigeon-toed strides. Final stretch, and he bowls to Mudassar – and he's out lbw! Well pitched-up, middle and off, and absolutely no hesitation from umpire Evans as the fielders went up in unison with Hendrick. And Mudassar is out second*

ball for nought, and Mike Hendrick has taken two wickets in three balls. And Pakistan are 27 for two."

In Hendrick's next over there was more mayhem, with Brian Johnston now the commentator: *"And it's Hendrick then, coming up now to bowl to Sadiq. In he comes, bowls this one – and that one bowls him! He's out. Sadiq is out. Hendrick's got his third wicket and Pakistan now are 28 for three…*

"And it's Hendrick running away from us. Comes up now and bowls to Haroon, who is caught at slip! A marvellous ball, that, outside edge, caught by Brearley at first slip. And Pakistan now 30 for four and this is a magnificent piece of bowling."

Hendrick had taken four wickets in eight balls. Ian Botham added the hugely important wickets of Zaheer Abbas and Javed Miandad and it was 34 for six. But then

'It wasn't a very large total, so we knew that someone was going to have to bowl well and that we were going to have to get wickets. And fortunately it was my day, my sort of conditions. It was overcast, it was slightly green, and I just happened to bowl that length and that pace and the line. The ball moved around all over the place and they got the edge or were bowled, and before I knew what was happening I'd got four for 15. I thoroughly enjoyed it.'

MIKE HENDRICK ON ENGLAND v PAKISTAN AT TRENT BRIDGE

Asif fought back, improvising skilfully to put on 52 with Wasim Raja and a further 29 with Imran Khan. When Asif was out, Imran and Wasim Bari added 20 more to take Pakistan within 20 runs of a dramatic victory. In the conditions, Mike Brearley needed another medium-pacer, in preference to Phil Edmonds' slow left arm, to finish the job. He turned to Geoff Boycott.

"Difficult pitch," Boycott recalls. "Bit of damp in it. Bit of uneven bounce – you expect that at Headingley. Very lively. I remember we were talking about who was going to bowl these extra overs, and they were talking about me bowling a few and who I was going to bowl at – Zaheer Abbas, Majid Khan, Asif Iqbal, Javed Miandad, all these great batsmen. I said to Botham and Willis, 'Hey, hang on, I'm a batsman, not a bowler. You're the best bowlers in England. You bowl at the batsmen, I'll bowl at the tail-enders.

"I snared Wasim Bari, inside edge, on to his pad, caught behind by Bob Taylor. Then another one, Sikander Bakht. He was playing with Imran, who was batting beautifully, and Imran was trying to coax him through as a number 11 – and they could still win it with Imran batting. And he lost his cool against me, did Sikander. Tried to slog me and in the end it went up in the air to my best fielder."

Christopher Martin-Jenkins: *"A real nail-biter, as Boycott bowls and Sikander hits it high on the off side. Hendrick trying to get underneath it. Catches it brilliantly! And that's the end of the match. England have won by 14 runs. Hendrick taking a superb catch, which I think will decide Brian Close to give him that Man of the Match. And the match ends at just after twenty to eight."*

GROUP A FINAL TABLE

	P	W	L	Pts
England	3	3	0	12
Pakistan	3	2	1	8
Australia	3	1	2	4
Canada	3	0	3	0

GROUP B FINAL TABLE

	P	W	L	NR	Pts
West Indies	3	2	0	1	10
New Zealand	3	2	1	0	8
Sri Lanka	3	1	1	1	6
India	3	0	3	0	0

· GROUP A ·

JUNE 9 AT LORD'S
England 160 for 4 (G A Gooch 53) **beat Australia** 159 for 9 by six wickets.

JUNE 9 AT HEADINGLEY
Pakistan 140 for 2 (Sadiq Mohammad 57*) **beat Canada** 139 for 9 (Sarfraz 3-26, Asif 3-28) by eight wickets.

JUNE 13-14 AT TRENT BRIDGE
Pakistan 286 for 7 (Majid J Khan 61, Asif Iqbal 61, Cosier 3-54) **beat Australia** 197 (A M J Hilditch 72, Sikander 3-34, Majid 3-53) by 89 runs.

JUNE 13-14 AT OLD TRAFFORD
England 46-2 **beat Canada** 45 (Old 4-8, Willis 4-11) by 8 wickets.

JUNE 16 AT HEADINGLEY
England 165 for 9 (Majid 3-27, Sikander 3-32) **beat Pakistan** 151 (Asif Iqbal 51, Hendrick 4-15) by 14 runs.

JUNE 16 AT EDGBASTON
Australia 106 for 3 **beat Canada** 105 (Hurst 5-21) by 7 wickets.

· GROUP B ·

JUNE 9 AT EDGBASTON
West Indies 194 for 1 (C G Greenidge 106*) **beat India** 190 (G R Viswanath 75, Holding 4-33) by nine wickets.

JUNE 9 AT TRENT BRIDGE
New Zealand 190 for 1 (G M Turner 83*, G P Howarth 63*) **beat Sri Lanka** 189 (A P B Tennekoon 59, McKechnie 3-25, Stott 3-48) by nine wickets.

JUNE 13-14 AT HEADINGLEY
New Zealand 183 for 2 (B A Edgar 84*) **beat India** 182 (S M Gavaskar 55, McKechnie 3-24, Cairns 3-36) by eight wickets.

JUNE 13, 14, 15 AT THE OVAL
West Indies v Sri Lanka abandoned without a ball being bowled. The teams were awarded two points each.

JUNE 16 AT TRENT BRIDGE
West Indies 244 for 7 (C H Lloyd 73*, C G Greenidge 65) **beat New Zealand** 212 for 9 (Roberts 3-43) by 32 runs.

JUNE 16 AT OLD TRAFFORD
Sri Lanka 238 for 5 (S R de S Wettimuny 67, R D Mendis 64, R L Dias 50, Amarnath 3-40) **beat India** 191 (D S de Silva 3-29, Opatha 3-31) by 47 runs.

1979

THE OVAL
·SEMI-FINAL·

So it was Pakistan who had drawn the short straw to meet the West Indies at The Oval on Wednesday June 20. Asif Iqbal invited them to bat first, and Gordon Greenidge and Desmond Haynes accepted the invitation to the feast gratefully, running up 132 before Asif himself got the breakthrough. In fact Asif, using himself as the sixth bowler, dismissed the first four in the order – but by then the West Indies were well past 200 and on their way to a big total. Greenidge 73, Haynes 65, Viv Richards 42 – the damage was done and the later batsmen tucked in. Clive Lloyd's 37 came from 38 balls and Collis King's 34 from only 25.

Pakistan found themselves chasing a score of 293 for six. Despite an early shock when Michael Holding had Sadiq Mohammad caught behind, Majid and Zaheer put Pakistan in the driving seat with a stand of 166 in 36 overs. A major upset seemed to be on the cards, but Colin Croft dismissed Zaheer for 93, Majid for 81, then trapped Javed Miandad lbw first ball, and suddenly it was game on.

Pakistan captain Asif Iqbal recalls: "We had a splendid start. Majid and Zaheer added 166, a big partnership, and it was almost certain that we were going to win that match – but the West Indies were so good at it. Almost every time, they went on to win their matches. It was a perfect execution. They let you get into this false sense of security, thinking that everything was rosy, everything is going smoothly for you. And when the run rate required reaches about six an over, one looks up and sees that Garner, Holding and Roberts have a few overs left to bowl and there's no way you can score six or seven off those bowlers."

The rest of the Pakistan batting, even with canny one-day hitters such as Imran and Asif, fell steadily behind the rate. Asif fell to a classic sucker punch: "Viv Richards was the only bowler I knew could get runs off. I remember going for a big hit and being dropped by Michael Holding on the boundary line, and the ball crossed the line for a six. So I repeated the shot – and this time I was caught. I got a lot of stick for that."

Pakistan were all out in the 57th over, 43 runs short, and Greenidge picked up his second Man of the Match award.

'Majid and Zaheer put Pakistan in the driving seat with a stand of 166 in 36 overs. A major upset seemed to be on the cards...'

Right: A narrow escape for Clive Lloyd as he avoids being run out. Opposite: Majid Khan scored 81 to take Pakistan to 176 for one. But Lloyd and his men were used to escaping from tricky situations

· SEMI-FINAL ·
THE OVAL • JUNE 20

WEST INDIES

C G Greenidge c Wasim Bari b Asif	73
D L Haynes c and b Asif	65
I V A Richards b Asif	42
*C H Lloyd c Mudassar b Asif	37
C L King c and b Sarfaz	34
A I Kallicharran b Imran	11
A M E Roberts not out	7
J Garner not out	1
Extras (B 1, l-b 17, w 1, n-b 4)	23
Total *(60 Overs, for 6 wickets)*	**293**

Did not bat: †D L Murray, M A Holding and C E H Croft

Fall of wickets: 1/132 2/165 3/233 4/236 5/285 6/285

Bowling: Imran 9-1-43-1; Sarfraz 12-1-71-1; Sikander 6-1-24-0; Mudassar 10-0-50-0; Majid 12-2-26-0; Asif 11-0-56-4.

PAKISTAN
won the toss

Majid J Khan c Kallicharran b Croft	81
Sadiq Mohammad c Murray b Holding	2
Zaheer Abbas c Murray b Croft	93
Haroon Rashid run out	15
Javed Miandad lbw b Croft	0
*Asif Iqbal c Holding b Richards	17
Mudassar Nazar c Kallicharran b Richards	2
Imran Khan c and b Richards	6
Sarfraz Nawaz c Haynes b Roberts	12
†Wasim Bari c Murray b Roberts	9
Sikander Bakht not out	1
Extras (L-b 9, w 2, n-b 1)	12
Total *(56.2 Overs)*	**250**

Fall of wickets: 1/10 2/176 3/187 4/187 5/203 6/220 7/221 8/228 9/246

Bowling: Roberts 9.2-2-41-2; Holding 9-1-28-1; Croft 11-0-29-3; Garner 12-1-47-0; King 7-0-41-0; Richards 8-0-52-3.

Umpires: D J Constant and W L Budd

Man of the Match: Gordon Greenidge

WEST INDIES
won by 43 runs

1979

THE OLD TRAFFORD
·SEMI-FINAL·

England had now formally abandoned the idea of five specialist bowlers, and for the semi-final at Old Trafford against New Zealand, Wayne Larkins was preferred to Phil Edmonds, as an extra batsman who could help Boycott and Gooch 'fiddle' the other 12 overs. After Boycott had gone cheaply in the ninth over, Larkins made only seven. It was a stand between Brearley and Gooch that got the innings going. They added 63, before Jeremy Coney had Brearley caught behind for 53.

After David Gower had been run out early, Gooch was joined by Ian Botham and they put on 47 in ten overs. When they had gone – Gooch for a magnificent 71 which took only 84 balls and included three sixes, and Botham for 21 – it was Derek Randall, pushed down the order by the inclusion of Larkins, who guided the total to something just about defendable, but not excessive – 221 for eight.

A lot now depended on the England bowlers. "It was a baking hot day," Mike Hendrick remembers. "The pitch was hard, but didn't have pace and bounce, and it was hard work bowling on it. It was flat. We'd got a reasonable total but then New Zealand got away to a very good start."

Chris Old had Bruce Edgar lbw when the score was 47, and the demon bowler Boycott did the same to Geoff Howarth, hitting him with a full toss on the ankle as he bowled round the wicket. But John Wright was going well until he encountered some Randall brilliance in the field.

Christopher Martin-Jenkins: *"In goes Willis and bowls, and that's played away by Wright off the leg stump towards square leg. He's got one run. Randall is haring in. Picks it up one-handed and they'll have to be quick! And he's got a runout!*

'A brilliant bit of fielding and a very unwise bit of running by Wright. And that is the wicket that England so badly needed. It seemed as though he just didn't sense the danger there. A sad end to a magnificent innings for New Zealand by John Wright."

The pressure of the chase now started to tell on the later New Zealand batsmen. Hendrick picked up three wickets and the captain, Mark Burgess, was run out. New Zealand were always one good over away from being on top and at the end the last pair needed to score 14 from the final over, bowled by Ian Botham. They managed only four.

Says Mike Hendrick: "I remember coming off that field at twenty to eight totally physically drained and mentally drained. In fact it wasn't until the following day that I began to exactly realise what had happened."

Left: Mike Hendrick took three wickets in a tense semi-final. Graham Gooch (right) was the top scorer and Man of the Match

· SEMI-FINAL ·
OLD TRAFFORD · JUNE 20

ENGLAND

*J M Brearley c Lees b Coney	53
G Boycott c Howarth b Hadlee	2
W Larkins c Coney b McKechnie	7
G A Gooch b McKechnie	71
D I Gower run out	1
I T Botham lbw b Cairns	21
D W Randall not out	42
C M Old c Lees b Troup	0
†R W Taylor run out	12
R G D Willis not out	1
Extras (L-b 8, w 3)	11

Total *(60 Overs, for 8 wickets)* **221**

Did not bat: M Hendrick

Fall of wickets: 1/13 2/38 3/96 4/98 5/145 6/177 7/178 8/219

Bowling: Hadlee 12-4-32-1; Troup 12-1-38-1; Cairns 12-2-47-1; Coney 12-0-47-1; McKechnie 12-1-46-2.

NEW ZEALAND
won the toss

J G Wright run out	69
B A Edgar lbw b Old	17
G P Howarth lbw b Boycott	7
J V Coney lbw b Hendrick	11
G M Turner lbw b Willis	30
*M G Burgess run out	10
R J Hadlee b Botham	15
†W K Lees b Hendrick	23
B L Cairns c Brearley b Hendrick	14
B J McKechnie not out	4
G B Troup not out	3
Extras (B 5, w 4)	9

Total *(60 Overs, for 9 wkts)* **212**

Fall of wickets: 1/47 2/58 3/104 4/112 5/132 6/162 7/180 8/195 9/208

Bowling: Botham 12-3-42-1; Hendrick 12-0-55-3; Old 12-1-33-1; Boycott 9-1-24-1; Gooch 3-1-8-0; Willis 12-1-41-1.

Umpires: J G Langridge and K E Palmer

Man of the Match: Graham Gooch

ENGLAND
won by nine runs

1979

·THE FINAL·

E ngland would meet the West Indies in Saturday's the Final at Lord's on Saturday June 23, before a packed house of 25,000. Everyone knew that that would be a tall order. Geoff Boycott: "We were going to have to play to our absolute best and perhaps catch them five per cent not at their best, or even ten per cent, because they were a very great side."

To make the job that bit harder, Bob Willis, the spearhead of the England attack, had been injured during Wednesday's semi-final and on the morning of the Final had to be ruled out. Phil Edmonds returned to fill his place, but the 'fifth bowler' would still have to be a combination of Boycott, Gooch and Larkins.

Brearley won the toss and put the West Indies in. The first breakthrough came in the ninth over, described on the radio by Tony Cozier:

"Twenty-two without loss. Haynes moving to 13 with that single. Old now to Greenidge and Greenidge plays it defensively on the on side. They go for a quick single. In comes Randall. Underarms the return. He's out! He has gone! Randall has run out Greenidge. A magnificent bit of fielding by Randall and a real blow to the West Indies. Greenidge pushed the ball down to midwicket very slowly, took off with a single, always was going to be struggling and Randall, very very fast indeed, underarming the return to the bowler's end, hitting the stumps and Greenidge is run out for nine. Twenty-two for one in the ninth over of the innings as Derek Randall strikes again for England."

Desmond Haynes was caught at second slip off Old for 20, Alvin Kallicharran bowled by Hendrick for four and Clive Lloyd, who had so dominated the first Final, caught and bowled by Old for 13. At 99 for four, there was a genuine feeling that England had a chance of surprising their doubters.

But Viv Richards was in and was now joined by a big-hitting Barbadian, Collis King. They tucked into the makeshift trio who were trying to carry 12 overs between them. King, facing only 66 balls and hitting ten fours and three sixes, made 86 of their fifth-wicket stand of 139 as

> 'Bob Willis, the spearhead of the England attack, had been injured during the semi-final and had to be ruled out. Phil Edmonds returned to fill his place, but the fifth bowler would still have to be a combination of Boycott, Gooch and Larkins'

Viv Richards bestrode the Lord's stage with a crushing 138 not out

the bowling of Boycott, Gooch and Larkins was taken apart to the tune of 86 runs. King was out in the 51st over, caught at deep square leg off Edmonds, but it still left Viv Richards at the crease.

Christopher Martin-Jenkins: *"There are nine overs left*

and now it's Old continuing from this Pavilion end, running in to bowl a ball of full length, in fact a full toss, to Richards. This could be his hundred. He plays it away from his legs, a typical Richards shot. It brings him to his hundred. He raises his bat and with his other hand he takes off his cap and waves it to the crowd. Deryck Murray quietly congratulates him, shakes him by the hand, and Viv Richards, this quiet master, looking as casual as if he's just going for a walk down the street in Antigua, reaches 101 not out, out of 243 for five, in the 52nd over."

In the quest for quick runs at the end, the new batsmen came and went, none more dramatically than when Brearley held a brilliantly judged catch looking back over his shoulder at deep mid-wicket to dismiss Roberts. But Richards remained to face the last ball of the innings.

Tony Cozier: "Richards to face the last ball of the West Indies innings. What will Hendrick do, what will Richards do? Brearley in long conversation with Hendrick. 280 for nine. Here is the last ball of the innings. Richards 132. Hendrick on the way. Richards gets a full toss – and hits a six over square leg! A fitting end to the innings. Richards 138 not out, ending the innings with a massive six over square leg. The West Indies are 286 for nine off their 60 overs."

Richards' magnificent 138 not out had

> 'I took rather a good catch in the Final from an Andy Roberts shot that went up a mile, running flat out looking over my shoulder. The funny thing is, I actually did not feel the ball in my hands. It was almost as if it was there from the beginning. There are occasions where you go for a catch with absolute conviction because you can somehow see it before it happens. That was one of them.'
>
> MIKE BREARLEY

'SIX. THANKS, VIV. WELL PLAYED, MATE'
Mike Hendrick on the 1979 World Cup Final

'Losing Bob Willis was a desperate blow, because we had fielded a consistent side throughout the World Cup. Bob was bowling quick and bowling well, but unfortunately he was ruled unfit on the morning of the game. That puts a lot of pressure on your four main bowlers – they've got to bowl extremely well to try and take the pressure off whoever was going to have to fulfil the fifth bowler's role. In our case we had Graham Gooch, Wayne Larkins and Geoff Boycott: three bowlers all of the same type, similar pace, and we had to get 12 overs out of them.

"I caught Desmond Haynes off Chris Old. I

A rueful Hendrick and Botham congratulate Richards as Colin Croft looks on

enjoyed that catch. A nice one, just about ankle height at second slip. And then I bowled Alvin Kallicharran round his legs, so they were three down for not many. You can imagine how we felt. This is great stuff, we were really in with a chance.

"Then Viv came in and the first ball I bowled to him, he just shuffled across his stumps, the way he did, to try to work the ball away on the leg side, and it nipped back a little bit and caught him below the knee roll. I thought it was plum. Absolutely plum. We appealed and the umpire said not out. To this day I can't believe it. I really can't.

"Richards was ruthless that day. Sometimes when I bowled at Viv, you could look at him and wink. And if you beat the bat, he would look at you. But what I remember about him that day was that he was so cold and calculating. I didn't get a word out of him at all. Before he hit that six off the last ball of the West Indies innings, I had bowled two or three balls at him. I was trying to get in the leg-stump yorker, and he knew that was what I was trying to do. So I was concentrating. I thought, I'm not going to get it leg stump this time. I want to get in an off-stump yorker, because I knew he was going to come across his stumps. So the less room I could give him, he can't get hold of it. He just walked across his stumps, swung his bat and everything seemed to happen in slow motion and the ball disappeared down St John's Wood Road. Six. Thanks, Viv. Well played, mate."

come off 157 balls, with three sixes and 11 fours. Now England needed a good start. They got a solid one from Boycott and Brearley, who put on 129 for the first wicket, but it was altogether *too* solid and the rate required was rising. It was even cynically suggested, when Boycott was dropped by Lloyd with the score on 107 in the 34th over, that the West Indies had decided to keep the pair in.

Michael Holding eventually persuaded each of them to loft it, Brearley for 64 and Boycott for 57. England were 135 for two; not too bad a score, but it was already the 40th over. 152 runs were wanted off the last 20 overs.

Geoff Boycott echoes Asif Iqbal's point about the difficulties of facing that West Indies attack. "I don't know many sides that played against the great West Indies of the late Seventies and early Eighties who could score much more than four an over off Michael Holding, Garner, Croft and Roberts. You could get four if you played well. You could get four and a bit, but you weren't ever going to get five. That was the difference, so the pressure mounted, you see.

"We got a good start. Mike Brearley and I played quite well. We got some runs, but you couldn't get that impetus you wanted because they didn't have so many weak bowlers. Collis King bowled fairly decent seamers. It was difficult.

"It was a good pitch, nothing wrong with the pitch. The day was lovely, sunshine, crowd on our side. We were proud of our performance in some ways. But as soon as the new batsmen came in trying to score four or five an over, Garner just yorked them, didn't he? How do you hit

The England team can only watch enviously as Clive Lloyd raises the Cup again

yorkers at about 80 miles an hour down at your boots? You just couldn't."

Gooch and Randall tried to get the runs flowing, as they added 48 quickly, but the pace needed was too great against this bowling. The giant figure of Joel Garner swept through England with a spell in which he took five for four in 11 balls, aided by a sensational catch on the long-on boundary by Viv Richards to remove Ian Botham, as five Englishmen registered ducks. The end came with shattering suddenness.

Tony Cozier: *"194 for nine. Croft now in to Hendrick. He's bowled him! That's it. The West Indies have retained the title.*

"Hendrick grabs a souvenir stump. Murray does so as well. Up comes Holding. The swarm coming over the ground and the players rushing for the safety of the Pavilion. Hundreds and hundreds of spectators. Joel Garner is being mobbed. This big man has been brought to the ground already. Five wickets and he's being surrounded, and the West Indies have retained the World Cup."

The West Indies had won by 92 runs, with England bowled out in the 51st over. On that June evening, after such a demonstration of cricketing power, it was difficult to imagine anyone else ever receiving the World Cup. Clive Lloyd held up the trophy on the Lord's balcony for the second time in four years and Vivian Richards was duly made Man of the Match.

Meeting just after the tournament, the International Cricket Conference now resolved that the World Cup should be staged every four years and that the next one – in 1983 – should yet again be in England.

'As soon as the new batsmen came in trying to score four or five an over, Garner just yorked them, didn't he? How do you hit yorkers at about 80 miles an hour down at your boots? You just couldn't.'

GEOFF BOYCOTT

The moment we lost the World Cup

THE 1975 WORLD CUP FINAL • ENGLAND v WEST INDIES

Two crucial tactical decisions have caused controversy ever since 1979.
The England captain admits he has regrets – but only about one of them

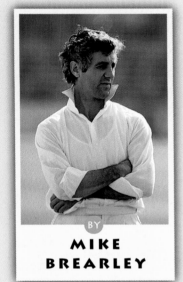

BY

**MIKE
BREARLEY**

*'Discussing the situation in
the dressing room, I was
inclined to have a real slog.
But I was talked out of it,
and there I was wrong'*

Being without our Packer players made a difference. I have a lot of time for Bob Taylor, but Alan Knott could score quick fifties and was at least as good a wicket-keeper; Tony Greig was a commanding one-day cricketer; and Derek Underwood was the best defensive slow bowler in the world. If the West Indies had been without their Packer players, they would have been considerably less of a team; so would Pakistan. But, although we were beaten by a West Indies side with all its Packer players, it never crossed my mind to feel bitter about it.

We had a good team attitude. Twelve of the England squad had been on the 1978-79 Ashes tour, which we won 5-1, so we knew each other well, which isn't always the case when you play at home. We stayed together throughout the World Cup and it was like a mini-tour within our own country.

Geoff Boycott had a good series with the ball. He turned his arm over in the nets more or less as a joke, but he bowled slow medium in-swingers with the odd straight ball, often from round the wicket, and that is quite difficult to get away unless you are a very strong player. There's no pace on the ball to run it to third man or fine leg, so you largely have to hit in front of the wicket or hit across the line and risk getting out. So Boycott was actually not a bad one-day bowler – as he would tell you himself. He was shrewd, mean, competitive … and surprising.

In the final group match against Pakistan, we were put in to bat and

we struggled. Headingley suited our bowlers, but it suited Pakistan too: Sikander, Imran, Majid, Zaheer and Asif were a useful attack for those conditions. It was frustrating that Majid took the wickets but, like Boycott, he was a medium-pacer who swung the ball a bit and was hard to get away. At 118 for eight we were down and out, but then Taylor got stuck in and made 20 not out and, remarkably, Willis got 24 to take us up to 165 for nine. No doubt Pakistan were kicking themselves.

We had got out of jail – but then so did they. Hendrick bowled quite beautifully to reduce them to six for 34, but then they hauled themselves to within 20 runs of the target with two wickets in hand. So jail was repeatedly occupied by each team at various stages of the match. It was a real ding-dong struggle which either side could have won. And then Boycott did the business when it was very tight, taking the last two wickets to give us a 14-run win.

Our semi-final opponents, New Zealand, were a shrewd team, and nearly beat us. They had one great attacking fast bowler in Richard Hadlee, whom they used parsimoniously. They faced the fact that the rest of their bowling was ordinary, so what they were going to do was bowl straight, bowl slower, so that the batsman had to hit the ball rather than use its pace, and set the field straight. They also made the best use of their batting. They didn't have many stars, but they worked the ball around, turning ones into twos. I admired how they played to their limitations.

There are two criticisms of our tactics in the Final. The first

Continued overleaf

concerns England's 'fifth bowler'. When you pick a team, you are constantly weighing a bit of extra strength in batting against a bit of extra strength in bowling. After the way Boycott had bowled throughout the tournament, and with Gooch being a decent back-up bowler, we thought it was a good gamble.

In the semi-final, it had worked well. We picked seven batsmen and four bowlers including Botham. Boycott bowled nine overs and took one for 24, Derek Randall batted at number seven and scored 42 not out, and we won by 38 runs. The fact that it didn't work in the Final doesn't mean it was wrong. I would certainly stand by that decision.

We won the toss, which was worth 20-30 runs, and we began well. Randall was worth his place for his fielding alone, and the first wicket came when he ran out Gordon Greenidge from square leg. We got three other wickets by about lunchtime and had them at 99 for four. They must have been worried. One more wicket and we were through to Deryck Murray and the tail. We were within an inch or two.

Brearley, Taylor, Old and Randall celebrate as Randall runs Greenidge out

In fact, if Viv had been given lbw second ball, which we all thought was out, we would probably have had them five down for 100. I remember seeing that ball on TV. It was pretty damn straight. But these things happen...

One trouble was, there was a short boundary at Lord's, which favoured the West Indies because of their sheer physical strength. Even their mishits would carry. To beat them you needed to play them on a big field – that was one of Ray Illingworth's perennial complaints. When Viv Richards and Collis King were batting, it was like playing on a postage stamp. They kept swinging through the ball and clearing the boundary. King's aggression also enabled Viv to play his ordinary game. 'Ordinary' for Viv was pretty pugnacious, but he didn't have to take any risks he didn't want to. They were two great innings.

We knew we had some task to get 287 against the West Indies bowlers. Their semi-final at The Oval had been played on an even better batting wicket than Lord's. Pakistan had a tremendously powerful middle order – Zaheer, Miandad, Asif Iqbal, Haroon, Imran – and they got to 176 for one but still fell 43 runs short of their target of 293.

One of Clive Lloyd 's greatest qualities as a captain was his realism. He had four very fast bowlers – and was prepared to select them. Other teams would have been more constrained by the aesthetics or cultural niceties and expectations of the game, which had always deemed that a well-balanced attack consisted of two fast bowlers, one medium-pacer and two spinners. The West Indies questioned that unwritten rule, and I admire that way of thinking.

In those days there was no restriction on fielding positions, so there was no such thing as a pinch hitter. We opened with our normal openers and thought we had started well. We were 79 for no wicket at tea, so we needed 193 runs off 35 overs; that's a reasonable target. It was better than being 90 for four, which they had been. Discussing the situation in the dressing room, I was inclined to have a real slog. But I was talked out of it, and there I think I was wrong. I myself should have taken every risk in the book, and I should have told Boycott to up his scoring rate too.

A couple of people said, in the old 'pro' way, "Don't get too excited, wickets in hand are very important, don't throw it away." Randall said it, in a supportive way, and probably Bob Willis, who was in effect the vice-captain. (As a fast bowler he was rather like a front-row forward who has slogged all the way up the touchline and doesn't want fancy play by the backs – the batsmen – if it means that they have to

Joel Garner's yorkers brought him five wickets in 11 balls

run back 70 yards and start defending again. So his general tendency was to say to batsmen: "Get your bloody heads down, don't throw your wicket away.") The whole mental attitude in those days was that if you had wickets in hand at the halfway stage, you could get a decent score. So we

carried on batting without sufficiently raising the tempo.

Richards was bowling after tea, doing the job that Boycott had done for us. We let him bowl ten overs for 35, and that was our chance gone. Not long after, when wickets had begun to fall and the light had got gloomier, Joel Garner bowled fast yorkers and took five wickets for about 20 runs. Botham was caught at wide long-on – a wonderful shot that might well have gone for six. In current cricket, that probably wouldn't happen because that fielder would be in the circle.

The end of the match was an anticlimax, and I remember feeling bad because I hadn't made the right decision. But you shouldn't forget that they had more powerful batsmen than us, and the most powerful fast bowling line-up the world had ever seen – bowling to deep-set fields with as many as six men back on the boundary. If you didn't have the strength to hit the likes of Holding and Roberts for six, you had to rely on shrewdness of placing and running ones and twos, disturbing them and changing things about – guerrilla warefare as against out and out frontal assault.

If you went in to chase 292 against the West Indies with that team on that pitch with those weather conditions, you could do it ten times and you might win once. So I don't think we did quite so badly. The best side won but we had our moments.

• *Michael Brearley is now a psychoanalyst practising in London. He writes from time to time about cricket, mainly for The Observer*

· THE FINAL ·
LORD'S • JUNE 23

WEST INDIES

C G Greenidge run out	9
D L Haynes c Hendrick b Old	20
I V A Richards not out	138
A I Kallicharran b Hendrick	4
* C H Lloyd c and b Old	13
C L King c Randall b Edmonds	86
†D L Murray c Gower b Edmonds	5
A M E Roberts c Brearley b Hendrick	0
J Garner c Taylor b Botham	0
M A Holding b Botham	0
C E H Croft not out	0
Extras (B 11)	11
Total *(60 Overs, for 9 wickets)*	**286**

Fall of wickets: 1/22 2/36 3/55 4/99 5/238 6/252 7/258 8/260 9/272

Bowling: Botham 12-2-44-2; Hendrick 12-2-50-2; Old 12-0-55-2; Boycott 6-0-38-0; Edmonds 12-2-40-2; Gooch 4-0-27-0; Larkins 2-0-21-0.

ENGLAND
won the toss

*J M Brearley c King b Holding	64
G Boycott c Kallicharran b Holding	57
D W Randall b Croft	15
G A Gooch b Garner	32
D I Gower b Garner	0
I T Botham c Richards b Croft	4
W Larkins b Garner	0
P H Edmonds not out	5
C M Old b Garner	0
†R W Taylor c Murray b Garner	0
M Hendrick b Croft	0
Extras (L-b 12, w 2, n-b 3)	17
Total *(51 Overs)*	**194**

Fall of wickets: 1/129 2/135 3/183 4/183 5/186 6/186 7/188 8/192 9/192

Bowling: Roberts 9-2-33-0; Holding 8-1-16-2; Croft 10-1-42-3; Garner 11-0-38-5; Richards 10-0-35-0; King 3-0-13-0.

Umpires: H D Bird and R J Meyer

Man of the Match: Vivian Richards

WEST INDIES
won by 92 runs

· 1979 STATISTICS ·

Highest totals

293 for 6   West Indies against Pakistan
286 for 7   Pakistan against Australia
286 for 9   West Indies against England
244 for 7   West Indies against New Zealand
238 for 5   Sri Lanka against India

Lowest totals (completed innings)

45   Canada against England
105   Canada against Australia
139-9   Canada against Pakistan
151   Pakistan against England
159-9   Australia against England

Highest winning margins

9 wickets   West Indies against India
9 wickets   New Zealand against Sri Lanka
8 wickets   New Zealand against India
8 wickets   Pakistan against Canada
8 wickets   England against Canada

Closest winning margins

9 runs   England against New Zealand
14 runs   England against Pakistan

Highest aggregates

543 for 16   West Indies v Pakistan
483 for 17   Pakistan v Australia
480 for 19   England v West Indies
456 for 16   West Indies v New Zealand
429 for 15   Sri Lanka v India

Wins by non-Test teams

Sri Lanka beat India by 47 runs

Centuries

138 n.o.   I V A Richards, W Indies v England (Final)
106   C G Greenidge, W Indies v India

Highest scores for each position

1   C G Greenidge, 106, West Indies v India
2   S R de S Wettimuny, 67, Sri Lanka v India
3   Zaheer Abbas, 93, Pakistan v West Indies
4   I V A Richards, 138 n.o., W Indies v Pakistan
5   C H Lloyd, 73 n.o., W Indies v New Zealand
6   Asif Iqbal, 61, Pakistan v Australia
7   Asif Iqbal, 51, Pakistan v England
8   R J Hadlee, 42, New Zealand v West Indies
9   Imran Khan 21 n.o., Pakistan v England
10   R G D Willis 24, England v Pakistan
11   B S Bedi 13, India v West Indies

Leading scorers

C G Greenidge, W Indies   253   Ave: 84.33
I V A Richards, W Indies   217   Ave: 108.50
G A Gooch, England   210   Ave: 52.50
G M Turner, New Zealand   176   Ave: 88.00
J G Wright, New Zealand   166   Ave: 41.50

Most wickets

10 at 14.90   M Hendrick, England
9 at 15.66   B J McKechnie, New Zealand
9 at 17.44   C M Old, England
9 at 17.44   Asif Iqbal
8 at 13.25   M A Holding, West Indies
8 at 17.50   C E H Croft, West Indies
8 at 21.50   J Garner, West Indies

Most wickets in a match

5-21   A G Hurst, Australia v Canada
5-38   J Garner, West Indies v England
4-8   C M Old, England v Canada
4-11   R G D Willis, England v Canada
4-15   M Hendrick, England v Pakistan
4-33   M A Holding, West Indies v India
4-56   Asif Iqbal, Pakistan v West Indies

Most dismissals by a wicketkeeper

7   (6ct, 1st)   Wasim Bari, Pakistan
7   (7ct)   D L Murray, West Indies
6   (6ct)   W K Lees, New Zealand
5   (5ct)   K J Wright, Australia
4   (4ct)   R W Taylor, England

Most catches by an outfielder

4   J M Brearley, England
4   Asif Iqbal, Pakistan
4   A I Kallicharran, West Indies
3   M Hendrick, England
3   I V A Richards, West Indies
3   C H Lloyd, West Indies
3   J V Coney, New Zealand
3   Sadiq Mohammad, Pakistan

Australia *batting*

	M	I	NO	Runs	HS	Avge	100	50	Ct	St
A.M.J.Hilditch	3	3	0	143	72	47.66	-	1	1	-
G.N.Yallop	3	3	1	60	37	30.00	-	-	-	-
K.J.Hughes	3	3	1	48	27*	24.00	-	-	1	-
A.R.Border	3	3	0	59	34	19.66	-	-	1	-
W.M.Darling	3	3	0	51	25	17.00	-	-	-	-
K.J.Wright	3	2	0	29	23	14.50	-	-	5	-
G.Dymock	3	2	1	14	10	14.00	-	-	-	-
T.J.Laughlin	1	1	0	8	8	8.00	-	-	-	-
J.K.Moss	1	1	0	7	7	7.00	-	-	2	-
G.J.Cosier	3	2	0	6	6	3.00	-	-	1	-
G.D.Porter	2	1	0	3	3	3.00	-	-	1	-
R.M.Hogg	2	1	0	0	0	0.00	-	-	-	-
A.G.Hurst	3	2	2	6	3*	-	-	-	-	-

Australia *bowling*

	O	M	R	W	Avge	Best	5w	Econ
G.D.Porter	18	5	33	3	11.00	2-13	-	1.83
G.Dymock	31	7	64	2	32.00	1-17	-	2.06
G.J.Cosier	27.2	4	95	5	19.00	3-54	-	3.47
A.G.Hurst	32	6	119	7	17.00	5-21	1	3.71
T.J.Laughlin	9.1	0	38	2	19.00	2-38	-	4.14
R.M.Hogg	11	1	51	1	51.00	1-25	-	4.63
G.N.Yallop	8	0	56	0	-	-	-	7.00
A.R.Border	4	0	38	1	38.00	1-38	-	9.50

Canada *batting*

	M	I	NO	Runs	HS	Avge	100	50	Ct	St
G.R.Sealy	3	3	0	73	45	24.33	-	-	-	-
F.A.Dennis	3	3	0	47	25	15.66	-	-	-	-
C.J.D.Chappell	3	3	0	38	19	12.66	-	-	-	-
J.C.B.Vaughan	3	3	0	30	29	10.00	-	-	-	-
B.M.Mauricette	3	3	0	20	15	6.66	-	-	-	-
C.C.Henry	2	2	1	6	5	6.00	-	-	-	-
M.P.Stead	2	2	0	10	10	5.00	-	-	-	-
C.A.Marshall	2	2	0	10	8	5.00	-	-	-	-
Tariq Javed	3	3	0	15	8	5.00	-	-	-	-
J.M.Patel	3	3	0	3	2	1.00	-	-	-	-
R.G.Callender	2	2	0	0	0	0.00	-	-	-	-
S.Baksh	1	1	0	0	0	0.00	-	-	-	-
J.N.Valentine	3	2	2	3	3*	-	-	-	-	1	-

Canada *bowling*

	O	M	R	W	Avge	Best	5w	Econ
R.G.Callender	9	1	26	1	26.00	1-14	-	2.88
J.M.Patel	15.1	0	47	0	-	-	-	3.09
J.C.B.Vaughan	11	1	36	0	-	-	-	3.27
J.N.Valentine	19	5	66	3	22.00	1-18	-	3.47
G.R.Sealy	6	0	21	0	-	-	-	3.50
C.C.Henry	15	0	53	2	26.50	2-27	-	3.53
M.P.Stead	4.5	0	24	0	-	-	-	4.96

England *batting*

	M	I	NO	Runs	HS	Avge	100	50	Ct	St
G.A.Gooch	5	5	1	210	71	52.50	-	2	-	-
J.M.Brearley	5	5	0	161	64	32.20	-	2	4	-
R.G.D.Willis	4	2	1	25	24	25.00	-	-	-	-
G.Boycott	5	5	1	92	57	23.00	-	1	-	-
I.T.Botham	5	4	1	65	22	21.66	-	-	2	-
D.I.Gower	5	4	1	50	27	16.66	-	-	1	-
R.W.Taylor	5	3	1	32	20*	16.00	-	-	4	-
D.W.Randall	5	5	1	64	42*	16.00	-	-	1	-
P.H.Edmonds	3	2	1	7	5*	7.00	-	-	-	-
W.Larkins	2	2	0	7	7	3.50	-	-	-	-
M.Hendrick	5	2	1	1	1*	1.00	-	-	3	-
C.M.Old	5	3	0	2	2	0.66	-	-	1	-
G.Miller	1	0	0	0	0	-	-	-	-	-

England *bowling*

	O	M	R	W	Avge	Best	5w	Econ
G.Miller	2	1	1	0	-	-	-	0.50
R.G.D.Willis	44.3	8	109	7	15.57	4-11	-	2.44
M.Hendrick	56	14	149	10	14.90	4-15	-	2.66
C.M.Old	58	10	157	9	17.44	4-8	-	2.70
P.H.Edmonds	26	3	73	3	24.33	2-40	-	2.80
I.T.Botham	53	13	168	6	28.00	2-38	-	3.16
G.Boycott	27	1	94	5	18.80	2-14	-	3.48
G.A.Gooch	8	1	36	0	-	-	-	4.50
W.Larkins	2	0	21	0	-	-	-	10.50

India *batting*

	M	I	NO	Runs	HS	Avge	100	50	Ct	St
G.R.Viswanath	3	3	0	106	75	35.33	-	1	-	-
S.M.Gavaskar	3	3	0	89	55	29.66	-	1	-	-
S.Venkataraghavan	3	3	2	23	13*	23.00	-	-	-	-
B.P.Patel	3	3	0	63	38	21.00	-	-	-	-
A.D.Gaekwad	3	3	0	54	33	18.00	-	-	1	-
Kapil Dev	3	3	0	53	25	17.66	-	-	-	-
D.B.Vengsarkar	3	3	0	44	36	14.66	-	-	1	-
K.D.Ghavri	3	3	0	35	20	11.66	-	-	-	-
B.S.Bedi	3	3	1	19	13	9.50	-	-	-	-
S.C.Khanna	3	3	0	17	10	5.66	-	-	1	-
M.Amarnath	3	3	0	16	8	5.33	-	-	2	-

India *bowling*

	O	M	R	W	Avge	Best	5w	Econ
S.Venkataraghavan	36	3	108	0	-	-	-	3.00
B.S.Bedi	36	3	114	0	-	-	-	3.16
K.D.Ghavri	32	3	112	0	-	-	-	3.50
M.Amarnath	31.3	4	114	4	28.50	3-40	-	3.61
Kapil Dev	33	6	137	2	68.50	1-46	-	4.15

New Zealand *batting*

	M	I	NO	Runs	HS	Avge	100	50	Ct	St
G.M.Turner	4	4	2	176	83*	88.00	-	1	2	-
G.P.Howarth	2	2	1	70	63*	70.00	-	1	1	-
B.A.Edgar	3	3	1	113	84*	56.50	-	1	1	-
J.G.Wright	4	4	0	166	69	41.50	-	1	1	-
R.J.Hadlee	4	2	0	57	42	28.50	-	-	-	-
J.V.Coney	4	2	0	47	36	23.50	-	-	3	-
M.G.Burgess	4	2	0	45	35	22.50	-	-	2	-
W.K.Lees	4	2	0	28	23	14.00	-	-	6	-
J.F.M.Morrison	2	1	0	11	11	11.00	-	-	1	-
B.L.Cairns	4	3	0	17	14	5.66	-	-	1	-
B.J.McKechnie	4	2	2	17	13*	-	-	-	1	-
G.B.Troup	3	1	1	3	3*	-	-	-	-	-
E.J.Chatfield	1	1	1	3	3*	-	-	-	-	-
L.W.Stott	1	0	0	0	0	-	-	-	1	-

New Zealand *bowling*

	O	M	R	W	Avge	Best	5w	Econ
R.J.Hadlee	45	11	117	5	23.40	2-20	-	2.60
B.J.McKechnie	45.5	4	141	9	15.66	3-24	-	3.07
G.B.Troup	32	3	104	4	26.00	2-36	-	3.25
B.L.Cairns	47.5	4	176	7	25.14	3-36	-	3.67
J.V.Coney	31	0	120	3	40.00	2-40	-	3.87
J.F.M.Morrison	8	0	31	0	-	-	-	3.87
L.W.Stott	12	1	48	3	16.00	3-48	-	4.00
E.J.Chatfield	11	0	45	1	45.00	1-45	-	4.09

Pakistan *batting*

	M	I	NO	Runs	HS	Avge	100	50	Ct	St
Asif Iqbal	4	3	0	129	61	43.00	-	2	4	-
Imran Khan	4	3	2	42	21*	42.00	-	-	-	-
Majid Khan	4	4	0	150	81	37.50	-	2	1	-
Zaheer Abbas	4	4	0	148	93	37.00	-	1	2	-
Sadiq Mohammad	4	4	1	104	57*	34.66	-	1	3	-
Haroon Rashid	4	4	1	69	37*	23.00	-	-	-	-
Wasim Raja	2	2	0	39	21	19.50	-	-	1	-
Javed Miandad	4	3	0	46	46	15.33	-	-	-	-
Wasim Bari	4	2	0	26	17	13.00	-	-	6	1
Sarfraz Nawaz	2	1	0	12	12	12.00	-	-	-	-
Sikander Bakht	4	2	1	3	2	3.00	-	-	1	-
Mudassar Nazar	4	3	1	3	2	1.50	-	-	1	-

Pakistan *bowling*

	O	M	R	W	Avge	Best	5w	Econ
Majid Khan	47	8	117	7	16.71	3-27	-	2.48
Sikander Bakht	41	10	108	7	15.42	3-32	-	2.63
Imran Khan	42.1	7	123	5	24.60	2-29	-	2.91
Mudassar Nazar	38	5	122	1	122.00	1-31	-	3.21
Asif Iqbal	47	5	157	9	17.44	4-56	-	3.34
Sarfraz Nawaz	22	2	97	4	24.25	3-26	-	4.40

Sri Lanka *batting*

	M	I	NO	Runs	HS	Avge	100	50	Ct	St
A.P.B.Tennekoon	1	1	0	59	59	59.00	-	1	1	-
S.de S.Wettimuny	2	2	0	83	67	41.50	-	1	-	-
L.R.D.Mendis	2	2	0	78	64	39.00	-	1	-	-
R.L.Dias	2	2	0	75	50	37.50	-	1	2	-
S.P.Pasqual	2	2	1	24	23*	24.00	-	-	-	-
B.Warnapura	2	2	0	38	20	19.00	-	-	2	-
A.R.M.Opatha	2	1	0	18	18	18.00	-	-	-	-
D.L.S.de Silva	2	1	0	10	10	10.00	-	-	1	-
D.S.de Silva	2	2	1	7	6	7.00	-	-	-	-
R.S.Madugalle	1	1	0	4	4	4.00	-	-	-	-
S.Jayasinghe	2	1	0	1	1	1.00	-	-	1	-
G.R.A.de Silva	1	1	1	2	2*	-	-	-	-	-
F.R.M.Goonetilleke	1	0	0	0	0	-	-	-	-	-

Sri Lanka *bowling*

	O	M	R	W	Avge	Best	5w	Econ
D.L.S.de Silva	20	2	54	2	27.00	2-36	-	2.70
G.R.A.de Silva	12	1	39	1	39.00	1-39	-	3.25
D.S.de Silva	20	1	71	3	23.66	3-29	-	3.55
A.R.M.Opatha	17.1	1	62	3	20.66	3-31	-	3.61
F.R.M.Goonetilleke	9	1	34	0	-	-	-	3.77
B.Warnapura	19	0	77	1	77.00	1-47	-	4.05
S.P.Pasqual	4.4	0	20	0	-	-	-	4.28

West Indies *batting*

	M	I	NO	Runs	HS	Avge	100	50	Ct	St
I.V.A.Richards	4	4	2	217	138*	108.50	1	-	3	-
C.G.Greenidge	4	4	1	253	106*	84.33	1	2	-	-
C.H.Lloyd	4	3	1	123	73*	61.50	-	1	3	-
C.L.King	4	3	0	132	86	44.00	-	1	2	-
D.L.Haynes	4	4	0	144	65	36.00	-	1	2	-
A.I.Kallicharran	4	3	0	54	39	18.00	-	-	4	-
J.Garner	4	3	2	10	9*	10.00	-	-	1	-
D.L.Murray	4	2	0	17	12	8.50	-	-	7	-
A.M.E.Roberts	4	3	1	8	7*	4.00	-	-	-	-
M.A.Holding	4	1	0	0	0	0.00	-	-	2	-
C.E.H.Croft	4	1	1	0	0*	-	-	-	-	-

West Indies *bowling*

	O	M	R	W	Avge	Best	5w	Econ
M.A.Holding	41	5	106	8	13.25	4-33	-	2.58
C.E.H.Croft	43	3	140	8	17.50	3-29	-	3.25
J.Garner	47	2	172	8	21.50	5-38	1	3.65
A.M.E.Roberts	39.3	6	149	7	21.28	3-43	-	3.77
C.L.King	32	2	128	2	64.00	1-36	-	4.00
I.V.A.Richards	18	0	87	3	29.00	3-52	-	4.83

Right: Mike Hendrick, the tournament's top wicket-taker, bowls to Gordon Greenidge, the tournament's top scorer

1983

THE PRUDENTIAL WORLD CUP

In England

SO FAR, ONLY ONE MAN HAD LIFTED THE PRUDENTIAL CUP. WITH GREENIDGE, RICHARDS, HOLDING, ROBERTS, MARSHALL AND GARNER IN HIS TEAM, NO ONE WAS BETTING AGAINST CLIVE LLOYD DOING IT AGAIN

Right: Scenes of jubilation at Lord's after a dramatic Final

AN INDIAN SUMMER OF SURPRISES

India had only ever won one World Cup match, yet suddenly they were contenders. Their inspired performance was just one of many shocks in this thrilling tournament. But whatever happened, the West Indies would still win in the end … wouldn't they?

It all started on a General Election day, Thursday June 9. If there was a surprise in Mrs Thatcher's majority that day, the cricket provided even more of a shock

In the interests of fairness – and probably not without some financial incentive – the World Cup was bigger than before. There were still eight teams in two groups, but now they would play each other twice at the group stage.

Sri Lanka were now in the tournament by right, having played their first Test match the previous year. Zimbabwe were making their debut, having won the ICC Trophy at their first attempt. There two groups were: Group A – England, New Zealand, Pakistan and Sri Lanka; and Group B – Australia, India, West Indies and Zimbabwe. This time, several matches were being moved away from Test venues.

Once more, the weather prior to the start was filthy – but, again, when play began, the sun shone. It all started on a General Election day, Thursday June 9. As voters were making their way to the polling stations to give Margaret Thatcher her second term as Prime Minister, crowds were also descending on The Oval, Old Trafford, Trent Bridge and Swansea. If there was a surprise in Mrs Thatcher's majority, the cricket provided even more of a shock.

At Trent Bridge, Zimbabwe were playing their first ever World Cup match – against mighty Australia. There was no hint of any reversal of form early on, as Zimbabwe were put in to face an awesome bowling line-up of Lillee, Thomson, Lawson and Hogg. At 94 for five they looked unlikely to make a challenging total. But their captain, Duncan Fletcher, was joined by Kevin Curran and they put on 70 in 15 overs before Rodney Hogg dismissed Curran for 27.

Then, with Ian Butchart, Fletcher added 75 over the last 12 overs. Fletcher was 69 not out in a score of 239 for six.

It was not a bad score, but surely no problem for Australia's finest against amateur bowling? It did not seem so, as Graeme Wood and Kepler Wessels put on 61 for the first wicket. Then Fletcher snatched the wickets of Wood and Kim Hughes – and 51 runs later he added Hookes and Graham Yallop to his hit list.

The Australians were making heavy weather against Zimbabwe's accurate bowlers and some quite sensational fielding. When Wessels, anxiously trying to push the run rate along, was run out by Jack Heron for 76 after a mix-up with Allan Border, the scoreboard read 138 for five – and Australia began to wake up to the awful possibility that they might lose. Rod Marsh laid about him for 50 not out, but the overs had all but run out and it fell to Bob Nixon, a dentist from Bulawayo and commentator for the Zimbabwe Broadcasting Corporation, to describe his country's achievement:

"And you would believe that this was either Harare or Bulawayo with this crowd. Well, it isn't. It's a Nottingham crowd and the most unbelievable start to the Prudential World Cup. As Rawson comes in from the far end to bowl to Marsh. Marsh pats it away and Zimbabwe have beaten Australia by 13 runs. 226 for seven Australia in reply to Zimbabwe's 239 for six."

If any bookmakers had taken bets at their declared odds of 1,000/1 against Zimbabwe winning the Cup, they might just have been a little worried. After the match the

minnows' odds were slashed to 100/1. It had been a great day for the former Lancashire League player, now captain of Zimbabwe and Man of the Match, Duncan Fletcher. "If we had failed miserably here, I think the TCCB would have been a bit worried about inviting the next winners of the ICC Trophy over," he said. "It's up to us to put up a good performance, to see that the sides that do keep winning that competition are given a chance in the senior competition."

England, meanwhile, were at The Oval to meet New Zealand, with a giant television screen installed for the first time on an English ground. This was to cause some controversy, when it showed the replay of a turned-down lbw appeal, contrary to the agreement. As it was situated fairly straight at the Vauxhall End, it also proved a distraction for left-hand

Zimbabwe celebrate as Duncan Fletcher takes his fourth wicket – that of David Hookes. Australia are 94 for five and starting to feel a little uncomfortable...

Allan Lamb of England is bowled out after hitting a buccaneering century against New Zealand at The Oval. Lamb's 102 came in only 103 balls. The bowler, Martin Snedden, conceded 105 runs, making him the first bowler to go for a century in a World Cup match

Cup game. It looked a foregone conclusion before the start.

That start was delayed by rain until after lunch on the Thursday, when Clive Lloyd put India in. His four fast bowlers – Roberts, Holding, Marshall and Garner – worked through the Indian batting to have them 141 for five, with Larry Gomes disposing of the dangerous Kapil Dev for six. But then Yashpal Sharma pulled and drove his way to 89, hitting nine fours, with support from Roger Binny and Madan Lal, to take the total up to 262 for eight.

Gordon Greenidge and Desmond Haynes took the score to 49 before Haynes was run out. With Greenidge bowled by Balwinder Sandhu, West Indies were 67 for two at Thursday's close. The early scalp of Viv Richards next morning for Binny gave India the ideal start and he later added the wickets of Lloyd and Jeffrey Dujon. Ravi Shastri came into the act and the West Indies decline continued apace. At 157 for nine with Joel Garner and Andy Roberts at the crease, there was no doubt the tournament was in for its second surprise.

But Garner had other ideas. The Big Bird hit a couple of large blows off Shastri, which took him out of the attack, and as the runs mounted, suddenly it began to look as if this game might slip away from India at the last gasp. The two giant West Indian bowlers put on an unlikely 71 runs and, with Garner slogging Sandeep Patil for a huge six, they were only 35 from victory with six overs to go. Kapil Dev, running out of options, brought Shastri back to face the music. In the radio box, Tony Cozier could scent an extraordinary West Indian win.

"Looking out there now, you feel that panic has set in a long time ago, whereas it shouldn't have. Shastri is in now to Garner, outside the leg stump. He's out! Stumped! Garner is out stumped. That's it, the end of the innings. India have won. Garner stumped down the leg side by Kirmani and India have won the match by 34 runs. West Indies being dismissed for 228. The first defeat they have ever suffered in World Cup cricket."

England's second match took them down to Taunton to play Sri Lanka. On a perfect day, the small ground was packed and David Gower obliged them in his most elegant form, watched by Sri Lankan commentator Lucien Wijesinghe:

"248 for five. Gower on 97. John walking resolutely back to the top of his bowling mark. Runs in now, bowls to Gower, Gower swings and that's it. It could be six! It's a tremendous shot. Six runs over midwicket and what a way to go to Gower's 100.

batsmen, and a further decree was laid down that it should be blanked when they were facing bowling from that end.

It certainly did not worry Allan Lamb, though. After Bob Willis had won the toss, he blasted 102 from 103 balls with two sixes and 12 fours. His fourth-wicket stand of 115 with Mike Gatting, who made 43, occupied only 16 overs. More long-handled batting took England to 322 for six.

By the time the 20-year-old Martin Crowe came in, New Zealand were 62 for four and, though he revealed his class – to many for the first time – in making 97, it never threatened England, who won by 106 runs. As Willis put it succinctly: "We outplayed New Zealand in every department."

An even bigger target was set at Swansea, where Pakistan were put in by Sri Lanka. After a slow start, Javed Miandad and Imran Khan shared a fourth-wicket stand of 96 in only nine overs – Miandad 72 from 54 balls, Imran 56 not out from 33 – to post an imposing 338 for five. Yet Sri Lanka were not daunted, and Brendon Kuruppu's 72 and an unbeaten 59 by wicketkeeper Guy de Alwis kept the margin down to 50 runs.

There was another shock the next morning at Old Trafford. India had only ever won one World Cup match, against East Africa. The West Indies had never lost a World

How David slew the Aussie Goliath

1983 GROUP MATCH AT TRENT BRIDGE • AUSTRALIA v ZIMBABWE

*Zimbabwe's first ever World Cup match was against Australia – Lillee, Thomson, Lawson and all.
The cricket world's minnows had no chance, surely?*

BY KEVIN CURRAN

Before Zimbabwe gained independence from Britain in 1980, Rhodesia had played in the South African Currie Cup, so the standard of cricket was strong – we had the likes of Mike Procter, Paddy Clift and Brian Davison. Once independence came, many of our talented cricketers left the country and we only had about 25 first-class players to pick from. Prior to the 1983 World Cup we had never played a major country. Facing all these world-class players was something you only dreamed of.

Duncan Fletcher was an outstanding captain. I remember him saying before we left for the World Cup: "This is a learning curve, let's just enjoy and be committed." Committed was an understatement. Coming from the Southern Hemisphere, we always had that hunger to win. We worked hard on our fielding to make up for what we lacked in batting and bowling.

Our first World Cup practice game was against Pakistan – and we beat them. That was a major boost.

Enter Trent Bridge. Our first ever World Cup match – against Australia. The legendary Dennis Lillee, Jeff Thomson, Allan Border. The closest we'd ever got to them was the TV screen. None of our players were pros. Duncan Fletcher was a computer analyst, John Traicos and Andy Pycroft both lawyers, Vince Hogg an insurance broker. Our opening batsmen Grant Paterson and Robin Brown were farmers. What a match – the farmers vs the two greatest quicks in the world.

Australia won the toss and put us in. Some of the players, faced with the prospect of batting against Dennis Lillee, thought we might

'It wasn't until we got to the last over, with Australia still needing 17 to win, that I first thought we were in with a chance'

be shot out for a low total, but we whittled away and managed to get to 239 for six, which was fantastic – although I'm sure the Aussies still thought they would win comfortably.

Kepler Wessels and Graeme Wood put on 61 for the first wicket, but our fielders were keeping them tied down, and they got a bit frustrated. Fletcher took four wickets as we slowly piled on the pressure. Even so, it wasn't until we got to the last over, with Australia seven wickets down and still needing 17 to win, that I first thought we were in with a chance.

I remember Peter Rawson bowling the final over to Rodney Marsh, with a tail-ender at the other end. He tried to hit the first ball for four, but it went straight to a fielder. A couple of balls later, they still needed 14 off three balls, so he went for the big hit. Didn't get it, didn't take the run, so they couldn't win and he just blocked the last two balls out.

It was such a fantastic feeling. Here were we, the minnows from Zimbabwe, and we'd beaten Australia. I ran and put my arm round Peter Rawson – I've got that picture in my benefit brochure. When we walked off and saw Dennis Lillee and those guys with their heads down, we just thought, what an achievement.

To this day, it is still the most exciting game I've ever played in. I'll treasure it for the rest of my life. The papers said we were the best fielding side in the 1983 tournament by a long way. We brought that into world cricket and it's something we can be proud of.

• Kevin Curran lives in England and plays for Northants. 1999 is his benefit year

'Taunton was looking magnificent. A packed ground, a beautiful wicket and of course short boundaries, and there was a run feast.

The only slight disappointment for the local crowd was that Ian Botham was run out for nought. We had the luxury of a huge total to defend, and the Sri Lankans all came in blazing. It enabled me to get some wickets: I picked up five as the Sri Lankans unavailingly tried to get close to the huge total of 333. It was a memorable occasion.'

VIC MARKS
on England v Sri Lanka

Gower 103 with a mighty blow over the midwicket boundary."

Gower's brilliant 130 was the impetus for the whole innings of 333 for nine, even when Gatting and the Somerset crowd's favourite, Ian Botham, were both run out cheaply. But the crowd had another Somerset man to cheer, as Vic Marks picked up five for 39 with his off spin. Sri Lanka were all out 47 runs short with two overs to go.

At Edgbaston, New Zealand ran into Abdul Qadir's World Cup debut for Pakistan. His mystical leg spin and googly collection brought him four for 21 as New Zealand were reduced to 120 for five, but they recovered to 238 for nine – and if that had not seemed enough, the first eight balls of the Pakistan innings made it appear more than adequate. Mohsin Khan and Zaheer Abbas fell in Richard Hadlee's first over, Mudassar Nazar went to Lance Cairns' second ball, and Pakistan were three down without a run on the board. It was a devastating start from which they never recovered. They were all out for 186 in the 56th over.

It was a dramatic Sunday in Leeds, too, where the game between Australia and the West Indies could not start until Saturday afternoon. Hogg and Lawson disposed of Haynes, Greenidge and Richards for only 32, but they recovered to 160 for five by the end of the day with 18 overs to go and their sheet anchor, Larry Gomes, still there. On Sunday he took his score to 78 and the tail-enders' enthusiastic contributions helped the West Indies to 252.

The scale of the problem for Australia in the face of the West Indian fast attack on a helpful Headingley pitch was underlined in the fourth over when Graeme Wood ducked into a short ball from Michael Holding and was taken to hospital with concussion.

But it was not to be Holding, nor Roberts or Daniel, who would cause the havoc, but a tall young man from St Vincent – Winston Davis. He had not started encouragingly: despite getting a wicket, his first five overs cost 37 runs. But Lloyd persisted with him and his next five-and-a-half overs brought him six more wickets for 14 runs to finish the Australian innings.

They had been bowled out in 30.3 overs for 151, with Davis taking the first seven-wicket haul in a one-day international.

The two first-round giant-killers met at Leicester – but Zimbabwe, after a damp morning, were bowled out for 155, with the Indian wicketkeeper, Syed Kirmani, taking five catches. India overhauled that in the 38th over.

England, the new favourites, met Pakistan at Lord's on Monday June 13. Bob Willis made early inroads after Imran Khan had decided to bat and the only real challenge came from Zaheer Abbas, with 83 not out in their 193 for eight. Graeme Fowler led the way with 78 not out as England knocked off the runs in 51 overs for the loss of just two wickets.

At Bristol that day Richard Hadlee took five wickets to bowl out Sri Lanka for 206. Geoff Howarth's 76 gave New Zealand victory in the 40th over by five wickets.

So Group A at the halfway point had England at the top with three wins, then New Zealand with two, Pakistan with one and Sri Lanka still looking for their first success.

Australia went into the third round of Group B matches in the same parlous state. They were playing India at Trent Bridge. Each team rested a great player out of form – Dennis Lillee and Sunil Gavaskar. Trevor Chappell replaced the injured Graeme Wood – and rode his luck in twice being dropped to make 110. With Kim Hughes' 52 and Graham Yallop's 66 not out, Australia passed 300 as for once the Indian medium-pace bowlers were collared. Ken MacLeay had been regarded as the ideal English-conditions seamer and this was his day. He took six for 39 to bowl India out in the 38th over and give Australia a 162-run win and their first points.

Zimbabwe now came up against their most fearsome opponents: the West Indies, at Worcester. A fifth-wicket stand of 92 between Fletcher and a future Zimbabwean captain, David Houghton, made sure of a respectable total of 217 for seven – and when Peter Rawson had Haynes caught behind and Richards lbw, the West Indies, at 23 for two, must have had visions of what had happened to Australia the previous

HALFWAY: GROUP A	P	W	L	Pts
England	3	3	0	12
New Zealand	3	2	1	8
Pakistan	3	1	2	4
Sri Lanka	3	0	3	0
GROUP B				
West Indies	3	2	1	8
India	3	2	1	8
Australia	3	1	2	4
Zimbabwe	3	1	2	4

Left: David Gower of England tucks into the New Zealand bowling at Edgbaston, where he scored a superb 92 not out from 96 deliveries – yet the match was won by New Zealand off the penultimate ball

THE BUSINESS

The third World Cup was, like the first two, sponsored by Prudential Assurance, who doubled their input to £500,000, and all the awards were doubled. The winning team received £20,000, the losing finalists £8,000, the losing semi-finalists £4,000 each, and group match-winning teams £1,000. Players winning the Man of the Match award received £600 in the Final, £400 in the semi-finals, and £200 in group matches. A total of 232,081 spectators watched the games, and paid £1,195,712. The Final was watched by 24,609 people. A surplus of over £1 million was distributed between the full and associate members of the ICC.

week. But Larry Gomes and Gordon Greenidge got the job done with no more alarms – Greenidge 105 not out and Gomes 75 in their eight-wicket win with 11 overs to spare.

Group B was looking tight: West Indies and India with two wins apiece, and Australia and Zimbabwe one each.

The second half of the group section got under way 48 hours later. At Edgbaston, England reverted to former foibles against New Zealand. Graeme Fowler's 69 got them off to a bright start but Botham, pushed up to number three to accelerate the scoring, hit a four and a huge six and then gave off-spinner John Bracewell a hard return catch for 12.

David Gower was still in vintage form, treating Richard Hadlee with scant respect as he made 92 not out in only 96 balls with four sixes. But at the other end wickets started to tumble and England were bowled out by Hadlee and Lance

Cairns four-and-a-half overs inside the distance for 234.

That did not seem to be a problem when Willis sent back both openers with only three runs on the board. But Howarth steadied the ship, and eventually four were needed off the last over. John Bracewell's boundary off the fifth ball gave New Zealand the match by two wickets.

Pakistan and Sri Lanka, who had set batting records in their first encounter, met the next day in rather different conditions at Headingley. Mendis put Pakistan in and it soon looked as if Sri Lanka might at last have their first win as Asantha de Mel and Rumesh Ratnayake reduced them to 43 for five. At that late stage Imran found support from Shahid Mahboob to frustrate the Sri Lankans. De Mel eventually removed Mahboob for 77, but Imran was 102 not out in Pakistan's 235 for seven. At 162 for two in reply,

Sri Lanka seemed to have a real chance, but Abdul Qadir's five wickets ended their dreams. The last pair had needed only 12 from ten balls when the final wicket fell.

In Group B, the West Indies were determined to exact revenge on India at The Oval. Viv Richards, hitherto not at his blistering best, came good now with a century, though there was a collapse to the apparently innocuous Indian medium pace. But 283 was still a stiff target.

Mohinder Amarnath put on 68 with Dilip Vengsarkar for the third wicket – but then Vengsarkar was laid out by a rearing delivery from Malcolm Marshall and had to retire on 32. Four years earlier, Amarnath had been knocked unconscious by a bouncer from Richard Hadlee, which dented his confidence as much as his skull. Now, in the age of the batting helmet, he had conquered his fear and went on to make a brave 80 against Roberts, Holding, Marshall and Davis. But the fast bowlers worked through his colleagues and they were all out 66 runs behind.

Next day it was Australia's turn to get their own back at Southampton, against Zimbabwe. Graeme Wood had been restored to health and made 73 in a useful total of 272 for seven. A sixth-wicket stand of 103 between Houghton and Curran began to worry the Australians, and it looked like they could suffer another embarrassing upset. But then Trevor Chappell and Rodney Hogg started a collapse which cost Zimbabwe four wickets for one run in eight balls, and Australia won by 32 runs.

A sunny Saturday saw Australia and the West Indies at Lord's and England taking on Pakistan at Old Trafford. The sensations of the day, though, were to be found on fields less accustomed to the limelight.

News of the first shocks started to come through in the morning from amongst the rhododendrons of Tunbridge

Desmond Haynes catches Kapil Dev as the West Indies get revenge at The Oval

Wells. Zimbabwe were at it again: India were 17 for five. Gavaskar had fallen first ball, lbw to Rawson. Two more wickets to him and two for Curran had brought India to this plight. Kapil Dev knew it was time for a captain's innings: "I just said to myself, come on mate, I want to play for 60 overs, not to go for runs. I only got 50 in the first 30 overs. I just got a lot of runs in the last 10 overs." A rather modest way to describe one of the most remarkable innings ever played in one-day cricket.

With Binny, and a measure of caution, Kapil added 60 for the sixth wicket, but two more wickets plunged India back in the mire at 78 for seven. Aggression was the only way out... Even Zimbabweans like commentator Bob Nixon were thrilled by it:

"And it is a lovely sight here with those rhododendrons in full bloom as Rawson comes in to Kapil Dev, who has 99. This one is nudged out on the offside. They go through for the single and he's got it. And there's going to be applause from all the Zimbabwe players, never mind all the Indian supporters here. What a glorious innings!"

Kapil Dev's hundred had come in the 49th over and at the end he was 175 not out in a score of 266 for eight, having hit six sixes – some right over the marquees – and 16 fours. It was the highest individual score thus far in limited-overs internationals … and as an inspiration to India for the rest of the tournament, it was also one of the most significant.

A good start from Brown and Paterson showed that Zimbabwe reckoned 267 was quite attainable. But two run-outs and the persistence of the Indian medium-pacers had them just about out of it at 113 for six. Now Kevin Curran started to play an innings that looked as if it might do what Kapil Dev had done for India. With five overs to go, Zimbabwe needed 41. Then Curran lobbed Madan Lal to mid-off to be out for a fine 73 and effectively sealed Zimbabwe's fate. Kapil Dev appropriately took the last wicket and India won by 31 runs.

At Derby, Sri Lanka took New Zealand by surprise. Asantha de Mel sent back Turner and Wright for only eight runs and when Rumesh Ratnayake disposed of Geoff Howarth and Martin Crowe it was 47 for four. New Zealand were down and out at 116 for nine before Martin Snedden and Ewan Chatfield put on 65 to give themselves something to bowl at.

At 129 for two, it looked as if Sri Lanka's victory was going to be a lot more straightforward than it eventually was. A clatter of wickets delayed Sri Lankan celebrations, but at last their commentator, Lucien Wijesinghe, had his moment:

"The Sri Lankan supporters are getting ready to charge into the middle when the winning runs are scored. Martin Snedden running in now. Bowls to Dias, and Dias plays it down to third man. This should be it. They've taken one, they're going for the second and that is Sri Lanka's victory! Sri Lanka win by three wickets, 182 for seven. Sri Lanka have registered their first win in this year's Prudential Trophy. Well played, Sri Lanka."

At Old Trafford, England restricted Pakistan to 232 for eight, after Vic Marks tempted Imran and Wasim Raja into lofting catches, and Javed Miandad was brilliantly run out by Botham for 67. With half the required 233 runs being knocked off by the opening partnership between the contrasting characters of Graeme Fowler and Chris Tavaré, England won by seven wickets to ensure a semi-final place.

There was a full house at Lord's for the repeat of the first World Cup Final between Australia and the West Indies. Malcolm Marshall removed Australia's openers, but Hughes and Hookes put on 101 for the second wicket and a big score looked likely before Larry Gomes' gentle medium pace accounted for both Hughes, for 69, and Border.

The ease with which the West Indies posted 200 with only one wicket down showed that the Australians' 273 was not enough. Greenidge made 90 and Richards an arrogant 95 not out, with nine fours and three sixes, when the match was won by seven wickets in the 58th over. The West Indies had secured their semi-final place as if it was their birthright.

The final group matches would include two head-to-

Right: Kapil Dev thunders towards 175 not out at Tunbridge Wells

· GROUP A ·

JUNE 9 AT THE OVAL
England 322 for 6 (A J Lamb 102) **beat**
New Zealand 216 (M D Crowe 97) **by 106 runs**

JUNE 9 AT SWANSEA
Pakistan 338 for 5 (Mohsin Khan 82, Zaheer Abbas
82, Javed Miandad 72, Imran Khan 56*)
beat Sri Lanka 288 for 9 (B Kuruppu 72,
R G de Alwis 59*, Sarfraz 3-40) **by 50 runs**

JUNE 11 AT TAUNTON
England 333 for 9 (D I Gower 130, A J Lamb 53)
beat Sri Lanka 286 (R G de Alwis 58*, L R D
Mendis 56, Marks 5-39, Dilley 4-45) **by 47 runs**

JUNE 11 AT EDGBASTON
New Zealand 238 for 9 (Qadir 4-21, Rashid 3-47)
beat Pakistan 186 (Hadlee 3-20, Coney 3-28)
by 52 runs

JUNE 13 AT LORD'S
England 199 for 2 (G Fowler 78*) **beat Pakistan**
193 for 8 (Zaheer Abbas 83*) **by eight wickets**

JUNE 13 AT BRISTOL
New Zealand 209 for 5 (G P Howarth 76,
G M Turner 50, de Mel 3-35) **beat Sri Lanka** 206
(R S Madugalle 60, Hadlee 5-25) **by five wickets**

JUNE 15 AT EDGBASTON
New Zealand 238 for 8 (J V Coney 66*,
G P Howarth 60, Willis 4-24) **beat England** 234
(D I Gower 92*, G Fowler 69, Hadlee 3-32,
Cairns 3-44) **by two wickets**

JUNE 16 AT HEADINGLEY
Pakistan 235 for 7 (Imran Khan 102*,
Shahid Mahboob 77, de Mel 5-39) **beat Sri Lanka**
224 (S Wettimuny 50, Qadir 5-44) **by 11 runs**

JUNE 18 AT OLD TRAFFORD
England 233 for 3 (G Fowler 69, C J Tavaré 58)
beat Pakistan 232 for 8 (Javed Miandad 67)
by seven wickets

JUNE 18 AT DERBY
Sri Lanka 184 for 7 (R L Dias 64*, B Kuruppu 62)
beat New Zealand 181 (de Mel 5-32)
by three wickets

JUNE 20 AT HEADINGLEY
England 137 for 1 (G Fowler 81*)
beat Sri Lanka 136 (Allott 3-41) **by nine wickets**

JUNE 20 AT TRENT BRIDGE
Pakistan 261 for 3 (Zaheer Abbas 103*,
Imran Khan 79*) **beat New Zealand** 250
(J V Coney 51, Mudassar 3-43) **by 11 runs**

Order, order! Right: Geoff Howarth cuts, Javed Miandad dances, in the decisive match at Trent Bridge. Opposite: Umpire Merv Kitchen defends the pitch against celebrating Pakistan supporters after their side went through by the narrowest of margins

head contests for a semi-final place. Group A had already been won by England, who wasted no time in demolishing Sri Lanka at Headingley. They bowled them out for 136 and then Fowler led the way home with 81 not out for a nine-wicket win in 25 overs.

Second place would be decided at Trent Bridge between New Zealand and Pakistan. New Zealand, with three wins, only needed a victory. Pakistan needed to win *and* improve their run rate above New Zealand's. An unbroken fourth-wicket stand between Zaheer Abbas, who made 103 not out, and Imran Khan gave them an overall scoring rate of 4.01 as opposed to New Zealand's 3.94 – just enough, provided they won the game.

New Zealand's roller-coaster of an innings was enough to give Kiwis in the crowd heart failure. It seemed when the eighth wicket fell at 187 in the 52nd over that it was Pakistan's match. But John Bracewell joined Jeremy Coney and they ran the fielders ragged. Sixteen runs were needed off 13 balls with two wickets in hand. Bracewell hooked Sarfraz for what looked like the six that would ease that equation, but the boundary catch, and the runout of Coney for 51, ended New Zealand's Cup. They were eliminated by the narrowest of margins – .08 of a run per over.

Zimbabwe's farewell to a competition that had done so much for their reputation was at Edgbaston, where Marshall, Garner and Daniel, and Richards' off-spin, dismissed them for 171 of which Curran made 62. Haynes opened with Faoud Bacchus and knocked off the runs in the 46th over.

At Chelmsford Australia met India to decide the last semi-final place, both having had up-and-down rides to here. Australia could only get through with a win and a better run rate than their opponents. India chose to bat and again lost Gavaskar early. Hogg

GROUP A FINAL TABLE

	P	W	L	Pts	*Run-rate
England	6	5	1	20	4.67
Pakistan	6	3	3	12	4.01
New Zealand	6	3	3	12	3.93
Sri Lanka	6	1	5	4	3.75

*Run-rate was the average number of runs per over

and Thomson each took three wickets in a no-more-than-adequate 247 all out.

The crowd expected Australia now to step up and claim their semi-final place. What followed was a remarkable exhibition of how useful the Indian medium-pace bowlers had become. Stars of the show were Madan Lal and Roger Binny. The Australian commentator Jim Maxwell looked on in horror:

"Binny moves up once more and Hookes is forward – he's bowled him! He's gone right through his defence. Inside edge on to his stumps. A great blow for India. Hookes bowled Binny for one. And all of a sudden Australia are in a bit of bother at 48 for three…

"Away goes Binny again from the river end. And Yallop swung at this, a top edge. *Binny's underneath it, he should catch it. He's waiting. He's got it! A leading edge, straight up in the air. Not a good shot and Binny has captured his third wicket. It's 52 for four."*

And so Australia slid rather ingloriously out of the World Cup, bowled out for 129 in the 39th over. The semi-finals would be England v India and West Indies v Pakistan.

GROUP B FINAL TABLE

	P	W	L	Pts	*Run-rate
West Indies	6	5	1	20	4.31
India	6	4	2	16	3.87
Australia	6	2	4	8	3.81
Zimbabwe	6	1	5	4	3.49

*Run-rate was the average number of runs per over

· GROUP B ·

JUNE 9 AT TRENT BRIDGE
Zimbabwe 239 for 6 (D A G Fletcher 69*) **beat Australia** 226 for 7 (K C Wessels 76, R W Marsh 50*, Fletcher 4-42) **by 13 runs**

JUNE 9-10 AT OLD TRAFFORD
India 262 for 8 (Yashpal Sharma 89) **beat West Indies** 228 (Shastri 3-26, Binny 3-48) **by 34 runs**

JUNE 11-12 AT HEADINGLEY
West Indies 252 for 9 (H A Gomes 78, Lawson 3-29) **beat Australia** 151 (Davis 7-51) **by 101 runs**

JUNE 11 AT LEICESTER
India 157 for 5 (S M Patil 50) **beat Zimbabwe** 155 (Madan Lal 3-27) **by five wickets**

JUNE 13 AT TRENT BRIDGE
Australia 320 for 9 (T M Chappell 110, G N Yallop 66*, K J Hughes 52 Kapil Dev 5-43) **beat India** 158 (MacLeay 6-39) **by 162 runs**

JUNE 13 AT WORCESTER
West Indies 218 for 2 (C G Greenidge 105*, H A Gomes 75*) **beat Zimbabwe** 217 for 7 (D A G Fletcher 71*, D L Houghton 54, Roberts 3-36) **by eight wickets**

JUNE 15 AT THE OVAL
West Indies 282 for 9 (I V A Richards 119, Binny 3-71) **beat India** 216 (M Amarnath 80, Holding 3-40) **by 66 runs**

JUNE 16 AT SOUTHAMPTON
Australia 272 for 7 (G M Wood 73) **beat Zimbabwe** 240 (D L Houghton 84, Hogg 3-40, Chappell 3-47) **by 32 runs**

JUNE 18 AT TUNBRIDGE WELLS
India 266 for 8 (Kapil Dev 175*, Rawson 3-47, Curran 3-65) **beat Zimbabwe** 235 (K M Curran 73, Madan Lal 3-42) **by 31 runs**

JUNE 18 AT LORD'S
West Indies 276 for 3 (I V A Richards 95*, C G Greenidge 90) **beat Australia** 273 for 6 (K J Hughes 69, D W Hookes 56, G N Yallop 52*) **by seven wickets**

JUNE 20 AT CHELMSFORD
India 247 (Hogg 3-40, Thomson 3-51) **beat Australia** 129 (Madan Lal 4-20, Binny 4-29) **by 118 runs**

JUNE 20 AT EDGBASTON
West Indies 172 for 0 (D L Haynes 88*, S F A Bacchus 80*) **beat Zimbabwe** 171 (K M Curran 62, Daniel 3-28, Richards 3-41) **by ten wickets**

THE OVAL
1983 ·SEMI-FINAL·

The West Indies were only too happy that their semi-final was at The Oval. On a fast bouncy pitch with a little cloud around, they put Pakistan in. Javed Miandad had gone down with flu overnight, but it probably made little difference. Apart from a fourth-wicket stand of 51 between Mohsin, who made 70, and Zaheer, with 30, there was little resistance to the fast quartet. Malcolm Marshall took three wickets in 14 balls, including Imran Khan, as Pakistan clawed their way to 184 for eight.

Imran had not bowled a ball throughout the tournament, due to a shin stress fracture. How Pakistan could have done with his bowling at The Oval. They soon discovered that Viv Richards had just come into form at the right time.

After Greenidge and Haynes had gone with 56 on the board, Richards, with the admirable foil of Gomes, eased his side home in the 49th over by eight wickets. Richards, the Man of the Match, was 80 and Gomes 50 as they claimed a spot in their third successive World Cup Final.

Above: Pakistan opener Mohsin Khan cuts Malcolm Marshall during his innings of 70.
Right: Mohsin's fellow opener Mudassar Nazar starts the thrash prematurely

Viv Richards was back to his best in a crushing innings of 80 not out which took the West Indies to the Final

· SEMI-FINAL ·
THE OVAL • JUNE 22

PAKISTAN

Mohsin Khan b Roberts	70
Mudassar Nazar c and b Garner	11
Ijaz Faqih c Dujon b Holding	5
Zaheer Abbas b Gomes	30
*Imran Khan c Dujon b Marshall	17
Wasim Raja lbw b Marshall	0
Shahid Mahboob c Richards b Marshall	6
Sarfraz Nawaz c Holding b Roberts	3
Abdul Qadir not out	10
†Wasim Bari not out	4
Extras (B 6, l-b 13, w 4, n-b 5)	28
Total (60 Overs, for 8 wickets)	**184**

Fall of wickets: 1/23 2/34 3/88 4/139 5/139 6/159 7/164 8/171

Bowling: Roberts 12-3-25-2; Garner 12-1-31-1; Marshall 12-2-28-3; Holding 12-1-25-1; Gomes 7-0-29-1; Richards 5-0-18-0.

WEST INDIES
won the toss

C G Greenidge lbw b Rashid	17
D L Haynes b Qadir	29
I V A Richards not out	80
H A Gomes not out	50
Extras (B 2, l-b 6, w 4)	12
Total (48.4 Overs, for 2 wickets)	**188**

Did not bat: *C H Lloyd, S F A Bacchus, †P J Dujon, A M E Roberts, M D Marshall, J Garner and M A Holding

Fall of wickets: 1/34 2/56

Bowling: Rashid 12-2-32-1; Sarfraz 8-0-23-0; Qadir 11-1-42-1; Mahboob 11-1-43-0; Raja 1-0-9-0; Zaheer 4.4-1-24-0; Mohsin 1-0-3-0.

Umpires: D J Constant and A G T Whitehead

Man of the Match: Vivian Richards

WEST INDIES
won by eight wickets

1983

THE OLD TRAFFORD
·SEMI-FINAL·

At Old Trafford there was little doubt, as the other semi-final started, that they were playing to meet the West Indies on Saturday. Few had much doubt that it would, in fact, be a repeat of the 1979 England-West Indies final.

Bob Willis won the toss, chose to bat and again Graeme Fowler and Chris Tavaré got England away to an impressive start – 69 in the first 17 overs. The opening spells of Kapil Dev and Balwinder Sandhu had been seen off and now England would surely accelerate. But again it was Roger Binny who made the breakthrough, bowling Fowler for 33 and having Tavaré caught behind for 32.

More unlikely was the sight of the even more gentle Mohinder Amarnath posing problems. He had David Gower caught behind, and bowled Mike Gatting. Ian Botham struggled fruitlessly for eight overs, finally resorting to the reverse sweep to take two runs off the off-spinner Kirti Azad, but he was bowled in the same over while making room to cut. Six runs to Botham, game to Azad.

With the agonising runouts of Lamb and Ian Gould, England were 175 for seven. Kapil Dev returned and bowled Marks for eight. Graham Dilley was helped by Paul Allott to add 25 for the ninth wicket, before Kapil finished the innings off for a fearfully disappointing 213.

Sunil Gavaskar chose this moment to make his highest score of the tournament, albeit it was only 25. India had a fair start, but the two openers, Gavaskar and Krishnamachari Srikkanth, were removed by Allott and Botham in successive overs and India were in hazard at 50 for two. The stand between Mohinder Amarnath and Yashpal Sharma gradually ended England's hopes. The Somerset pair of Botham and Marks made it hard for them for a time, but

> 'We taught them a lesson.'
> KAPIL DEV

Right: A crucial wicket for India as England's last real batting hope, Allan Lamb, is run out for 29, leaving the home team teetering on 160 for six

'WE THOUGHT: BUSINESS AS USUAL'

Vic Marks on the Old Trafford semi-final

'I remember the whole thing starting off perfectly well. Fowler and Tavaré put on over 60 and we thought: 'Well, this is business as usual. Everything is going according to plan.' We had only had one defeat and all the other games had gone very smoothly.

"But it doesn't always work out like that. India's medium pacers, bowlers that you will never lose sleep about, whittled away. They bowled very accurately. Allan Lamb was run out just as he was set.

"We were bundled out for 213 – fifty or sixty short of what we thought we would get and what we should have got – and that caused us considerable problems. We had our moments in the field, but we were always up against it. Amarnath and Sharma got runs and we were never able to put them under extreme pressure.

"So after all that hard work and success in the preliminary rounds, where everything had

Mohinder Amarnath, Man of the Match

gone very, very smoothly and we couldn't have played much better, we slightly crumpled when it mattered, at Old Trafford."

when they broke the shackles, the issue was not in doubt. Yashpal hit two sixes in his 61 and Amarnath another in his 46 – which, along with his two crucial wickets, won him the Man of the Match award.

After he was out, Sandeep Patil was just the man, with an unbeaten half-century, to see India to their first World Cup Final. They

had won by six wickets, with more than five overs to spare.

Kapil Dev reacted angrily to the way his team had been written off before the game by telling anyone who would listen: "We taught them a lesson." But that didn't stop everyone writing off India's chances in the forthcoming battle against the mighty West Indies…

· SEMI-FINAL ·

OLD TRAFFORD · JUNE 22

ENGLAND
won the toss

G Fowler b Binny	33
C J Tavaré c Kirmani b Binny	32
D I Gower c Kirmani b Amarnath	17
A J Lamb run out	29
M W Gatting b Amarnath	18
I T Botham b Azad	6
†I J Gould run out	13
V J Marks b Kapil Dev	8
G R Dilley not out	20
P J W Allott c Patil b Kapil Dev	8
*R G D Willis b Kapil Dev	0
Extras (B 1, l-b 17, w 7, n-b 4)	29
Total *(60 Overs)*	**213**

Fall of wickets: 1/69 2/84 3/107 4/141 5/150 6/160 7/175 8/177 9/202

Bowling: Kapil Dev 11-1-35-3; Sandhu 8-1-36-0; Binny 12-1-43-2; Madan Lal 5-0-15-0; Azad 12-1-28-1; Amarnath 12-1-27-2.

INDIA

S M Gavaskar c Gould b Allott	25
K Srikkanth c Willis b Botham	19
M Amarnath run out	46
Yashpal Sharma c Allott b Willis	61
S M Patil not out	51
*Kapil Dev not out	1
Extras (B 5, l-b 6, w 1, n-b 2)	14
Total *(54.4 Overs, for 4 wickets)*	**217**

Did not bat: K B J Azad, R M H Binny, Madan Lal, †S M H Kirmani and B S Sandhu

Fall of wickets: 1/46 2/50 3/142 4/205

Bowling: Willis 10.4-2-42-1; Dilley 11-0-43-0; Allott 10-3-40-1; Botham 11-4-40-1; Marks 12-1-38-0.

Umpires: D O Oslear and D G L Evans

Man of the Match: Mohinder Amarnath

INDIA
won by six wickets

1983

LORD'S
·THE FINAL·

After the ruthless execution of Pakistan by his four fast bowlers, Clive Lloyd was full of confidence as he waxed lyrical about the skills of his youngest paceman: "Malcolm seems to get quicker all the time. He is probably as fast now as Michael Holding was at his peak a few years ago. When Joel Garner is in the side, he sometimes gets that much more bounce from the new ball with his extra height. Malcolm shows better control with the shine off a bit."

The Indians knew that their necks were on the line. Yashpal Sharma nervously admitted: "We don't want grass left on the Lord's pitch, because that would suit the West Indian fast bowlers and leave the game one-sided." But Kapil Dev, their inspirational captain aged just 24, was looking forward to the fight: "I like to play cricket with the

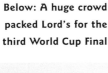

Below: A huge crowd packed Lord's for the third World Cup Final

hard men," he said, and he was about to get his wish…

Dawn on Saturday June 25 saw a huge noisy excited crowd at the Grace Gates at Lord's. Many were there to support the surprise finalists, India, unworried by the bookmakers making West Indies 4/1 on favourites. India had beaten England and Australia already that week. What did bookies know?

For the West Indians, it was the old routine. Lloyd won the toss and put India in, and in the opening assault Gavaskar was caught behind off Roberts with only two runs on the board. Mohinder Amarnath and Krishnamachari Srikkanth added 57 and got some impetus, with Srikkanth bravely pulling Roberts for six and hitting seven fours in his 38. Yashpal Sharma helped Amarnath add another 31.

India were 90 for two approaching the halfway point of their innings. But, instead of the necessary acceleration at that point, there came collapse. In seven overs either side of lunch, five wickets were lost for 40 runs. Most crucially for Indian supporters, Kapil Dev had gone just when he had

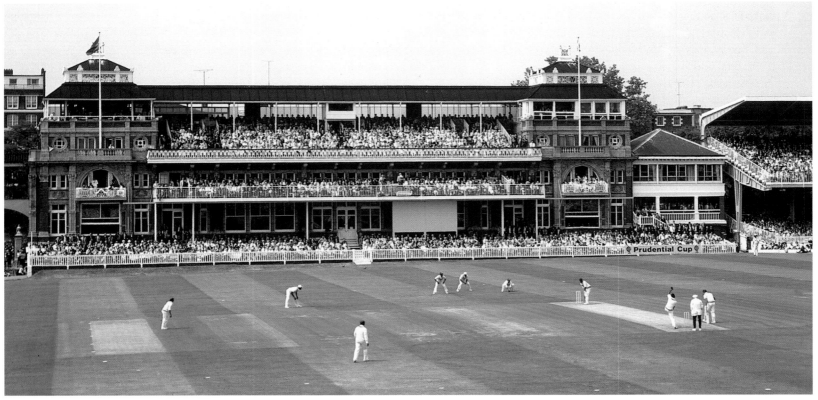

Either Sandip Patil has just played a snick through the slips, or he and Jeff Dujon have suddenly spotted a streaker

looked like getting into his stride. Madan Lal, Syed Kirmani and Balwinder Sandhu managed to scramble the score up to 183, but it surely couldn't be enough. The West Indian fast bowlers had done their work as efficiently as ever.

The wicket had not turned out to be the flat track that Yashpal Sharma had hoped for – but now the Indian seamers began to show that they could move the ball around too, albeit at a somewhat slower pace. In the West Indies' fourth over, Gordon Greenidge left a ball from Sandhu alone and was bowled for one. But that was obviously just a minor hiccup, as Viv Richards started to treat the bowling with his customary lack of respect in company with Desmond Haynes.

Tony Cozier: *"Fifty for one in the 12th over of the innings. Desmond Haynes to take strike from Madan Lal. Here is Madan Lal, in to him now. Haynes drives uppishly – and he's out, caught! Binny at extra cover takes the catch. A comfortable catch. Haynes comes forward looking for the drive. Not being to the pitch of the ball and giving a simple catch to wide cover. Binny took it in his lap. The West Indies have lost their second wicket for 50 in the 12th over of the innings."*

Now came Clive Lloyd, and West Indians felt that this must be the start of the real destruction of the Indian attack.

However, a quick run to get Lloyd off the mark tweaked a groin muscle and he had to send for a runner.

But Richards was winning the game on his own. A problem for Kapil Dev's captaincy: "In that over Vivian Richards hit two cover drives to Madan Lal and he said to me, what to do? I said just bowl a good line, because I was happy how he was playing. When a batsman like Vivian Richards is trying every ball to hit out of the ground, to try to get a quick 100 or finish the game before tea, I said we have nothing to lose." And so it proved…

Christopher Martin-Jenkins: *"Richards has played quite flawlessly so far. In comes Madan Lal, and Richards swings it high. It could be caught! Kapil Dev, going back, catches it. And that is a remarkable turn of events in this match, and the Indian spectators can't control themselves for joy as they run on to the field.*

"It was a very good catch. It was swirling. It came off high on the bat as he went to hook over midwicket. It swirled out about 40 yards and Kapil Dev, running back, took a vital catch, which has made this match not such a foregone conclusion after all.

"We were just saying how impeccably Richards had played. He's out for 33 and it's 57 for three. Lloyd batting with a runner. Only 13 overs gone. Suddenly the match is alive again."

Kapil recalls: "It wasn't a bad shot. He tried to pull and

'Kapil Dev, India's inspirational captain aged just 24, was looking forward to the fight: "I like to play cricket with the hard men," he said, and he was about to get his wish…'

Above: Kapil Dev raises the World Cup as India's triumph caps a tournament full of surprises. Right: Viv Richards mis-times a hook shot off Madan Lal, and sees Kapil Dev take a tricky catch on the midwicket boundary. Opposite: Kapil Dev congratulates Man of the Match Mohinder Amarnath, who cradles the Prudential Cup – the last time that particular trophy would be presented

went for a top edge. I saw the ball leave the bat. People said to me again and again, 'That was a very difficult catch,' but it wasn't that difficult for me."

Difficult or not, Kapil Dev's catch to dismiss the Master Blaster was a turning point. The match was very much alive as Madan Lal had Gomes caught at slip for five in the 18th over. The next over it was the handicapped Lloyd who was caught at extra cover off Roger Binny, to send the West Indies to tea in disarray at 76 for five from 25 overs.

In the first over after the interval, Faoud Bacchus had a rush of blood, chased a wide one from Sandhu, and was caught behind. It was 76 for six.

Dire as that sounded, only three runs an over were needed still and Jeff Dujon and Marshall kept their heads, adding 43. But then Kapil Dev made an inspired bowling change, bringing back Amarnath – who somehow induced Dujon to play his first ball on to his stumps. Nervously, five runs were added before Marshall, too, fell to Amarnath.

Kapil himself had Andy Roberts lbw and Indians prepared to celebrate, not least the huge radio audience worldwide listening to Christopher Martin-Jenkins.

"140 for nine. Forty-four needed to win. This is the 52nd over. In comes Amarnath again. Oh, it could be lbw. He's out lbw! He pulled across the line, Holding, and India have caused one of the greatest upsets in the history of all sport.

"They have won the third Prudential World Cup, beating the hot favourites, the 4/1 on favourites, West Indies."

Amarnath's gutsy 26 runs and three wickets for 12 won him his second consecutive Man of the Match award.

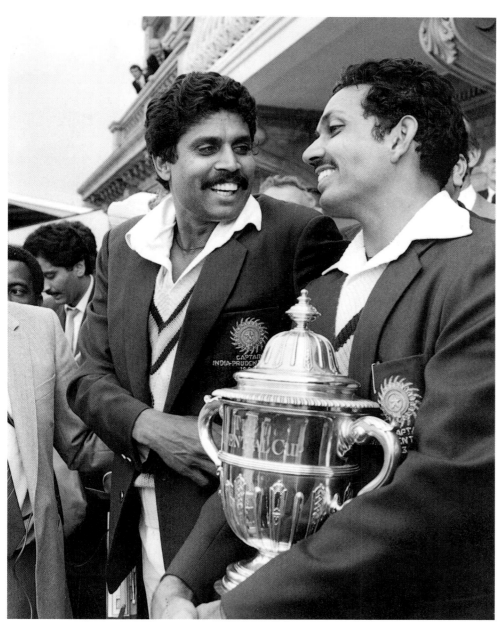

· THE FINAL ·
LORD'S • JUNE 25

INDIA

S M Gavaskar c Dujon b Roberts	2
K Srikkanth lbw b Marshall	38
M Amarnath b Holding	26
Yashpal Sharma c sub b Gomes	11
S M Patil c Gomes b Garner	27
*Kapil Dev c Holding b Gomes	15
K B J Azad c Garner b Roberts	0
R M H Binny c Garner b Roberts	2
Madan Lal b Marshall	17
†S M H Kirmani b Holding	14
B S Sandhu not out	11
Extras (B 5, l-b 5, w 9, n-b 1)	20
Total *(54.4 Overs)*	**183**

Fall of wickets: 1/2 2/59 3/90 4/92 5/110 6/111 7/130 8/153 9/161

Bowling: Roberts 10-3-32-3; Garner 12-4-24-1; Marshall 11-1-24-2; Holding 9.4-2-26-2; Gomes 11-1-49-2; Richards 1-0-8-0.

WEST INDIES
won the toss

C G Greenidge b Sandhu	1
D L Haynes c Binny b Madan Lal	13
I V A Richards c Kapil Dev b Madan Lal	33
*C H Lloyd c Kapil Dev b Binny	8
H A Gomes c Gavaskar b Madan Lal	5
S F A Bacchus c Kirmani b Sandhu	8
†P J Dujon b Amarnath	25
M D Marshall c Gavaskar b Amarnath	18
A M E Roberts lbw b Kapil Dev	4
J Garner not out	5
M A Holding lbw b Amarnath	6
Extras (L-b 4, w 10)	14
Total *(52 Overs)*	**140**

Fall of wickets: 1/5 2/50 3/57 4/66 5/66 6/76 7/119 8/124 9/126

Bowling: Kapil Dev 11-4-21-1; Sandhu 9-1-32-2; Madan Lal 12-2-31-3; Binny 10-1-23-1; Amarnath 7-0-12-3; Azad 3-0-7-0.

Umpires: H D Bird and B J Meyer

Man of the Match: Mohinder Amarnath

INDIA
won by 43 runs

India could scarcely believe their triumph by 43 runs themselves, but no one could deny they deserved it. The West Indies, undefeated in World Cup matches before this tournament, had now lost twice – and both times to Kapil Dev's team. The scenes of joyous celebration at Lord's were repeated in cities all over India.

After the match Clive Lloyd, the dominant figure of the first three World Cups, announced his retirement. He soon changed his mind, but the very suggestion showed that this was the end of an era indeed.

· 1983 STATISTICS ·

Highest totals

338 for 5   Pakistan against Sri Lanka
333 for 9   England against Sri Lanka
322 for 6   England against New Zealand
320 for 9   Australia against India
288 for 9   Sri Lanka against Pakistan

Lowest totals (completed innings)

129   Australia against India
136   Sri Lanka against England
140   West Indies against India
155   Zimbabwe against India
171   Zimbabwe against West Indies

Highest winning margins

10 wickets   West Indies against Zimbabwe
9 wickets   England against Sri Lanka
8 wickets   England against Pakistan
8 wickets   West Indies against Zimbabwe
8 wickets   West Indies against Pakistan
162 runs   Australia against India
118 runs   India against Australia
106 runs   England against New Zealand
101 runs   West Indies against Australia

Closest winning margins

2 wickets   New Zealand against England
11 runs   Pakistan against New Zealand
11 runs   Pakistan against Sri Lanka
13 runs   Zimbabwe against Australia

Highest match aggregates

626 for 14   Pakistan v Sri Lanka
619 for 19   England v Sri Lanka
549 for 9   West Indies v Australia
538 for 16   England v New Zealand
512 for 17   Australia v Zimbabwe

Wins by non-Test teams

Zimbabwe beat Australia by 13 runs

Centuries

175 n.o.   Kapil Dev, India v Zimbabwe
130   D I Gower, England v Sri Lanka
119   I V A Richards, West Indies v India
110   T M Chappell, Australia v India
105 n.o.   C G Greenidge, West Indies v Zimbabwe
103 n.o.   Zaheer Abbas, Pakistan v New Zealand
102 n.o.   Imran Khan, Pakistan v Sri Lanka
102   A J Lamb, England v New Zealand

Highest scores for each position

1   C G Greenidge, 105 n.o., W Indies v Zimbabwe
2   T M Chappell, 110, Australia v India
3   D I Gower, 130, England v Sri Lanka
4   Zaheer Abbas, 103 n.o., Pakistan v NZ
5   Imran Khan, 102 n.o., Pakistan v Sri Lanka
6   Kapil Dev, 175 n.o., India v Zimbabwe
7   Shahid Mahboob, 77, Pakistan v Sri Lanka
8   R G de Alwis 58 n.o., Sri Lanka v England
9   R G de Alwis 59 n.o., Sri Lanka v Pakistan
10   M C Snedden, 40, New Zealand v Sri Lanka
11   E J Chatfield, 19 n.o., New Zealand v Sri Lanka

Leading scorers

D I Gower, England   384   Ave: 76.80
I V A Richards, W Indies   367   Ave: 73.40
G Fowler, England   360   Ave: 72.00
Zaheer Abbas, Pakistan   313   Ave: 62.60
Kapil Dev, India   303   Ave: 60.60

Most wickets

18   at 18.66   R M H Binny, India
17   at 15.58   A L F de Mel, Sri Lanka
17   at 16.76   Madan Lal, India
14   at 12.85   R J Hadlee, New Zealand
13   at 18.92   V J Marks, England

Most wickets in a match

7-51   W W Davis, West Indies v Australia
6-39   K H MacLeay, Australia v India
5-25   R J Hadlee, New Zealand v Sri Lanka
5-32   A L F de Mel, Sri Lanka v New Zealand
5-39   V J Marks, England v Sri Lanka
5-39   A L F de Mel, Sri Lanka v Pakistan
5-43   Kapil Dev, India v Australia

Most dismissals by a wicketkeeper

16   (15ct, 1st)   P J L Dujon, West Indies
14   (12ct, 2st)   S H Kirmani, India
12   (11ct, 1st)   I J Gould, England
9   (6ct, 3st)   Wasim Bari, Pakistan
8   (8ct)   R W Marsh, Australia

Most catches by an outfielder

7   Kapil Dev, India
6   A J Lamb, England
5   D L Haynes, West Indies
5   C H Lloyd, West Indies
4   I T Botham, England
4   R G D Willis, England
4   B A Edgar, New Zealand
4   Imran Khan, Pakistan
4   I V A Richards, West Indies

Australia *batting*

	M	I	NO	Runs	HS	Avge	100	50	Ct	St
G.N.Yallop	6	6	2	187	66*	46.75	-	2	-	-
G.M.Wood	5	5	1	144	73	36.00	-	1	1	-
R.W.Marsh	6	6	2	142	50*	35.50	-	1	8	-
T.M.Chappell	4	4	0	139	110	34.75	1	-	1	-
K.J.Hughes	5	5	0	170	69	34.00	-	2	2	-
K.C.Wessels	3	3	0	92	76	30.66	-	1	1	-
A.R.Border	6	6	0	150	43	25.00	-	-	3	-
D.W.Hookes	6	6	0	133	56	22.16	-	1	3	-
T.G.Hogan	4	4	2	24	11	12.00	-	-	2	-
G.F.Lawson	4	4	0	24	16	6.00	-	-	-	-
K.H.MacLeay	4	4	0	19	9	4.75	-	-	1	-
D.K.Lillee	4	1	0	0	0	0.00	-	-	-	-
J.R.Thomson	3	1	0	0	0	0.00	-	-	-	-
R.M.Hogg	6	4	4	29	19*	-	-	-	1	-

Australia *bowling*

	O	M	R	W	Avge	Best	5w	Econ
R.M.Hogg	67	8	220	9	24.44	3-40	-	3.28
G.F.Lawson	38	7	127	5	25.40	3-29	-	3.34
K.H.MacLeay	44.5	6	163	8	20.37	6-39	1	3.63
T.G.Hogan	47	2	172	6	28.66	2-33	-	3.65
A.R.Border	23	1	85	1	85.00	1-11	-	3.69
G.N.Yallop	14	0	54	3	18.00	2-28	-	3.85
D.K.Lillee	45	2	177	4	44.25	2-47	-	3.93
J.R.Thomson	32.5	1	161	3	53.66	3-51	-	4.90
T.M.Chappell	19.4	0	98	4	24.50	3-47	-	4.98

England *batting*

	M	I	NO	Runs	HS	Avge	100	50	Ct	St
D.I.Gower	7	7	2	384	130	76.80	1	1	1	-
G.Fowler	7	7	2	360	81*	72.00	-	4	-	-
A.J.Lamb	7	6	2	278	102	69.50	1	1	6	-
G.R.Dilley	6	4	2	90	31*	45.00	-	-	1	-
C.J.Tavare	7	7	0	212	58	30.28	-	1	2	-
I.J.Gould	7	4	1	66	35	22.00	-	-	11	1
M.W.Gatting	7	5	1	83	43	20.75	-	-	2	-
I.T.Botham	7	4	0	40	22	10.00	-	-	4	-
V.J.Marks	7	3	0	18	8	6.00	-	-	2	-
P.J.W.Allott	7	3	1	8	8	4.00	-	-	1	-
R.G.D.Willis	7	2	0	0	0	0.00	-	-	4	-
N.G.Cowans	1	0	0	0	0	-	-	-	1	-

England *bowling*

	O	M	R	W	Avge	Best	5w	Econ
N.G.Cowans	12	3	31	2	15.50	2-31	-	2.58
R.G.D.Willis	73.4	19	206	11	18.72	4-42	-	2.79
V.J.Marks	78	9	246	13	18.92	5-39	1	3.15
I.T.Botham	80	13	288	8	36.00	2-12	-	3.60
G.R.Dilley	66	4	243	7	34.71	4-45	-	3.68
M.W.Gatting	12	3	48	1	48.00	1-35	-	4.00
P.J.W.Allott	80.3	10	335	8	41.87	3-41	-	4.16

India *batting*

	M	I	NO	Runs	HS	Avge	100	50	Ct	St
Kapil Dev	8	8	3	303	175*	60.60	1	-	7	-
D.B.Vengsarkar	2	2	1	37	32*	37.00	-	-	1	-
Yashpal Sharma	8	8	1	240	89	34.28	-	2	2	-
Madan Lal	8	6	3	102	27	34.00	-	-	1	-
S.M.Patil	8	8	1	216	51*	30.85	-	2	2	-
M.Amarnath	8	8	0	237	80	29.62	-	1	-	-
K.Srikkanth	8	8	0	156	39	19.50	-	-	3	-
B.S.Sandhu	8	4	2	28	11*	14.00	-	-	2	-
S.M.H.Kirmani	8	6	1	61	24*	12.20	-	-	12	2
R.M.H.Binny	8	6	0	73	27	12.16	-	-	2	-
R.J.Shastri	5	5	1	40	17	10.00	-	-	3	-
S.M.Gavaskar	6	6	0	59	25	9.83	-	-	3	-
K.Azad	3	2	0	15	15	7.50	-	-	-	-

India *bowling*

	O	M	R	W	Avge	Best	5w	Econ
K.Azad	17	1	42	1	42.00	1-28	-	2.47
Kapil Dev	84	13	245	12	20.41	5-43	1	2.91
Madan Lal	83	8	285	17	16.76	4-20	-	3.43
B.S.Sandhu	83	10	297	8	37.12	2-26	-	3.57
M.Amarnath	49	2	178	8	22.25	3-12	-	3.63
R.M.H.Binny	88	9	336	18	18.66	4-29	-	3.81
R.J.Shastri	20.1	1	87	4	21.75	3-26	-	4.31
S.M.Patil	9	0	61	0	-	-	-	6.77

New Zealand *batting*

	M	I	NO	Runs	HS	Avge	100	50	Ct	St
J.V.Coney	6	6	2	197	66*	49.25	-	2	1	-
G.P.Howarth	6	6	0	224	76	37.33	-	2	1	-
M.D.Crowe	6	6	0	202	97	33.66	-	1	1	-
M.C.Snedden	3	2	0	61	40	30.50	-	-	2	-
J.G.Bracewell	3	3	1	41	34	20.50	-	-	1	-
W.K.Lees	4	4	1	60	26	20.00	-	-	4	-
J.J.Crowe	2	2	0	40	23	20.00	-	-	2	-
G.M.Turner	6	6	0	103	50	17.16	-	1	-	-
J.G.Wright	5	5	0	83	45	16.60	-	-	1	-
B.A.Edgar	5	5	0	81	44	16.20	-	-	4	-
R.J.Hadlee	6	5	0	71	31	14.20	-	-	2	-
I.D.S.Smith	2	2	1	8	4*	8.00	-	-	1	-
B.L.Cairns	6	5	0	16	6	3.20	-	-	3	-
E.J.Chatfield	6	4	4	37	19*	-	-	-	1	-

New Zealand *bowling*

	O	M	R	W	Avge	Best	5w	Econ
R.J.Hadlee	65.1	17	180	14	12.85	5-25	1	2.76
J.V.Coney	58	7	183	9	20.33	3-28	-	3.15
E.J.Chatfield	70.2	8	249	8	31.12	2-24	-	3.54
B.L.Cairns	61.2	10	237	7	33.85	3-44	-	3.86
J.G.Bracewell	35	2	155	1	155.00	1-66	-	4.42
M.C.Snedden	32.5	3	201	5	40.20	2-58	-	6.12
M.D.Crowe	17	2	110	1	110.00	1-15	-	6.47

Pakistan *batting*

	M	I	NO	Runs	HS	Avge	100	50	Ct	St
Imran Khan	7	7	3	283	102*	70.75	1	2	4	-
Zaheer Abbas	7	7	2	313	103*	62.60	1	2	2	-
Wasim Bari	7	4	3	58	34	58.00	-	-	6	3
Javed Miandad	6	6	0	220	72	36.66	-	2	3	-
Shahid Mahboob	5	3	0	100	77	33.33	-	1	1	-
Mohsin Khan	7	7	0	223	82	31.85	-	2	3	-
Abdul Qadir	6	5	3	62	41*	31.00	-	-	1	-
Mudassar Nazar	6	6	0	106	36	17.66	-	-	2	-
Ijaz Faqih	6	5	1	61	42*	15.25	-	-	1	-
Sarfraz Nawaz	7	5	0	53	17	10.60	-	-	1	-
Rashid Khan	7	1	0	9	9	9.00	-	-	1	-
Wasim Raja	3	3	0	24	15	8.00	-	-	1	-
Mansoor Akhtar	2	2	0	9	6	4.50	-	-	-	-
Tahir Naqqash	1	1	1	0	0*	-	-	-	1	-

Pakistan *bowling*

	O	M	R	W	Avge	Best	5w	Econ
Mohsin Khan	1	0	3	0	-	-	-	3.00
Sarfraz Nawaz	73	12	231	7	33.00	3-40	-	3.16
Ijaz Faqih	37	2	125	0	-	-	-	3.37
Mudassar Nazar	48	3	165	6	27.50	3-43	-	3.43
Rashid Khan	71	11	266	8	33.25	3-47	-	3.74
Zaheer Abbas	19.4	2	74	2	37.00	1-8	-	3.76
Abdul Qadir	67.4	6	264	12	22.00	5-44	1	3.90
Mansoor Akhtar	13	2	52	1	52.00	1-44	-	4.00
Shahid Mahboob	52	4	228	4	57.00	1-37	-	4.38
Wasim Raja	4	0	23	0	-	-	-	5.75
Tahir Naqqash	8	0	49	1	49.00	1-49	-	6.12

Sri Lanka *batting*

	M	I	NO	Runs	HS	Avge	100	50	Ct	St
R.G.de Alwis	6	6	3	167	59*	55.66	-	2	5	-
D.S.B.P.Kuruppu	6	6	0	182	72	30.33	-	2	1	-
R.L.Dias	6	6	1	150	64*	30.00	-	1	3	-
L.R.D.Mendis	6	6	0	158	56	26.33	-	1	1	-
S.Wettimuny	6	6	0	128	50	21.33	-	1	-	-
R.S.Madugalle	5	5	0	104	60	20.80	-	1	3	-
V.B.John	5	5	3	35	15	17.50	-	-	-	-
D.S.de Silva	6	6	0	94	35	15.66	-	-	2	-
R.J.Ratnayake	6	5	1	54	20*	13.50	-	-	-	-
A.Ranatunga	6	6	0	80	34	13.33	-	-	3	-
A.L.F.de Mel	6	5	0	66	27	13.20	-	-	-	-
M.A.R.Samarasekera	2	2	0	5	5	2.50	-	-	1	-

Sri Lanka *bowling*

	O	M	R	W	Avge	Best	5w	Econ
A.L.F.de Mel	66	13	265	17	15.58	5-32	2	4.01
D.S.de Silva	58	6	238	3	79.33	2-11	-	4.10
R.J.Ratnayake	64	6	274	8	34.25	2-18	-	4.28
M.A.R.Samarasekera	16.2	2	71	0	-	-	-	4.34
V.B.John	50.2	3	251	3	83.66	1-49	-	4.98
S.Wettimuny	3	0	15	0	-	-	-	5.00
A.Ranatunga	44.1	2	240	1	240.00	1-65	-	5.43

West Indies *batting*

	M	I	NO	Runs	HS	Avge	100	50	Ct	St
I.V.A.Richards	8	7	2	367	119	73.40	1	2	4	-
H.A.Gomes	8	7	3	258	78	64.50	-	3	3	-
J.Garner	4	2	1	42	37	42.00	-	-	3	-
C.G.Greenidge	7	7	1	250	105*	41.66	1	1	1	-
S.F.A.Bacchus	8	5	1	157	80*	39.25	-	1	-	-
D.L.Haynes	8	8	1	240	88*	34.28	-	1	5	-
C.H.Lloyd	8	5	1	112	41	28.00	-	-	5	-
A.M.E.Roberts	7	4	1	53	37*	17.66	-	-	-	-
P.J.Dujon	8	4	0	53	25	13.25	-	-	15	1
M.A.Holding	7	4	0	36	20	9.00	-	-	3	-
M.D.Marshall	6	3	0	24	18	8.00	-	-	-	-
W.W.Daniel	3	1	1	16	16*	-	-	-	-	-
A.L.Logie	1	0	0	0	0	-	-	-	-	-
W.W.Davis	5	1	1	0	0*	-	-	-	-	-

West Indies *bowling*

	O	M	R	W	Avge	Best	5w	Econ
M.D.Marshall	70	10	175	12	14.58	3-28	-	2.50
J.Garner	43	10	117	5	23.40	2-13	-	2.72
M.A.Holding	74.5	11	235	12	19.58	3-40	-	3.14
A.M.E.Roberts	74	12	238	11	21.63	3-32	-	3.21
W.W.Daniel	24	6	84	3	28.00	3-28	-	3.50
W.W.Davis	54.3	6	206	8	25.75	7-51	1	3.77
I.V.A.Richards	24	2	93	3	31.00	3-41	-	3.87
H.A.Gomes	74	4	304	9	33.77	2-46	-	4.10

Zimbabwe *batting*

	M	I	NO	Runs	HS	Avge	100	50	Ct	St
D.A.G.Fletcher	6	6	2	191	71*	47.75	-	2	-	-
K.M.Curran	6	6	0	212	73	35.33	-	2	-	-
D.L.Houghton	6	6	0	176	84	29.33	-	2	7	-
R.D.Brown	4	4	0	93	38	23.25	-	-	2	-
I.P.Butchart	6	6	2	82	34*	20.50	-	-	2	-
G.A.Paterson	6	6	0	99	27	16.50	-	-	-	-
G.E.Peckover	3	3	1	33	16*	16.50	-	-	-	-
A.J.Pycroft	6	6	0	71	21	11.83	-	-	3	-
A.H.Shah	3	3	0	26	16	8.66	-	-	1	-
J.G.Heron	6	6	0	50	18	8.33	-	-	1	-
A.J.Traicos	6	4	1	25	19	8.33	-	-	2	-
P.W.E.Rawson	6	4	1	24	19	8.00	-	-	2	-
V.R.Hogg	2	1	1	7	7*	-	-	-	-	-

Zimbabwe *bowling*

A.J.Traicos	68	6	202	4	50.50	2-28	-	2.97
V.R.Hogg	15	4	49	0	-	-	-	3.26
P.W.E.Rawson	62.1	10	239	8	29.87	3-47	-	3.84
I.P.Butchart	50	4	213	3	71.00	2-52	-	4.26
D.A.G.Fletcher	50.1	5	221	7	31.57	4-42	-	4.40
K.M.Curran	58.2	3	274	5	54.80	3-65	-	4.69
A.H.Shah	7.3	0	40	1	40.00	1-17	-	5.33

**Left: Zimbabwe captain Duncan Fletcher scored 191 runs
to top his team's averages, as well as taking seven wickets**

1987

THE RELIANCE CUP

In India and Pakistan

ALLAN BORDER TOOK HIS TEAM
TO THE FOURTH WORLD CUP AS
NO-HOPERS. ENGLAND LOOKED
STRONG, WHILE THE WEST INDIES
WERE PROVEN WINNERS. BUT THE
MILLIONS ON THE SUB-CONTINENT
WERE LOOKING NO FURTHER
THAN AN INDIA-PAKISTAN FINAL

Right: Allan Border gets carried away at Eden Gardens, Calcutta

BORDER SKIRMISHES AND AN AUSTRALIAN RENAISSANCE

The World Cup came to the sub-continent. Politicians hoped it would ease the tensions between India and Pakistan — and, despite stone-throwing crowds and huge security, it did. All the two cricket-mad nations wanted was a chance to fight it out in the Final…

India, the Cup-holders, and Imran's Pakistan team of unpredictable talents would reap a big advantage from playing on the sub-continent with its heat, its vast distances, its volatile crowds and its health hazards'

Right: A crossroads in Calcutta welcomes visitors to the '4th World Cricket Championship 87'. The World Cup theme was 'Cricket For Peace', represented by a cricketing dove (above)

A t the end of the 1983 World Cup in England, the International Cricket Conference had asked for tenders from countries wanting to stage the next competition. Although England had expressed a willingness to do it for a fourth time, there was a natural desire to move the tournament around as a true World Cup. Substantial financial guarantees to the participants decided the vote in favour of a joint entry from India, the holders, and Pakistan. The cricket world held its breath about the logistics of the event; the thousands of miles of travelling required would make this World Cup more than twice as long as its predecessors.

Delhi, at the end of its long summer, was still oppressively hot as the teams gathered there at the end of September before dispersing to their first matches. The format would be as in 1983: two groups of four, each playing the others twice to decide the semi-finalists. Due to the length of daylight, matches would be 50 overs a side. And for the first time, a World Cup would have 30-yard fielding circles. Four men plus bowler and wicketkeeper must be inside the circle.

The two home teams started as favourites. India, reigning World Cup champions, and Imran Khan's Pakistan team of

unpredictable talents would reap a big advantage from playing on the sub-continent with its heat, vast distances, volatile crowds and health hazards (though, ironically, one of the first players to miss a playing session with an upset stomach was Imran himself). The West Indies could never be discounted, though an attack relying heavily on Patrick Patterson was no match for 1983's Roberts-Marshall-Garner-Holding – and at this World Cup, unlike those in England, spin bowlers were expected to play a major role.

Mike Gatting's England were now confident tourists, having won three one-day tournaments the previous winter in Australia, though they had come without Ian Botham and David Gower. Allan Border's Australia looked unlikely to reach the semi-finals…

Group A, based in India, included the hosts along with Australia, New Zealand and Zimbabwe. Pakistan would mostly host group B, which included England, Sri Lanka and the West Indies. The dream of all cricket fans on the sub-continent was that India and Pakistan would top their groups, avoid each other in the semi-finals, and then meet for a cataclysmic confrontation in the Final.

Pakistan, it was, who opened proceedings on October 8 in

Hyderabad, where they batted first against Sri Lanka. Their score of 267 for seven was based on two innings: Rameez Raja, who opened with a solid 76, and Javed Miandad, whose 103 came off 100 balls. For a time it seemed that Sri Lanka, steered by Roshan Mahanama's 89, might pull off an unlikely win, but they were all out in the final over, 15 runs short.

Among the delirious home crowd was Pakistan's Prime Minister – whose absence from the National Assembly drew criticism from one member. But in this cricket-mad country, the MP knew his complaint would fall on deaf ears, as the Speaker, too, had been seen watching the match…

England and the West Indies were out of their Lahore hotel before dawn next day to travel in armed convoy the fifty-odd miles to Gujranwala. As the sun rose, it became a stifling day, but by the time it was high the West Indies, put in to bat, were on their way to a par score of 243 for seven.

Their last ten overs realised 92 runs thanks to the strokeplay of Gus Logie, Jeff Dujon and Roger Harper. Neil Foster took three wickets but Derek Pringle's ten overs went for 83.

England's innings always seemed to be off the pace. At 153 for six after 40 overs their task was surely impossible. They would need to keep scoring at nine an over. But Allan Lamb was still there and finding imaginative support from the tail. John Emburey scored 22 from 15 balls, followed by Phil DeFreitas with 23 from 21 balls. Thirty-five were needed off the last three overs with only two wickets standing.

Now Neil Foster was there to try to nurse an exhausted Lamb through. Lamb managed to take 15 off the 48th, bowled by Courtney Walsh. The 49th brought six runs; 13 were needed from the last over. Christopher Martin-Jenkins had a precarious perch in a lofty radio commentary box.

"Thirteen runs needed now. Lamb has done it before. Can he

**Left: Allan Border and
his team were written
off by most observers
before the World Cup**

do it again? He's 60 not out. Walsh bowls to him. Short. Lamb pulls it away towards the deep square leg boundary, but it's going up to midwicket and it's stopped. He's coming back for the second, the throw is on its way and there's a possibility of overthrows as it misses the stumps at this end, with Foster desperately racing to make his ground. It's two runs, Lamb has kept the strike. Eleven to win off five balls.

"A sort of milky sunlight now as the sun starts to set. In comes Walsh, a full toss – and it's four runs! Hit away off a thick outside edge, past the diving short third man. Lamb gave himself room. Now he and England need just seven off the last four."

Peter Roebuck: *"Courtney Walsh still reaching for those leg-stump yorkers. He might be better off just bowling normally."*

CMJ: *"Here comes Walsh. Bowls to him again. It's surely a wide. Down the leg side. It's going to be four byes! I would think it's four wides actually. And he's given four wides, quite rightly too. Four wides. The scoreboard has now lost count. Three to win.*

"Lamb 70 not out and Walsh tries to gather himself. He runs in again, he bowls to Lamb. Good length. Lamb hits it away. It's going up towards deep midwicket. It was a no-ball! They needn't run for this. And Walsh I'm afraid has rather lost his head. There are four balls to go and England need only two runs off them with two wickets standing. Foster however is now facing."

Peter Roebuck: *"I think Richards is doing the right thing. He's calling all of his men in, which is Viv Richards's only tactic."*

CMJ: *"One man back at fine leg, that's all. Foster comes down and slides it down past third man, and England have won! It's gone for four. England have won with three balls to go. They have more or less come back from the dead in this match."*

A more dead-than-alive dehydrated Allan Lamb had to be helped from the ground and then back on to the field to receive the Man of the Match award.

Conditions were no less steamy in Madras, where the holders, India, met Australia in the first Group A match. It turned out to be even closer than the thriller in Gujranwala. On this ground a year earlier, the two teams had fought out only the second tie in Test history. No one dreamed that this one-day game would be almost as close…

Put in to bat, the Australians got off to a superb start. David Boon and Geoff Marsh put on 110 for the first wicket, with Marsh going on to make 110 himself. Dean Jones made 37 from 35 balls – a score which was promoted

to 39 between innings when Kapil Dev agreed that one of his four boundaries had in fact cleared the boundary for his second six. It was to be a crucial alteration.

India set off at such a rate in pursuit of 271 to win that that change seemed academic. Krishnamachari Srikkanth and Navjot Sidhu each passed 70 at nearly a run a ball. Craig McDermott returned with renewed vigour to take four wickets, but by the 47th over India needed 15 to win from 24 balls with four wickets in hand. The match was at their mercy.

But two runouts made it tighter, and by the start of the last over the last pair were in, needing just six to win. They managed to get the target down to two from two balls – but last man Maninder Singh was bowled by Steve Waugh to give Australia victory by one run with one ball to spare. A mortified Kapil Dev admitted: "We should not have lost."

Next day, the other two teams in Group A started their campaign in the southern Indian city of Hyderabad. Zimbabwe put New Zealand in and, despite Martin Snedden's 64 and Martin Crowe's 72, kept them to 242 for seven. Their reply depended almost entirely on David Houghton. At 104 for seven his lone cause seemed lost, but he was joined in a stand of 117 by Ian Butchart. It ended in the 47th over, with Houghton out for 141 from only 137 balls, with no fewer than six sixes and 13 fours. Twenty-two were still needed, and then six by the last pair off the final over. But the romantic dream was ended on the fourth ball when Butchart was run out in a chaotic mix-up and New Zealand were home by three runs.

After his heroic innings in the punishing conditions, Houghton said: "I don't know how much weight I lost during the day, but I needed to diet and that was the quickest way of doing it. I felt dizzy, dehydrated, and had cramps in both legs. I wanted to drink gallons – and when I did get off the field I couldn't walk for an hour."

The threat of terrorism brought a force of commandos to Pakistan's game against England at Rawalpindi, where five people had died the month before in a bomb attack at the bus station blamed on Afghanistan. But it was the weather that delayed the match until the following morning, when England put Pakistan in and restricted them to 239 for seven, Javed Miandad showing his astonishment at the rare experience of being given out lbw in his own country.

England set off in pursuit of their target in convincing

'A more dead-than-alive dehydrated Allan Lamb had to be helped from the ground at Gujranwala and then back on to the field to receive the Man of the Match award.'

THE BUSINESS

The fourth World Cup was sponsored by Reliance Industries, an Indian textile company, who paid £1.3 million. Prize money was increased by 50 per cent. The Final was watched by 70,000 people.

lost by 191 runs. Their captain Duleep Mendis described Richards' apocalyptic effort as like "penance for past sins".

In Madras, Australia were put in by Zimbabwe, and had visions of 1983 when they were 20 for two. Border had a 'life' early on, before restoring the situation with a century partnership with Geoff Marsh. Even so, 235 for nine was less than they would have wanted. With accurate seam bowling, though, it proved enough, Simon O'Donnell's four wickets owing much to the meanness of McDermott, Reid and Waugh. Australia in the end won comfortably by 96 runs.

New Zealand had moved further south to Bangalore, where they put India in to bat and quickly ran out both openers. But, from 21 for three, Sidhu made a swift 75 and then Kapil Dev hit 72 not out from only 58 balls. New Zealand, chasing 253, ended 16 runs short.

Back in Pakistan, the West Indies had a cliff-hanger of a match against their hosts in Lahore. Deciding to bat first, they were bowled out in the 50th over for 216, with Imran finishing off the tail for figures of four for 37.

That slender total looked enough when Pakistan slumped to 110 for five with only 15 overs to go. Imran and wicket-keeper Salim Yousuf dragged Pakistan back into it, putting on 73 in 11 overs. But Courtney Walsh removed them both, and the 49th over seemed to seal it when Patterson had Wasim Akram caught and Tauseef Ahmed was run out.

Abdul Qadir and Saleem Jaffer, Pakistan's last pair, would need 14 off the last over, to be bowled by Walsh. Four came of the first three balls, but then Qadir set the 50,000 crowd alight with straight-driven six. Qadir got another two – two runs were now needed off the last ball.

Then came a true moment of sportsmanship. As Walsh was running in to bowl, he found Jaffer backing up too far. He could have run him out and won the match. Instead, he stopped and held the ball over the stumps as a warning while the sheepish Jaffer crept back to his ground. Walsh's generosity was not rewarded. Qadir hit the next ball for a scrambled two and Pakistan were in by one wicket off the last ball.

Such excitement could not be matched by Sri Lanka and England up on the North West Frontier, in Peshawar. Gooch, Gatting and Lamb helped themselves to runs and, after rain, Sri Lanka fell well short of a revised target of 267 off 45 overs.

Group B was now at its halfway point, with Pakistan top

style, Graham Gooch and Chris Broad putting on 52 in 14 overs. But after Gooch was out, Tim Robinson became becalmed. Ninety-nine were needed off the last 15 overs, but there were eight wickets in hand. Sixty-five runs came off 11 overs for the loss of only two more wickets, but then panic seemed to set in. Three runouts and the wiles of Abdul Qadir – who took two wickets in an eventful over in which he was stung by a wasp – brought the last six wickets crashing for 15 in 16 balls. Pakistan won by 18 runs, with eight balls to go.

Meanwhile Viv Richards was blasting the Sri Lankan bowlers to all parts of Karachi. He made 181 from 125 balls and hit six sixes and 16 fours – the highest score in a World Cup, overshadowing Desmond Haynes' 105 from 109 balls in the same innings. Facing a total of 360 for four, Sri Lanka

Left: Heavy rain in Rawalpindi turned the outfield into a mudbath. Play between England and Pakistan was delayed until the next day, when England's batsmen managed to get trapped in a morass of their own making

'Sri Lanka captain
Duleep Mendis
described Richards'
apocalyptic effort
as like "penance
for past sins".'

with three wins out of three, England second with two and the West Indies having beaten only Sri Lanka.

Group A reached halfway with India overwhelming Zimbabwe at Bombay, where the medium pace of Prabhakar (4-19) and left-arm spin of Maninder Singh (3-21) proved decisive. Kapil Dev boldly declared: "I am now confident of making the semi-finals. And we shall continue to play with three spinners."

Australia met New Zealand at Indore in a tight contest, reduced by rain to 30 overs a side. Australia made 199 thanks to a swashbuckling 87 in as many balls by David Boon. John Wright and Ken Rutherford gave New Zealand a blistering start with 83 in 12 overs, but Australia kept chipping away and New Zealand were three runs short with one wicket left at the end.

The second close win for Australia put them top of Group A at halfway with three victories. India had two wins and New Zealand one, over Zimbabwe.

England now had to play Pakistan again, in Karachi. A third-wicket stand of 135 between Bill Athey (86) and Mike Gatting (60) should have led to a bigger total, but Imran and Qadir, those thorns in England's flesh, kept them to 244 for nine. A century by Ramiz Raja, and Salim Malik's 88, made something of a mockery of that. A stone-throwing crowd stopped play temporarily, but Pakistan cruised in with seven wickets to spare.

Athey's dismissal had come when he was bowled by Tauseef Ahmed while attempting a reverse sweep – a stroke invented by Gatting which had entered the repertoires of several England players. Athey's folly sparked a chorus of disapproval, but England's players showed no sign of giving the stroke up...

The rest of England's group matches would be in India, where the West Indies and Sri Lanka were meeting in Kanpur. Despite their previous experience, Sri Lanka put the opposition in, but this was not a pitch for strokeplay

India's Maninder Singh skittled Australia

and Simmons had to bat for most of the innings to make his 89 out of 236 for eight. The innings of the match was played by Arjuna Ranatunga, but his 86 not out from 92 balls was not enough. Sri Lanka finished 25 runs short.

Australia and India were to meet next in Delhi. For a magic night, one of the Indian capital's largest hotels played host to most of the teams. England and the West Indies were passing through en route to Jaipur, Sri Lanka were heading back to Pakistan, and contact was made between many cricket folk who had thus far been separated by the dusty miles of the great sub-continent.

India, desperate to avoid coming second in the group and thus going against the pre-ordained script by having to meet Pakistan in Pakistan for the semi-final, needed to beat Australia. A total of 289 gave them every chance, with Gavaskar, Sidhu, Vengsarkar and Azharuddin all passing 50.

Marsh and Boon began the chase in fine form, but India's secret weapon was the two slow left-arm bowlers, Ravi Shastri and Maninder Singh, and they accounted for both the openers. Then they stifled the rest of the Australian batting, Maninder taking three for 34, so that they were all out in the penultimate over for 233. India had improved their chance of reaching that all-important Bombay semi-final.

In Calcutta next day, three Zimbabwean batsmen, Arnott, Houghton and Pycroft, made half-centuries in their total of 227 for five against New Zealand. But the Crowe brothers ensured there would be no shock result. Martin made 58, Jeff followed with 88 and they won by seven wickets with two-and-a-half overs to spare.

This was the first match at Eden Gardens, where the Final was to be held, and it was still being prepared for business. The new electronic scoreboard was not working, and Jeff Crowe complained: "It was difficult to know what was going on out there." Yet 50,000 people watched the game,

Left: The pink city of
Jaipur witnessed a
thrilling match
between England
and the West Indies

'The lack of accuracy
the West Indian
bowlers displayed
against England was
so unexpected that it
was difficult to bear.'
CLIVE LLOYD
writing in *The Times* of India

'Some of our players
who have been around
for a few years and
enjoyed the good
times are finding it
very hard to lose.
They are depressed
because they are not
used to it'
CLYDE WALCOTT
West Indies manager

and an impressed Clive Lloyd declared that Eden Gardens was now the best cricket stadium in the world.

Pakistan maintained their unbeaten run with a 113-run win over Sri Lanka in Faisalabad, where Salim Malik made a hundred and Abdul Qadir took three wickets.

On a blisteringly hot day at the pink city of Jaipur, England and the West Indies met in a match that was vital for both teams' prospects. Richards put England in, but found Graham Gooch in a mood to plunder his wayward bowlers. England posted 150 in the 30th over. It was Richards himself, with his off-spin, who put the brake on. Patterson returned to the attack to have Gooch caught for 92 but, with a generous donation of 22 in wides, England still reached 269 for seven.

Enter the master blaster, Viv Richards – and today he was in blasting mood. I was fortunate enough to be watching the mayhem from the BBC commentary box:

"Now Viv Richards down there, a daunting prospect to bowl at for Hemmings as he comes in now – and Richards swings him over square leg for six! An enormous six into the second tier of the grandstand away to our right. A huge blow and he picked it up so lazily and easily. They're looking for the ball above those dark blue shamianas there. And he's now 42. That's his second six and it's 135 for two in the 29th over.

"Hemmings bowls again and Richards again swings – and he's going to be caught, is he? No, it goes over the head of DeFreitas at backward square leg – six more! Again the two Antiguans punch gloves above their heads, and that takes Richards up to 48. He's catching Richardson all the time and 141 for two is the West Indies score in the 29th over. Two sixes of successive balls. Both in the square leg area."

England's total was starting to look distinctly vulnerable.

· GROUP A ·

OCTOBER 9 AT MADRAS
Australia 270 for 6 (G R Marsh 110) **beat India** 269
(N S Sidhu 73, K Srikkanth 70, McDermott 4-56)
by one run

OCTOBER 10 AT HYDERABAD
New Zealand 242 for 7 (M D Crowe 72,
M C Snedden 64) **beat Zimbabwe** 239
(D L Houghton 141, I P Butchart 54) **by three runs**

OCTOBER 13 AT MADRAS
Australia 235 for 9 (A R Border 67, G R Marsh 62)
beat Zimbabwe 139 (O'Donnell 4-39) **by 96 runs**

OCTOBER 14 AT BANGALORE
India 252 for 7 (N S Sidhu 75, Kapil Dev 72*,
Patel 3-36) **beat New Zealand** 236 for 8
(K R Rutherford 75, A H Jones 64) **by 16 runs**

OCTOBER 17 AT BOMBAY
India 136 for 2 **beat Zimbabwe** 135 (A J Pycroft 61,
Prabhakar 4-19, Maninder 3-21) **by eight wickets**

OCTOBER 18 AT INDORE
Australia 199 for 4 (D C Boon 87, D M Jones 52)
beat New Zealand 196 for 9 (M D Crowe 58)
by three runs

OCTOBER 22 AT NEW DELHI
India 289 for 6 (D B Vengsarkar 63, S M Gavaskar 61,
M Azharuddin 54*, N S Sidhu 51, McDermott 3-61)
beat Australia 233 (D C Boon 62, Azharuddin 3-19,
Maninder 3-34) **by 56 runs**

OCTOBER 23 AT CALCUTTA
New Zealand 228 for 6 (J J Crowe 88*, M D Crowe
58) **beat Zimbabwe** 227 for 5 (A J Pycroft 52*,
K J Arnott 51, D L Houghton 50) **by four wickets**

OCTOBER 26 AT AHMEDABAD
India 194 for 3 (N S Sidhu 55, S M Gavaskar 50)
beat Zimbabwe 191 for 7 (K J Arnott 60)
by seven wickets

OCTOBER 27 AT CHANDIGARH
Australia 251 for 8 (G R Marsh 126*, D M Jones 56)
beat New Zealand 234 (J G Wright 61) **by 17 runs**

OCTOBER 30 AT CUTTACK
Australia 266 for 5 (D C Boon 93, D M Jones 58)
beat Zimbabwe 196 for 6 **by 70 runs**

OCTOBER 31 AT NAGPUR
India 224 for 1 (S M Gavaskar 103*, K Srikkanth 75)
beat New Zealand 221 for 9 (Sharma 3-51)
by nine wickets

But cometh the hour, cometh the man.

"Hemmings comes in again to bowl to Richards, who makes room – and he's bowled! Hemmings may well raise his hand above his head in triumph. That is a tremendous blow for England. Viv Richards is out for 51. The end of a treat for unpartisan spectators and a tremendous blow for the England camp."

And Hemmings was not finished.

"It's going to be Gladstone Small to bowl the 44th over of the West Indies innings. Fifty-one needed to win, 219 for six is the West Indies score. And he comes in to bowl to Harper now. Harper dabs down on that one into the ground. A throw – he's run out, Harper, at the far end! A throw from Eddie Hemmings, who can do no wrong at the moment."

Richie Richardson was caught behind off Small for 93 and the West Indies were all out in the 49th over for 235. After being in every World Cup Final so far, they would have to beat Pakistan in Karachi and hope that England, in their final group match, lost to Sri Lanka. But even their staunchest supporters could not see that happening.

Hasib Ahsan, the manager of their next opponents, Pakistan, gleefully observed: "It takes a very long time to build a good team but it can take only five minutes for that team to fall apart. The West Indies disintegrated against England, didn't they?"

The England-Sri Lanka match was at

FINAL GROUP A TABLE

	P	W	L	Pts	Run-rate*
India	6	5	1	20	5.39
Australia	6	5	1	20	5.19
New Zealand	6	2	4	8	4.88
Zimbabwe	6	0	6	0	3.76

*Run-rate was the average number of runs per over

Pune, formerly known as Poona, in the hills inland from Bombay. Sri Lanka had cottoned on to the fact that teams batting first tended to win in this World Cup and, on winning the toss, chose to do just that. Roy Dias, after being dropped behind the wicket on one – one of four lapses in the field – went on to make 80 as Sri Lanka reached 218 for seven.

An opening stand of 123 inside the first half of England's reply largely put the issue beyond doubt. Gooch, having dislocated a finger in missing a catch early in the day, made 61, and Robinson 55 as England won by eight wickets with eight overs to spare.

England could travel the short distance back to Bombay knowing that they would be playing their semi-final there in six days' time.

They had needed that win, because in Karachi the West Indies, led by the two Antiguans, Richardson and Richards, had a good win over Pakistan. Richardson made 110, Richards 67, in a score of 258 for seven. Pakistan finished 28 runs adrift.

Once more, the game was interrupted by stone-throwing, and police fired tear gas into the crowd. As the home team subsided to defeat, the mood grew angrier – even though Pakistan were already through to the semi-finals, in which they would meet the runners-up of Group A in Lahore.

That would be either Australia or India, who were level on points and were both eager to ensure a berth in the Bombay semi by winning the group. Australia were making a strong claim for that honour at Cuttack, near India's eastern coast.

On a sub-standard pitch, David Boon's 93 led them to a total of 266 for five against Zimbabwe. Worries about the pitch were endorsed early in Zimbabwe's reply, when Andy Waller was hit in the face by a sharply rising ball from Bruce Reid. Scoring at the required rate proved impossible against the Australian attack, though Waller did return to make a brave 38. Zimbabwe ran out of overs still 70 runs behind.

So, in Nagpur next day, India knew that to take their coveted place in Bombay, they would have not only to beat New Zealand, but to score their runs at five-and-a-quarter an over. New Zealand won the toss and batted. Their total of 221 for nine might have been more, had not Chetan Sharma, in the 42nd over, taken the first ever World Cup hat-trick. Ken Rutherford, Ian Smith and Ewan Chatfield were the victims – all bowled – and it ended New Zealand's resistance.

India knew they had to get 222 in 42 overs and two balls. The determination not to have to go to Lahore brought out the very best in Sunil Gavaskar. Krishnamachari Srikkanth was no stranger to outrageous hitting, but Gavaskar did not shrink in comparison. Off four successive balls from Chatfield he hit two sixes and then two fours. The pair brought up the 100 in the 14th over and Srikkanth's 75 came off only 58 balls, with nine fours and three sixes.

Gavaskar, the man who had battled through 60 overs for 36 not out in the first World Cup, reached his first one-day hundred in 85 balls. He was 103 not out when India won in the 33rd over. They had achieved their run-rate target with over ten overs in hand.

The Australians, waiting in Delhi to see where they were going for their semi-final, set off for Lahore, while the relieved Indians knew that they would be in front of a noisy home crowd in Bombay.

West Indian Richie Richardson went out of the World Cup fighting, with scores of 93 and 110

FINAL GROUP B TABLE

	P	W	L	Pts	Run-rate*
Pakistan	6	5	1	20	5.01
England	6	4	2	16	5.12
West Indies	6	3	3	12	5.16
Sri Lanka	6	0	6	0	4.04

*Run-rate was the average number of runs per over

· GROUP B ·

OCTOBER 8 AT HYDERABAD
Pakistan 267 for 6 (Javed Miandad 103, Ramiz Raja 76) **beat Sri Lanka** 252 (R S Mahanama 89) **by 15 runs**

OCTOBER 9 AT GUJRANWALA
England 246 for 8 (A J Lamb 67*, Hooper 3-42) **beat West Indies** 243 for 7 (R B Richardson 53, Foster 3-53) **by two wickets**

OCTOBER 12, 13 AT RAWALPINDI
Pakistan 239 for 7 (Salim Malik 65, Ijaz Ahmed 59, DeFreitas 3-42) **beat England** 221 (Qadir 4-31) **by 18 runs**

OCTOBER 13 AT KARACHI
West Indies 360 for 4 (I V A Richards 181, D L Haynes 105) **beat Sri Lanka** 169 for 4 (A Ranatunga 52*) **by 191 runs**

OCTOBER 16 AT LAHORE
Pakistan 217 for 9 (Salim Yousuf 56, Walsh 4-40) **beat West Indies** 216 (I V A Richards 51, P V Simmons 50, Imran 4-37) **by one wicket**

OCTOBER 17 AT PESHAWAR
England 296 for 4 (G A Gooch 84, A J Lamb 76, M W Gatting 58) **beat Sri Lanka** 158 for 8 **by 109 runs**

OCTOBER 20 AT KARACHI
Pakistan 247 for 3 (Ramiz Raja 113, Salim Malik 88) **beat England** 244 for 9 (C W J Athey 86, M W Gatting 60, Imran 4-37, Qadir 3-31) **by seven wickets**

OCTOBER 21 AT KANPUR
West Indies 236 for 8 (P V Simmons 89, A L Logie 65*, Ratnayeke 3-41) **beat Sri Lanka** 211 for 8 (A Ranatunga 86*, Patterson 3-31) **by 25 runs**

OCTOBER 25 AT FAISALABAD
Pakistan 297 for 7 (Salim Malik 100) **beat Sri Lanka** 184 for 8 (L R D Mendis 58, A Ranatunga 50, Qadir 3-40) **by 113 runs**

OCTOBER 26 AT JAIPUR
England 269 for 5 (G A Gooch 92, Patterson 3-56) **beat West Indies** 235 (R B Richardson 93, I V A Richards 51, DeFreitas 3-28) **by 34 runs**

OCTOBER 30 AT PUNE
England 219 for 2 (G A Gooch 61, R T Robinson 55) **beat Sri Lanka** 218 for 7 (R L Dias 80, Hemmings 3-57) **by eight wickets**

OCTOBER 30 AT KARACHI
West Indies 258 for 7 (R B Richardson 110, I V A Richards 67, Wasim 3-45, Imran 3-57) **beat Pakistan** 230 for 9 (Ramiz Raja 70, Patterson 3-34, Benjamin 3-69) **by 28 runs**

1987
THE LAHORE
·SEMI-FINAL·

Imran Khan had vowed that the semi-final against Australia would be his last game on home soil before retiring later in the year. On the eve of the most emotional game of his life, he admitted that his team had room for improvement: "We must do something about our fielding; too many dropped catches, too many runs given away." But he added: "Our bowling is the best in the competition. Qadir is our trump card – the only aggressive spinner left in cricket. Batsmen are now scared to play an attacking shot against him."

Australia coach Bobby Simpson responded: "We Australians were brought up on leg spinners." He was happy to acknowledge that his team were the underdogs, pointing out what a burden of expectation that put on Pakistan. On November 4, at the Gaddafi Stadium, Allan Border won the toss and decided to bat.

It was a solid performance by the Australian top six. The openers, Geoff Marsh and David Boon, put on 73 in 18 overs, before Marsh was run out by Salim Malik, throwing with only one stump to aim at. Boon was joined by Dean Jones and they added another 82 together.

Javed Miandad had taken over as wicketkeeper when Salim Yousuf took a blow in the face, and he now got a stumping – Boon out for 65, off Salim Malik's bowling. Jones followed next over for 38. The innings was in the balance, but they had provided the platform for an assault by the likes of Mike Veletta and Steve Waugh, though Imran prevented things getting too out of hand with three wickets at the end. In this competition, however, 267 for eight ought to be a winning score.

It certainly looked that way when Pakistan slumped to 38 for three in the 11th over of their reply, but over the next 26 overs the contrasting styles and characters of Javed and Imran pulled Pakistan back into the match with a stand of 112. But the asking rate was over seven-and-a-half an over.

The turning point came when Imran was caught behind off the part-time bowling of Border for 58. But Miandad kept his side's hopes alive until, in the 44th over, he was bowled playing an extravagant shot at Reid for 70. McDermott was now let loose on the tail, and the dénouement was described for radio listeners by Christopher Martin-Jenkins:

"So just one ball to come of this penultimate over from the red-haired bull from Brisbane, Craig McDermott. Nineteen runs still required. McDermott bowls to Tauseef Ahmed and he just jabs it – and he's caught behind! It's all over. Australia have won by 18 runs. McDermott throws his hands in the air. He's embraced by David Boon. They have got to the Final, upsetting the odds against Pakistan in their own back yard. 267 for eight their score. Pakistan in reply all out for 249."

Craig McDermott, with five for 44, was named Man of the Match.

Australia were in the Final and Allan Border pugnaciously attributed their success to the way the team had been talked down. "There weren't too many people who gave us any chance. In an odd way that has been a spur for us. A lot of discussion at our team meetings has centred on the fact that everyone has written us off.

"I have kept repeating it to the players, hoping that

Left: Dean jones is bowled by Tauseef Ahmed for 38

Salim Malik (above) was out for 25, but Javed Miandad made the game's top score to revive Pakistan's hopes

> 'Imran, meanwhile, went off into retirement with just one nagging doubt in his mind. Maybe he could have one more crack at winning the World Cup…'

it would make them more determined to prove people wrong.

"When Zaheer Abbas, the former Pakistan captain, called us a bunch of club cricketers, I knew we would be sparking today. I brought myself on to bowl simply to try to keep things tight. Getting Imran's wicket was a pleasant surprise."

Imran, meanwhile, went off into retirement with just one nagging doubt in his mind. Maybe he could have one more crack at winning the World Cup…

· SEMI-FINAL ·
LAHORE • NOVEMBER 4

AUSTRALIA
won the toss

G R Marsh run out	31
D C Boon st Miandad b Malik	65
D M Jones b Tauseef	38
*A R Border run out	18
M R J Veletta b Imran	48
S R Waugh not out	32
S P O'Donnell run out	0
†G C Dyer b Imran	0
C J McDermott b Imran	1
T B A May not out	0
Extras (B 1, l-b 19, w 13, n-b 1)	34
Total (50 Overs, for 8 wickets)	**267**

Did not bat: B A Reid

Fall of wickets: 1/73 2/155 3/155 4/215 5/236 6/236 7/241 8/249

Bowling: Imran 10-1-36-3; Jaffer 6-0-57-0; Wasim 10-0-54-0; Qadir 10-0-39-0; Tauseef 10-1-39-1; Malik 4-0-22-1.

PAKISTAN

Ramiz Raja run out	1
Mansoor Akhtar b McDermott	9
Salim Malik c McDermott b Waugh	25
Javed Miandad b Reid	70
*Imran Khan c Dyer b Border	58
Wasim Akram b McDermott	20
Ijaz Ahmed c Jones b Reid	8
†Salim Yousuf c Dyer b McDermott	21
Abdul Qadir not out	20
Saleem Jaffer c Dyer b McDermott	0
Tauseef Ahmed c Dyer b McDermott	1
Extras (L-b 6, w 10)	16
Total (49 Overs)	**249**

Fall of wickets: 1/2 2/37 3/38 4/150 5/177 6/192 7/212 8/236 9/247

Bowling: McDermott 10-0-44-5; Reid 10-2-41-2; Waugh 9-1-51-1; O'Donnell 10-1-45-0; May 6-0-36-0; Border 4-0-26-1.

Umpires: H D Bird and D R Shepherd

Man of the Match: Craig McDermott

AUSTRALIA
won by 18 runs

1987 · THE BOMBAY SEMI-FINAL ·

Graham Gooch sweeps yet again during one of the most remarkable innings in a World Cup

Allan Lamb feels the heat during his rapid 32

Australia's opponents were to be decided next day in Bombay. Like Australia, whose victory against popular expectation was quite heartening for them, England knew they were supposed just to turn up for the home side to beat them. Much was made beforehand of the restricting power of the two Indian slow left-armers, Ravi Shastri and Maninder Singh, but it was in the hope of early success from seam and swing that Kapil Dev put England in.

It was Maninder, though, who made the breakthrough, having Robinson stumped for 13. The dismissal of Athey by Chetan Sharma brought in Mike Gatting at 79 for two. With Graham Gooch he added 117 in 19 overs, both men taking on the two slow left-armers by sweeping almost every ball through the leg side – a bewildering tactic to which the Indians had no answer. Gatting was bowled by Maninder in the 41st over for 56. Henry Blofeld was commentating as Gooch neared his landmark:

"Here is Kapil Dev. In now, bowls to Gooch – and there it is!

How we swept into the World Cup Final

THE 1987 WORLD CUP SEMI-FINAL • INDIA v ENGLAND

The local nets bowler wondered why England's top batsman spent an entire morning practising his sweep.
Next day, the world found out…

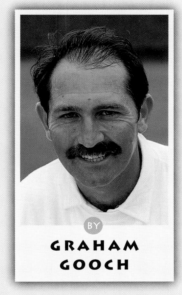

BY

**GRAHAM
GOOCH**

'The strange thing was that Kapil Dev didn't change the field. He kept a deep cover throughout, and that man only fielded the ball once'

After our first game in the 1987 tournament against the West Indies, where we played the medium pacers, it became evident throughout the competition that most sides were playing two spinners, because the wickets were flat and bare and it was easier to control the game with a couple of spinners. We played Eddie Hemmings and John Emburey and India had the two slow left-armers, Ravi Shastri and Maninder Singh.

The pitch for the semi-final was a used wicket. It had quite a few holes in it and looked as if it might turn. So we weren't displeased that Kapil Dev put us in. We had watched their spinners bowl in previous matches and they had bowled to a set off-side field, so I had decided to adopt a plan of trying to sweep them because they had just four men on the on-side.

The day before, I had taken a couple of left-arm spinners aside in the nets and practised for an hour or so, just playing different variations of the sweep. There was the slog-sweep, which is the shot that goes for four or six over square leg, then there's the normal sweep for one and a little fine sweep maybe for two.

The strange think about my innings that day, as it progressed, is that Kapil Dev didn't really change his field at all. He kept a long off and a deep cover throughout the 20 overs that the left-armers bowled and the deep cover fielder, I think, only fielded the ball once.

When Mike Gatting came in he adopted a similar policy to mine

and they just kept bowling to the same field. It was a plan that was hatched and it's nice for once when it is successful. We put on 117 together, with Gatt reaching 56 before he was bowled trying to sweep a ball by Maninder from outside his off stump. Two overs later, I was caught by Srikkanth on the midwicket boundary for 115, and then Allan Lamb made 32 off 29 balls to take us over the 250.

The Indians had an attacking middle order, but they kept losing wickets and if you do that you lose continuity. The crucial wicket was when Kapil Dev went for a big six over midwicket and was caught by Gatt off Eddie Hemmings. They were all out 35 runs short.

Australia and ourselves upset the plan completely, because it was all geared to an India-Pakistan Final, but it wasn't to be. It wasn't the one the locals wanted, but we deserved to be in the Final, if I do say so myself, because we played some excellent cricket throughout. We had beaten the West Indies twice, and that first match in Gujranwala rates as the hottest day I've ever played on. It was like a cauldron and the 47 I scored must be the hardest forty I've ever made. That game set the tone for the whole competition for us.

We played very well and it's galling that in the three World Cups I played in, the one match when we were out of sorts was the Final.

• *Graham Gooch is now an England Test selector and was manager of the 1998/9 England tour of Australia*

'Eddie came back
after being whacked
around a bit.
He did us proud.'

MIKE GATTING
on Eddie Hemmings

He goes back, hammers it through the gap, down to Sidhu at long on. And Gooch has got his 100. The crowd comes to life all round the ground, standing clapping him. Gooch holds up his bat, the face pointing towards the England dressing room. The Indian players, led by Srikkanth, give him a nice round of applause. Well, it has been a marvellous innings. An heroic innings in this heat. It must have taken quite a toll of him. But he has shown himself to be absolutely at the top of his form once again."

Maninder Singh finally got Gooch's wicket in the 43rd over for 115, but by then Allan Lamb had embarked on a rapid innings of 32 to boost England past the 250 mark. After 50 overs they had made 254 for seven.

The early dismissal of Sunil Gavaskar, bowled by Phil DeFreitas, was a huge blow for India. Srikkanth and Sidhu, confidently expected by their supporters to take England's attack apart, were unable to break the shackles of accurate bowling. They added 51, but were followed by Azharuddin and Pandit, who did start to take the initiative at last against Hemmings. Neil Foster ended that by having Pandit lbw, which brought in a potential match-winner in Kapil Dev.

England celebrate after Eddie Hemmings, centre, bowls India's last man, Ravi Shastri

The firecrackers were going off in the enclosing stands as Kapil boosted the scoring rate and it began to look as if he might turn the tide.

Henry Blofeld: *"Hemmings again, in to Kapil Dev. He bowls. Kapil swings this away. It's high in the air. Gatting is underneath it there at deep midwicket – and catches it! He has held it, he throws the ball in the air, and England have got themselves back into the game at jolly nearly the last gasp."*

It was 168 for five and it was the beginning of the end for India. Eddie Hemmings had Mohammed Azharuddin lbw for 64 and added the wickets of Ravi Shasti and Chetan Sharma as India were all out in the 46th over

'Kapil Dev said gloomily of his conquerors: "Whatever they may be, they are a thoroughly professional side and they know their one-day cricket".'

for 219. England had won by 35 runs. Gooch was inevitably Man of the Match. Gatting called his innings "a wonderful achievement", but had praise for Hemmings as well: "Eddie came back after being whacked around a bit. He did us proud."

Kapil Dev said gloomily of his conquerors: "Whatever they may be, they are a thoroughly professional side and they know their one-day cricket."

There were riots on the streets of Calcutta in which 28 people were hurt as the Indians tried to exorcise their disbelief. Against all prediction – and the organisers' script – England would meet Australia in the Calcutta Final on November 8.

· SEMI-FINAL ·
BOMBAY • NOVEMBER 5

ENGLAND

G A Gooch c Srikkanth b Maninder	115
R T Robinson st More b Maninder	13
C W J Athey c More b Sharma	4
*M W Gatting b Maninder	56
A J Lamb not out	32
J E Emburey lbw b Kapil Dev	6
P A J DeFreitas b Kapil Dev	7
†P R Downton not out	1
Extras (B 1, l-b 18, w 1)	20
Total (*50 Overs, for 6 wickets*)	**254**

Did not bat: N A Foster, G C Small and E E Hemmings

Fall of wickets: 1/40 2/79 3/196 4/203 5/219 6/231

Bowling: Kapil Dev 10-1-38-2; Prabhakar 9-1-40-0; Maninder 10-0-54-3; Sharma 9-0-41-1; Shastri 10-0-49-0; Azharuddin 2-0-13-0.

INDIA
won the toss

K Srikkanth b Foster	31
S M Gavaskar b DeFreitas	4
N S Sidhu c Athey b Foster	22
M Azharuddin lbw b Hemmings	64
C S Pandit lbw b Foster	24
*Kapil Dev c Gatting b Hemmings	30
R J Shastri c Downton b Hemmings	21
†K S More c and b Emburey	0
M Prabhakar c Downton b Small	4
Chetan Sharma c Lamb b Hemmings	0
Maninder Singh not out	0
Extras (B 1, l-b 9, w 6, n-b 3)	19
Total (*45.3 Overs*)	**219**

Fall of wickets: 1/7 2/58 3/73 4/121 5/168 6/204 7/205 8/218 9/219

Bowling: DeFreitas 7-0-37-1; Small 6-0-22-1; Emburey 10-1-35-1; Foster 10-0-47-3; Hemmings 9.3-1-52-4; Gooch 3-0-16-0.

Umpires: A R Crafter and S J Woodward

Man of the Match: Graham Gooch

ENGLAND
won by 35 runs

1987

EDEN GARDENS
·THE FINAL·

Eden Gardens was packed to the rafters. Right: David Boon on his way to 75. Playing as an opener, Boon was Australia's top scorer in the tournament

Eden Gardens was just as full for the encounter between two foreign teams as it would have been for the dream ticket of India v Pakistan, and the press attention and public discussion hardly less feverish. So it was into a cauldron of din that Mike Gatting and Allan Border ventured to toss. It was important to Australia to win that – and they did. Australia would bat.

They made a good start, too, with 52 runs coming from the first ten overs. Neil Foster applied the brake, bowling Geoff Marsh for 24. It was 75 for one in the 18th over. David Boon had enjoyed good form throughout the tournament and he and Dean Jones now added another 76.

After Eddie Hemmings had removed Jones for 33, Craig McDermott came in to have a swing at the bowling. He only lasted eight balls, but two of them went for four and he made 14 before Graham Gooch bowled him. With Hemmings having Boon caught behind for 75, England had an opening to restrict Australia, but now Border and Mike Veletta weighed in, adding 73 at better than a run a ball;

Border 31 and Veletta 45 not out at the end. Australia had made 253 for five. Not a huge total, but one that had not been passed by any team batting second in this competition.

If that was daunting, it was made more so by the loss of Tim Robinson, lbw to McDermott, in the first over. Bill Athey and Gooch took the score to 66 in the 18th over, when Gooch was lbw to Simon O'Donnell for 35. Gatting joined Athey and they added 69 over the next 13 overs. It

That reverse sweep was the turning point

THE 1987 WORLD CUP FINAL • AUSTRALIA v ENGLAND

The first Australian captain to lift the World Cup remembers
a day of disaster for his opposite number

BY

ALLAN BORDER

It was amazing in that tournament how we grew in stature following the first game against India in Madras, which we won by one run. That was the catalyst for a turnaround in our game. It gave us a bit of self-belief. We worked very hard. Bob Simpson, our coach, was a hard taskmaster in the basic areas, so we were a very good fielding side and did all the little things well.

We arrived in Calcutta for the Final on a bit of a high, having beaten Pakistan in Pakistan. I suppose we felt it was easier to be playing England than India, because of the local support. When we got there we found that most of the support was for Australia. If there were 100,000 in the ground, I reckon 98,000 were going for the Aussies. That support really was helpful.

With two teams going well, it's little things that turn a match. Two or three situations just went our way. It was an advantage to bat first, because the wickets started dry and flat and hard, so you had the best conditions. Then your quicker men would get a bit of low bounce, and your spinners got a little more purchase – which all made batting second more difficult. You're never totally satisfied with the number of runs you've scored, but I was quite happy with the 253.

Getting Goochie was a big wicket, and then there were a couple of crunch moments. There was a very, very close call on Bill Athey for the runout – remember this was before the days of the third umpire. Subsequently it has been shown that he was out, but in live action it would have been a tough call for the umpire. It went in our favour and that was a big call for us, because he was batting really well.

'The game was getting away from us and I had to do something different. I thought Gatting might just err on the side of caution if I brought myself on to bowl...'

Then of course there was the infamous reverse sweep of Mike Gatting. I have to cop the accolades for bringing myself on to bowl, but the game was getting away from us and I had to do something different and I thought to myself that he might just err on the side of caution if I came on to bowl. He might say to himself that you don't want to do anything silly against the old part-time spinner. But straight away, the way the field was set – because it's always a premeditated shot – he decided to play the reverse sweep. I was thinking, "I've got a stronger on-side field than off-side, so we've got to keep it in tight to him," and I dragged it way down the leg side. But Michael was committed in his reverse sweep, so he ended up catching the top edge on to his shoulder and it was caught by Greg Dyer, the wicketkeeper.

That was a big turning point, and from then on we were right in the box seat. But then Phil DeFreitas came in and hit those boundaries and I did start to panic a little bit, thinking, "A couple more big blows and England will be right back in it." But Steve Waugh was the ice-man in those days and Craig McDermott was a very good bowler to finish off the innings as well.

So the Australian resurgence came via the one-day game. Up to that time we hadn't really targeted one-day cricket. We were still struggling a little bit in the Test match arena, but we began to form a nucleus of good young players and you could just sense that the turnaround was happening.

• Allan Border is now an Australian Test selector and television commentator

'Well, that really was an absolute disaster. Gatting played the reverse sweep. He got the edge. It went on to the pad, up in the air, and was taken there by Dyer running round to square short leg.'

HENRY BLOFELD

Above: Greg Dyer is delighted at catching Mike Gatting off Allan Border's first ball. Right: The reverse sweep that, in many people's eyes, ended England's hopes of winning the World Cup

was 135 for two after 31 overs. England were in a comfortable position. In an uncomfortable position in the radio commentary box, Peter Roebuck was covering the change of commentators as Henry Blofeld squeezed into his place:

'Allan Border's bringing himself on to bowl. He's done this very effectively in one or two of the previous games when the scoring rate goes up above six an over. He reckons if he can bowl slow and straight, the batsmen will have to take risks, and he might pick up a couple of wickets. Because really there's nothing like wickets at this stage of an innings, just as it's bubbling towards its climax, to interrupt the flow of a team.

"He's bowling with naturally a very deeply set field. He hasn't contributed much with the bat, but here he can win the World Cup for Australia by taking a couple of wickets. He runs in to bowl to Mike Gatting. His first ball. He tries to sweep. It booms up above the wicket. It's skied and Gatting is out!"

Henry Blofeld: *"Well, that really was an absolute disaster. Gatting played the reverse sweep. He got the edge. It went on to the pad, up in the air, and was taken there by Dyer running round to square short leg. And Gatting is out in a way that, when you go for that shot, it looks terrible."*

Ironically, after the semi-final Gatting had rubbed salt into Kapil Dev's wounds by saying *he* had got out to an irresponsible shot. This really was a case of the biter bit.

But Allan Lamb was still there – and he had won matches for England from worse situations than this. Thirty-five more runs came before another decisive blow was struck.

Jack Bannister: *"Reid bowling to Athey. Athey looking to place that ball. Does it nicely. There are certainly two runs in it as Waugh chases from mid-on. Athey looking for a third and taking*

it, as Waugh misfielded. It will be tight. And a diving Athey has been given out! Run out on the third.

"Well, it was a misfield by Waugh. Athey saw it. Decided to take his chance. Waugh was up like a flash. A quick, hard, low return to the bowle. Reid had the bails off as Athey arrived in a flurry of bat and pads and diving. And in the end umpire Gupta decided that was that. So Bill Athey run out for 58."

Another 18 runs were added before Paul Downton became Border's second victim. The 200 came up in the 44th over with five wickets down. Forty-six runs were needed off the last five overs, but that became altogether a taller order when Lamb had his off stump knocked back by Steve Waugh in the 47th.

England's last hope was the hard-hitting Phil DeFreitas. In the 48th over he hit McDermott for a six and two fours. Maybe this match was going to have another twist as England's supporters began to believe that victory was possible after all. But Steve Waugh ended such fanciful notions by having DeFreitas caught in the deep in the penultimate over for 17 and that over cost only two.

Seventeen would be needed off the last over – an unlikely possibility. Henry Blofeld relayed the end of the match to an audience at opposite ends of the planet:

"And all of you listening round your radios wherever in Australia, you really can charge those glasses now. I give you my final permission. England are now 244 for eight. Therefore ten are needed off one ball. And even Professor Roebuck is scratching his head, thinking how that could be done.

"You've just never seen anything like this. All round the ground people standing up, yelling, just thrilled to be here, to have taken part. Bonfires are going in the stands at the far end,

Left: Allan Border, Australia's captain and driving force, proudly holds up the Reliance Cup

'You've just never seen anything like this. All round the ground people standing up, yelling, just thrilled to be here, to have taken part. Bonfires are going in the stands at the far end, flares are being lit. My goodness me!'

HENRY BLOFELD

flares are being lit. My goodness me! Here comes McDermott. The last ball. He bowls. Foster swings it away. It's going for four, I think, to backward point. Or will Veletta stop it? He stops it, they get two. That is the end! 246 for eight.

"Australia have won by seven runs. They jump into each other's arms, rip up the bails and stumps as souvenirs. Bobby Simpson is there and they're all hugging each other – and well they might. Australia have won the 1987 Cup Final in Calcutta."

After so many disappointments throughout the Eighties, Australia had triumphed and opened a new era of prolonged success.

· THE FINAL ·
CALCUTTA · 8 NOVEMBER

AUSTRALIA
won the toss

D C Boon c Downton b Hemmings	75
G R Marsh b Foster	24
D M Jones c Athey b Hemmings	33
C J McDermott b Gooch	14
*A R Border run out	31
M R J Veletta not out	45
S R Waugh not out	5
Extras (B 1, l-b 13, w 5, n-b 7)	26
Total (50 Overs, for 5 wickets)	**253**

Did not bat: S P O'Donnell, †G C Dyer, T B A May and B A Reid

Fall of wickets: 1/75 2/151 3/166 4/168 5/241

Bowling: De Freitas 6-1-34-0; Small 6-0-33-0; Foster 10-0-38-1; Hemmings 10-1-48-2; Emburey 10-0-44-0; Gooch 8-1-42-1.

ENGLAND

G A Gooch lbw b O'Donnell	35
R T Robinson lbw b McDermott	0
C W J Athey run out	58
*M W Gatting c Dyer b Border	41
A J Lamb b Waugh	45
†P R Downton c O'Donnell b Border	9
J E Emburey run out	10
P A J Defreitas c Reid b Waugh	17
N A Foster not out	7
G C Small not out	3
Extras (B 1, l-b 14, w 2, n-b 4)	21
Total (50 Overs, for 8 wickets)	**246**

Did not bat: E E Hemmings

Fall of wickets: 1/1 2/66 3/135 4/170 5/188 6/218 7/220 8/235

Bowling: McDermott 10-1-51-1; Reid 10-0-43-0; Waugh 9-0-37-2; O'Donnell 10-1-35-1; May 4-0-27-0; Border 7-0-38-2.

Umpires: R B Gupta and Mahboob Shah

Man of the Match: David Boon

AUSTRALIA
won by 7 runs

· 1987 STATISTICS ·

Matches now reduced to a maximum of 50 overs per side from 60

Highest totals

360 for 4   West Indies against Sri Lanka
297 for 7   Pakistan against Sri Lanka
296 for 4   England against Sri Lanka
289 for 6   India against Australia
270 for 6   Australia against India

Lowest totals (completed innings)

135   Zimbabwe against India
139   Zimbabwe against Australia
158 for 8   Sri Lanka against England
169 for 4   Sri Lanka against West Indies
184 for 8   Sri Lanka against Pakistan

Highest winning margins

9 wickets   India against New Zealand
8 wickets   India against Zimbabwe
8 wickets   England against Sri Lanka
191 runs   West Indies against Sri Lanka
113 runs   Pakistan against Sri Lanka
109 runs   England against Sri Lanka
96 runs   Australia against Zimbabwe
70 runs   Australia against Zimbabwe

Closest winning margins

1 wicket   Pakistan against West Indies
2 wickets   England against West Indies
1 run   Australia against India
3 runs   New Zealand against Zimbabwe
3 runs   Australia against New Zealand
7 runs   Australia against England
15 runs   Pakistan against Sri Lanka

Highest match aggregates

539 for 16   Australia v India
529 for 8   West Indies v Sri Lanka
522 for 16   India v Australia
519 for 16   Pakistan v Sri Lanka
516 for 18   Australia v Pakistan

Wins by non-Test nations   0

Centuries

181   I V A Richards, West Indies v Sri Lanka
142   D L Houghton, Zimbabwe v New Zealand
126 n.o.   G R Marsh, Australia v New Zealand
115   G A Gooch, England v India
113   Ramiz Raja, Pakistan v England
110   G R Marsh, Australia v India
110   R B Richardson, West Indies v Pakistan
105   D L Haynes, West Indies v Sri Lanka
103 n.o.   S M Gavaskar, India v New Zealand
103   Javed Miandad, Pakistan v Sri Lanka
100   Salim Malik, Pakistan v Sri Lanka

Highest Scores for each position

1   G R Marsh 126 n.o., Australia v New Zealand
2   G R Marsh, 110, Australia v India
3   D L Houghton, 142, Zimbabwe v New Zealand
4   I V A Richards, 181, West Indies v Sri Lanka
5   J J Crowe 88 n.o., New Zealand v Zimbabwe
6   M Azharuddin, 54 n.o. India v Australia
7   Kapil Dev, 72 n.o., India v New Zealand
8   I D S Smith 29, New Zealand v Zimbabwe
9   I P Butchart 54, Zimbabwe v New Zealand
10   W Watson 12 n.o. New Zealand v India
11   M P Jarvis, 8 n.o., Zimbabwe v India
     Saleem Jaffer, 8 n.o., Pakistan v West Indies

Most runs in tournament

471 at 58.87   G A Gooch, England
447 at 55.87   D C Boon, Australia
428 at 61.14   G R Marsh, Australia
391 at 65.16   I V A Richards, West Indies
354 at 50.57   M W Gatting, England

Most wickets

18 at 18.94   C J McDermott, Australia
17 at 13.05   Imran Khan, Pakistan
14 at 20.00   Maninder Singh, India
14 at 18.07   B P Patterson, West Indies
13 at 21.07   E E Hemmings, England

Most wickets in a match

5-44   C J McDermott, Australia v Pakistan
4-19   M Prabhakar, India v Zimbabwe
4-31   Abdul Qadir, Pakistan v England
4-37   Imran Khan, Pakistan v West Indies
4-37   Imran Khan, Pakistan v England
4-39   S P O'Donnell, Australia v Zimbabwe
4-40   C A Walsh, West Indies v Pakistan
4-52   E E Hemmings, England v India
4-56   C J McDermott, Australia v India

Hat-trick

C Sharma, India v New Zealand

Most dismissals by a wicketkeeper

11 (6ct, 5st)   K S More, India
11 (9ct, 2st)   G C Dyer, Australia
9 (8ct, 1st)   P R Downton, England
9 (9ct)   Salim Yousuf, Pakistan
5 (3ct, 2st)   D L Houghton, Zimbabwe

Most catches by an outfielder

5   Kapil Dev, India
4   D M Jones, Australia
4   S P O'Donnell, Australia
4   B A Reid, Australia
4   C W J Athey, England
4   M D Crowe, New Zealand
4   C L Hooper, West Indies

Australia *batting*

	M	I	NO	Runs	HS	Avge	100	50	Ct	St
G.R.Marsh	8	8	1	428	126*	61.14	2	1	2	-
D.C.Boon	8	8	0	447	93	55.87	-	5	2	-
S.R.Waugh	8	8	5	167	45	55.66	-	-	3	-
M.R.J.Veletta	4	4	1	136	48	45.33	-	-	-	-
D.M.Jones	8	8	1	314	58*	44.85	-	3	4	-
A.R.Border	8	8	0	183	67	22.87	-	1	1	-
G.C.Dyer	8	4	0	50	27	12.50	-	-	9	2
T.B.A.May	6	3	1	16	15	8.00	-	-	1	-
C.J.McDermott	8	6	0	34	14	5.66	-	-	2	-
T.M.Moody	3	3	1	10	8	5.00	-	-	1	-
S.P.O'Donnell	7	4	0	15	7	3.75	-	-	4	-
B.A.Reid	8	1	0	1	1	1.00	-	-	4	-
P.L.Taylor	2	1	1	17	17*	-	-	-	-	-
A.K.Zesers	2	2	2	10	8*	-	-	-	1	-

Australia *bowling*

	O	M	R	W	Avge	Best	5w	Econ
S.P.O'Donnell	60.4	6	261	9	29.00	4-39	-	4.30
B.A.Reid	68	7	303	6	50.50	2-38	-	4.45
S.R.Waugh	63.3	4	288	11	26.18	2-36	-	4.53
C.J.McDermott	73	3	341	18	18.94	5-44	1	4.67
T.B.A.May	44	1	213	4	53.25	2-29	-	4.84
A.K.Zesers	15	1	74	1	74.00	1-37	-	4.93
D.M.Jones	1	0	5	0	-	-	-	5.00
A.R.Border	32	0	166	6	27.66	2-27	-	5.18
P.L.Taylor	10	0	71	1	71.00	1-46	-	7.10
T.M.Moody	2	0	15	0	-	-	-	7.50
D.C.Boon	1	0	17	0	-	-	-	17.00

England *batting*

	M	I	NO	Runs	HS	Avge	100	50	Ct	St
A.J.Lamb	8	7	2	299	76	59.80	-	2	2	-
G.A.Gooch	8	8	0	471	115	58.87	1	3	2	-
C.W.J.Athey	6	6	2	211	86	52.75	-	2	4	-
M.W.Gatting	8	8	1	354	60	50.57	-	3	1	-
N.A.Foster	7	4	3	42	20*	42.00	-	-	1	-
B.C.Broad	3	3	0	67	36	22.33	-	-	1	-
R.T.Robinson	7	7	0	142	55	20.28	-	1	1	-
P.A.J.DeFreitas	8	6	2	79	23	19.75	-	-	-	-
J.E.Emburey	8	7	2	96	30*	19.20	-	-	3	-
D.R.Pringle	3	2	0	20	12	10.00	-	-	-	-
P.R.Downton	8	5	1	19	9	4.75	-	-	8	1
G.C.Small	8	3	1	3	3*	1.50	-	-	-	-
E.E.Hemmings	6	1	1	4	4*	-	-	-	2	-

England *bowling*

	O	M	R	W	Avge	Best	5w	Econ
A.J.Lamb	1	0	3	0	-	-	-	3.00
J.E.Emburey	79	4	295	6	49.16	2-26	-	3.73
P.A.J.DeFreitas	69.1	12	283	12	23.58	3-28	-	4.09
N.A.Foster	70	1	313	9	34.77	3-47	-	4.47
E.E.Hemmings	59.3	4	274	13	21.07	4-52	-	4.60
G.C.Small	68	2	331	6	55.16	2-47	-	4.86
G.A.Gooch	15	1	79	1	79.00	1-42	-	5.26
B.C.Broad	1	0	6	0	-	-	-	6.00
D.R.Pringle	24	0	148	1	148.00	1-11	-	6.16
C.W.J.Athey	1	0	10	0	-	-	-	10.00

'Let's make it a fun Final, Mike.' 'You have a bowl, Al, and give us all a laugh'

India *batting*

	M	I	NO	Runs	HS	Avge	100	50	Ct	St
M.Azharuddin	7	5	2	190	64	63.33	-	2	2	-
K.S.More	6	4	3	59	42*	59.00	-	-	6	5
D.B.Vengsarkar	6	5	2	171	63	57.00	-	1	1	-
N.S.Sidhu	7	5	0	276	75	55.20	-	4	3	-
Kapil Dev	7	5	2	152	72*	50.66	-	1	5	-
S.M.Gavaskar	7	7	1	300	103*	50.00	1	2	1	-
K.Srikkanth	7	7	0	248	75	35.42	-	2	2	-
C.S.Pandit	2	1	0	24	24	24.00	-	-	1	-
R.J.Shastri	7	4	0	63	22	15.75	-	-	2	-
M.Prabhakar	7	4	1	23	11*	7.66	-	-	1	-
Maninder Singh	7	2	1	4	4	4.00	-	-	1	-
R.M.H.Binny	1	1	0	0	0	0.00	-	-	-	-
C.Sharma	4	1	0	0	0	0.00	-	-	-	-
L.Sivaramakrishnan	2	0	0	0	0	-	-	-	1	-

India *bowling*

	O	M	R	W	Avge	Best	5w	Econ
M.Prabhakar	59	4	235	9	26.11	4-19	-	3.98
Maninder Singh	70	1	280	14	20.00	3-21	-	4.00
R.J.Shastri	68.2	1	274	7	39.14	2-45	-	4.00
L.Sivaramakrishnan	17	0	70	1	70.00	1-36	-	4.11
Kapil Dev	62	6	259	5	51.80	2-38	-	4.17
M.Azharuddin	23.5	0	109	5	21.80	3-19	-	4.57
C.Sharma	36.1	2	170	6	28.33	3-51	-	4.70
R.M.H.Binny	7	0	46	1	46.00	1-46	-	6.57

Pakistan *batting*

	M	I	NO	Runs	HS	Avge	100	50	Ct	St
Salim Malik	7	7	1	323	100	53.83	1	2	1	-
Ramiz Raja	7	7	0	349	113	49.85	1	2	-	-
Javed Miandad	7	7	1	274	103	45.66	1	1	1	1
Mudassar Nazar	2	1	0	40	40	40.00	-	-	3	-
Salim Yousuf	7	6	3	112	56	37.33	-	1	9	-
Imran Khan	7	6	0	147	58	24.50	-	1	1	-
Ijaz Ahmed	7	7	1	129	59	21.50	-	1	1	-
Mansoor Akhtar	6	6	0	99	33	16.50	-	-	2	-
Wasim Akram	7	6	0	85	39	14.16	-	-	1	-
Salim Jaffer	5	3	2	9	8*	9.00	-	-	-	-
Tausif Ahmed	6	2	0	1	1	0.50	-	-	1	-
Shoaib Mohammad	1	1	0	0	0	0.00	-	-	-	-
Abdul Qadir	7	4	4	56	20*	-	-	-	2	-
Manzoor Elahi	1	1	1	4	4*	-	-	-	-	-

Pakistan *bowling*

	O	M	R	W	Avge	Best	5w	Econ
Javed Miandad	3	0	5	1	5.00	1-5	-	1.66
Manzoor Elahi	9.4	0	32	1	32.00	1-32	-	3.31
Abdul Qadir	68	2	242	12	20.16	4-31	-	3.55
Tausif Ahmed	60	4	230	5	46.00	1-35	-	3.83
Imran Khan	49.5	6	222	17	13.05	4-37	-	4.45
Wasim Akram	63.2	1	295	7	42.14	3-45	-	4.65
Salim Malik	31	1	157	1	157.00	1-22	-	5.06
Salim Jaffer	39.4	0	210	5	42.00	3-30	-	5.29
Mansoor Akhtar	4	0	23	1	23.00	1-7	-	5.75
Mudassar Nazar	19	0	110	1	110.00	1-47	-	5.78

New Zealand *batting*

	M	I	NO	Runs	HS	Avge	100	50	Ct	St
K.R.Rutherford	5	5	0	204	75	40.80	-	1	2	-
M.D.Crowe	6	6	0	222	72	37.00	-	3	4	-
J.J.Crowe	6	6	1	180	88*	36.00	-	1	2	-
J.G.Wright	5	5	0	172	61	34.40	-	1	1	-
M.C.Snedden	6	6	0	157	64	26.16	-	1	-	-
W.Watson	6	4	3	24	12*	24.00	-	-	1	-
A.H.Jones	4	4	0	94	64	23.50	-	1	1	-
S.L.Boock	4	3	2	19	12	19.00	-	-	2	-
P.A.Horne	1	1	0	18	18	18.00	-	-	-	-
I.D.S.Smith	6	6	1	69	29	13.80	-	-	3	-
J.G.Bracewell	4	4	1	39	13*	13.00	-	-	-	-
D.N.Patel	6	6	0	58	40	9.66	-	-	1	-
E.J.Chatfield	6	3	2	5	5*	5.00	-	-	1	-
D.K.Morrison	1	0	0	0	0	-	-	-	-	-

New Zealand *bowling*

	O	M	R	W	Avge	Best	5w	Econ
E.J.Chatfield	50.1	8	231	5	46.20	2-52	-	4.60
S.L.Boock	32.4	2	157	4	39.25	2-42	-	4.80
W.Watson	53	3	270	7	38.57	2-36	-	5.09
D.N.Patel	43	1	222	4	55.50	3-36	-	5.16
M.C.Snedden	49	3	253	5	50.60	2-35	-	5.16
J.G.Bracewell	24	0	154	0	-	-	-	6.41
D.K.Morrison	10	0	69	0	-	-	-	6.90

Sri Lanka *batting*

	M	I	NO	Runs	HS	Avge	100	50	Ct	St
A.Ranatunga	5	5	2	252	86*	84.00	-	3	1	-
R.L.Dias	2	2	0	85	80	42.50	-	1	-	-
L.R.D.Mendis	6	6	1	136	58	27.20	-	1	-	-
A.P.Gurusinha	4	4	0	108	37	27.00	-	-	-	-
P.A.de Silva	6	6	2	101	42	25.25	-	-	2	-
R.S.Mahanama	6	6	0	134	89	22.33	-	1	2	-
R.S.Madugalle	5	4	0	85	30	21.25	-	-	1	-
D.S.B.P.Kuruppu	5	5	0	69	33	13.80	-	-	3	1
R.J.Ratnayake	3	3	1	27	14*	13.50	-	-	3	-
S.Jeganathan	3	3	1	24	20*	12.00	-	-	1	-
J.R.Ratnayeke	6	5	0	52	22	10.40	-	-	-	-
A.L.F.de Mel	3	2	0	0	0	0.00	-	-	-	-
S.D.Anurasiri	6	1	0	0	0	0.00	-	-	2	-
V.B.John	6	4	4	11	8*	-	-	-	1	-

Sri Lanka *bowling*

	O	M	R	W	Avge	Best	5w	Econ
S.Jeganathan	29	2	123	4	30.75	2-45	-	4.24
V.B.John	49	7	226	1	226.00	1-53	-	4.61
S.D.Anurasiri	55	1	271	4	67.75	1-44	-	4.92
P.A.de Silva	42	0	217	3	72.33	2-43	-	5.16
J.R.Ratnayeke	54	2	313	10	31.30	3-41	-	5.79
R.J.Ratnayake	25	0	163	4	40.75	2-64	-	6.52
A.Ranatunga	8	0	58	0	-	-	-	7.25
A.L.F.de Mel	24.2	0	184	1	184.00	1-97	-	7.56
A.P.Gurusinha	5	0	51	1	51.00	1-43	-	10.20

West Indies *batting*

	M	I	NO	Runs	HS	Avge	100	50	Ct	St
I.V.A.Richards	6	6	0	391	181	65.16	1	3	2	-
A.L.Logie	6	6	2	181	65*	45.25	-	1	1	-
R.B.Richardson	6	6	0	271	110	45.16	1	2	2	-
P.V.Simmons	4	4	0	170	89	42.50	-	2	-	-
D.L.Haynes	6	6	0	219	105	36.50	1	-	1	-
P.J.L.Dujon	6	5	1	59	46	14.75	-	-	4	-
E.A.E.Baptiste	1	1	0	14	14	14.00	-	-	1	-
C.L.Hooper	6	5	2	42	22	14.00	-	-	4	-
C.A.Best	2	2	0	23	18	11.50	-	-	1	-
C.A.Walsh	6	3	1	18	9*	9.00	-	-	1	-
R.A.Harper	6	6	1	37	24	7.40	-	-	2	-
W.K.M.Benjamin	5	4	1	15	8	5.00	-	-	-	-
B.P.Patterson	6	2	2	4	4*	-	-	-	1	-

West Indies *bowling*

	O	M	R	W	Avge	Best	5w	Econ
R.A.Harper	60	4	206	4	51.50	1-28	-	3.43
I.V.A.Richards	31	0	126	1	126.00	1-32	-	4.06
E.A.E.Baptiste	8	1	33	0	-	-	-	4.12
C.A.Walsh	55.3	6	229	9	25.44	4-40	-	4.12
C.L.Hooper	41	0	181	7	25.85	3-42	-	4.41
B.P.Patterson	56	2	253	14	18.07	3-31	-	4.51
W.K.M.Benjamin	44	2	218	4	54.50	3-69	-	4.95
R.B.Richardson	4	0	24	0	-	-	-	6.00

Zimbabwe *batting*

	M	I	NO	Runs	HS	Avge	100	50	Ct	St
D.L.Houghton	6	6	0	225	141	37.50	1	1	3	2
K.J.Arnott	4	3	0	112	60	37.33	-	2	1	-
A.J.Pycroft	6	6	1	174	61	34.80	-	2	-	-
P.W.E.Rawson	4	4	2	56	24*	28.00	-	-	2	-
A.C.Waller	6	6	1	125	39	25.00	-	-	1	-
E.A.Brandes	4	3	2	21	18*	21.00	-	-	2	-
I.P.Butchart	6	5	0	98	54	19.60	-	1	2	-
M.A.Meman	1	1	0	19	19	19.00	-	-	-	-
K.M.Curran	5	5	0	75	30	15.00	-	-	1	-
A.H.Shah	6	6	0	80	41	13.33	-	-	1	-
G.A.Paterson	4	4	0	24	16	6.00	-	-	2	-
R.D.Brown	3	3	0	17	13	5.66	-	-	3	-
A.J.Traicos	6	3	1	10	6	5.00	-	-	-	-
M.P.Jarvis	5	2	2	9	8*	-	-	-	1	-

Zimbabwe *bowling*

	O	M	R	W	Avge	Best	5w	Econ
A.J.Traicos	58	2	218	6	36.33	2-27	-	3.75
M.P.Jarvis	35.4	1	155	2	77.50	1-21	-	4.34
A.H.Shah	40	0	179	5	35.80	2-34	-	4.47
E.A.Brandes	33	4	153	2	76.50	2-44	-	4.63
K.M.Curran	26	0	124	4	31.00	2-29	-	4.76
M.A.Meman	6.5	0	34	0	-	-	-	4.97
P.W.E.Rawson	33	0	188	4	47.00	2-46	-	5.69
I.P.Butchart	35	1	222	3	74.00	2-59	-	6.34

1992

THE BENSON & HEDGES WORLD CUP

In Australia and New Zealand

AN ALL-WEATHER WORLD CUP,
PLAYED IN TROPICAL QUEENSLAND
AND CHILLY DUNEDIN, UNDER
THE FLOODLIGHTS OF MELBOURNE
AND GREY SKIES OF WELLINGTON.
BUT ON THE FIELD OF PLAY,
IT WAS ALL HOT STUFF

Right: Sunset over the Melbourne Cricket Ground during the Final

THE YEAR OF THE TIGER AND THE CROWE

What a series! South Africa's debut. India's wonderkids. New Zealand's secret weapon. Botham, Gooch, Imran and Javed – the old gun-slingers in the last chance saloon. Pinch-hitting! The rain rule that spread havoc. Oh yes, and Australia were favourites…

'The competition was launched by the two host nations playing in Auckland, following a noisy opening pageant with dancing girls, carnival floats, and toy trumpets for all 20,000 spectators'

It had been a New Zealand initiative to bring the World Cup to Australasia, after the success of the Rugby World Cup in the same two countries. This one was the biggest yet, because South Africa were back after 22 years in the wilderness as a result of the world's abhorrence of apartheid.

In October 1991 the World Cup organisers had had to rewrite the fixture list to accommodate them and in February 1992 there they were, lining up with Australia, England, India, New Zealand, Pakistan, Sri Lanka, West Indies and Zimbabwe for the publicity launch on Sydney Harbour. Their late inclusion caused comparatively little disruption because, for the first time, the lead-up to the semi-finals was not organised in groups. Each team would now play the other eight, with the top four qualifying. It would also be the first World Cup to include day/night games and the first played in coloured clothing.

Australia had had its usual Test and one-day international

Sydney Harbour welcomes the massed ranks of 126 cricketers

programme in full, making no concession to the fact that it was also staging a World Cup and thus pushing the tournament very late in the season. It might make the rules for rain interruption play more of a part. And those rules had changed. A recent example of how a simple calculation based on run-rate could produce an unfair target had convinced the Australian administrators that a different system was needed.

Little notice was taken of an early bizarre application of the rule they had come up with, when India, playing a warm-up game, had bowled a Victorian Country XI out for 156. They were cruising to their target at 129 for three in the 31st over, when it rained and they were declared to have lost under these new calculations. It was a rule they were to meet again soon.

The competition was launched by the two host nations playing in Auckland, following a noisy opening pageant with dancing girls, carnival floats, and toy trumpets for all 20,000 spectators. The World Cup-holders, Australia were regarded

Left: The first blow is struck in a match that transcended cricket – Pakistan celebrate as India's Krishnamachari Srikkanth departs

'Loiter at almost any of the main airports in Australia or New Zealand of a morning and you will see one or more of the teams coming or going. The teams' travel dress, in some cases, is indicative. England wear tracksuits, hardly elegant but at least a uniform, and a revealing one. Pakistan's players wear team blazers – but there, it seems, ends their obligation to conform. Few wear ties, some have floral shirts, and Imran yesterday sported jeans, sandals and no socks. They are in appearance as they are on the field, diverse and often disunited.'

ALAN LEE
writing in The Times

as the best one-day side in the world, while New Zealand had just been beaten soundly at home by England in Tests and one-dayers. It looked a foregone conclusion. But a New Zealander had just made headlines by winning their first ever Olympic skiing medal and if that could happen…

Matters seemed to be going as predicted when New Zealand were struggling at 53 for three, but Martin Crowe found support from Ken Rutherford in adding 118. Crowe, batting at his best, went on to 100 not out. Three dropped catches and the lack of the right plan to defend the peculiar shape of the boundaries at Eden Park helped the total to 248 for six. But that was surely well within the Aussies' range.

Lance Cairns opened the bowling for New Zealand, but then Crowe astonished onlookers and opposition alike by

summoning Dipak Patel, the off-spinner, to bowl the second over. On a pitch which had lost its early bounce, Patel, whose first seven overs cost only 19, and the phalanx of slow medium-pacers who followed him proved difficult to hit.

As the Australians tried to accelerate from a sound – if slow – start, the wickets started to tumble. Geoff Marsh had faced 53 balls for his 19 when he was the first to go. At 125 for five, the alarm bells started ringing. Steve Waugh tried valiantly to retrieve the situation, hitting three fours and a six in his 38, but in the 46th over, with more than ten an over needed, he was brilliantly caught and bowled by Gavin Larsen. When Bruce Reid skied Chris Harris in the 49th over, New Zealand had pulled off the first surprise by 37 runs. Crowe said jubilantly: "This win was my greatest thrill."

THAT 1992 RAIN RULE

The 1992 rain rule was originally put forward by Richie Benaud, who cannot have dreamed it would prove so controversial. Here is the key part of the rule:

If the team batting second has not had the opportunity to complete the agreed
 number of overs, and neither has been all out, nor has passed its opponent's
 score, the result shall be decided as follows:
(a) The runs scored by the team batting second shall be compared with the runs scored
 by the team batting first from the equivalent number of highest scoring overs.
(b) If, due to a suspension of play, the number of overs in the innings of the team
 batting second has to be revised, their target score shall be the runs scored by
 the team batting first from the equivalent number of overs, plus one.

'We had our bottoms kicked. We've got to try and recapture the feeling we had in 1987. There is more pressure on us this time because we are favourites.'

ALLAN BORDER
on Australia's opening day
defeat by New Zealand

Right: New Zealand off-spinner Dipak Patel is overjoyed at taking the crucial wicket of Allan Border in the opening game against Australia. The Aussies – and onlookers – were amazed to see Patel opening the bowling

By the time the news of Australia's defeat was relayed to Perth, the floodlit match between England and India was into its opening overs. The England captain, Graham Gooch, was playing his 100th one-day international, having agreed to make one last overseas tour at the age of 38 in the hope of finally coming home with a World Cup winner's medal. But it was 36-year-old Ian Botham who grabbed the pre-match headlines by asking to open the innings with Gooch. England's reliance on two veterans made a marked contrast with India's faith in its new batting stars, 18-year-old Sachin Tendulkar and 19-year-old Vinod Kambli. Would youth outgun experience?

Botham's promotion was not, in fact, a success, but when he had gone for nine, Gooch and Robin Smith laid the platform for a big score with a stand of 110 in 21 overs. Smith had pulled two huge sixes when he was caught off a cut for 91 and, from 197 for three, England were a little disappointed with the 50-over score of 236 for nine. It included 13 wides, which could prove expensive.

A third-wicket partnership between Sachin Tendulkar

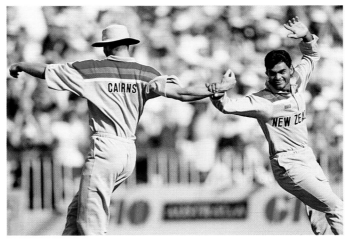

and Ravi Shastri took India into a threatening position at 126 for two. Now Gooch turned to Botham, who removed Tendulkar, caught behind for 35, and Kambli, caught at mid on for three. Game, set and match to experience.

England were back in the game, and when it came to the final over, 11 runs were needed with the last pair together. One run came off the first ball, but next ball Botham – again – with a throw from extra cover, ran out Javagal Srinath and England had scraped in by nine runs.

Where England had Gooch and Botham, Pakistan had Imran Khan and Javed Miandad – the only two men to play in all of the first five World Cups. Imran had 'retired' after the previous tournament but, like Gooch, found the lure of the World Cup too much to resist. His team's first match was the next day in Melbourne, but their preparations had been thrown into disarray by injuries. The explosive fast bowler Waqar Younis had withdrawn, and Imran would miss the match himself with a damaged shoulder.

They were put in by the West Indies and, with Ramiz Raja making 102, might have expected more than their 220 for two. The West Indies opened with the 22-year-old Brian Lara alongside Desmond Haynes and the pair put the result beyond doubt by rattling the score up to 175. Lara had hit 88, including 11 fours, when he was forced to retire hurt after Wasim Akram hit him painfully on the toe. Haynes, who was dropped twice, was 93 when his team won by ten wickets. West Indies manager Deryck Murray admitted this win meant a lot to a team who had rather lost their way in one-day internationals: "We feel we have turned a corner."

Meanwhile a remarkable game was going on in New Zealand. At New Plymouth, in a match not considered worthy of television coverage, Zimbabwe were put in by Sri Lanka. At first there seemed nothing unusual, until

Zimbabwe's Andy Waller came in and the ball started flying to all parts. He hit three sixes and nine fours and his 50 came from only 32 balls, a new World Cup record. His example inspired Andy Flower, who was also flying to his hundred now. They added 145 unbeaten for the fifth wicket (also a World Cup record), Waller contributing 83 from 45 balls. Flower finished with 115 not out and Zimbabwe had made an astonishing 312 for four.

Undaunted, Samarasekera and Mahanama set off at a cracking pace and soon had three figures on the board. Samarasekera's 75 came from only 61 balls, but they were parted at 128 when the veteran spinner John Traicos put a brake on the scoring. As wickets fell, Sri Lanka's cause began to look hopeless, but in came Arjuna Ranatunga. He seemed to set out to eclipse the innings of Waller, reaching his fifty in one ball more. By the last over, Sri Lanka needed only three to win and he hammered a four through the leg side for a three-wicket win. Ranatunga was 88 not out from 61 balls when Sri Lanka became the first side to score as many as 313 to win a World Cup match batting second.

Two days later, at Hamilton, Sri Lanka met New Zealand and found their diet of nagging medium-pacers harder to hit. The home team overhauled their total of 206 for nine with six wickets in hand, and Ken Rutherford – who had been dropped on nought – 65 not out from 71 balls.

All the teams had now made their entry to the tournament except one. South Africa's return to world cricket, although they had already played India, would be a big occasion. It was scheduled for Sydney with Australia the opposition. To add to the drama, South Africa were being led by a man who, in the years of isolation, had played a World Cup for Australia – Kepler Wessels.

Ticket touts were operating outside the SCG for the start of the day/night game as Australia chose to bat first. No one in the crowd was seriously contemplating a South African win. It was just good to witness a historic occasion.

Inside ten overs Australia's openers had 42 on the board. Then Boon was run out and the next ten overs brought only 34 runs as Richard Snell bowled a tight spell. It was Adrian Kuiper who made the most telling breakthrough, with Rod Marsh caught behind and Allan Border bowled next ball. Allan Donald's second spell brought him three for 14, and Australia finished on a fragile 170 for nine.

Now, would the occasion perhaps get to the reborn South Africa? Not with an experienced head like Wessels opening the innings. With Hudson he put on 74, and was then joined by another old hand in Peter Kirsten. I was in the commentary box as South Africa claimed a momentous victory:

"Wessels is 76. Kirsten is 49. Reid is on his way to bowl to Wessels. Wessels drives at that one through the off side. The scores are going to be level after this. That will be four runs to Kepler Wessels and he goes to 80. What a sensational re-entry to world cricket. In comes Reid to bowl to Kepler Wessels. Off the back foot he runs it down to third man. Whitney fields, but it really doesn't matter. They've taken the single.

"Kepler Wessels punches the air. He shakes hands with the Australian players. Allan Border puts an arm round his shoulders. That's very nice. Two old Queensland colleagues. Two Australian colleagues. And now they're pleased, I think, for their old friend Kepler Wessels. But they must be very disappointed for themselves. Australia have been beaten.

"South Africa have won this match by nine wickets. You couldn't really have got in the end an easier victory."

While South Africans celebrated, Australians were stunned. Border proclaimed that "the New Zealand match

Left: Allan Border and Craig McDermott congratulate their former teammate Kepler Wessels after South Africa's shock victory over Australia

'It's a great night for South Africa and a great night for all the guys. They've tried hard, worked hard. It's very nice to be back in Australia, and the way that people have been towards me has been terrific. So I did enjoy it.'
KEPLER WESSELS

was bad enough, but this was a shocker. It's all gone haywire. We've got a lot of soul-searching to do very quickly." The champions were in trouble.

Next day at the Bellerive Oval, just outside Hobart, Pakistan secured their first points after Zimbabwe put them in. Aamir Sohail was dropped four times in making 114 and Javed Miandad made 89 in a score of 254 for four. The Zimbabwean batsmen who had passed 300 four days before found that this attack posed more of a problem, and Pakistan won by 53 runs.

England's second game was a day/nighter in Melbourne against the West Indies, who struggled to score against the medium pace attack. Chris Lewis had Lara caught behind second ball and Richie Richardson caught at slip for five. With Ian Botham having Carl Hooper caught, it was 36 for three. Keith Arthurton rode his luck with two dropped catches to make 54, but the West Indies were all out in the final over for 157.

An opening stand of 50 by England was dominated by Gooch to the extent that Botham made only eight of them, before Winston Benjamin had him caught behind. But Hick showed his authority with 54 from 55 balls as England won by six wickets with more than ten overs to spare. A happy Graham Gooch said: "In our first game we won without playing particularly well. Today we played very well."

The next day at Mackay, in tropical Queensland, the efforts of enthusiastic local helpers were dashed by the weather. Only two balls were bowled before the downpour; India and Sri Lanka shared the points.

Further south in Brisbane, the weather was finer, as the West Indies met Zimbabwe in a clash of maroon and pillarbox red. Put in, the West Indies ran up 264 for eight, with Lara making 72 off as many balls. At no point did Zimbabwe look likely to get near to that; nor, indeed, did they seem to try. The West Indies won by 75 runs.

At the same time, in Auckland, the South Africans were meeting the other host country. Crowe again opened the New Zealand bowling with Patel, whose first seven overs cost just 15 runs. He also bowled Andrew Hudson and soon South Africa were 29 for three. Peter Kirsten and Dave Richardson added 79 before Cairns took a hand, dismissing Richardson and Jonty Rhodes. He then had Kuiper caught behind, only to find that – unbeknown to Kuiper – the square leg umpire had signalled no-ball for a bouncer. But Kuiper had left his crease; he tried to scramble back, but was run out. South Africa could only manage 190 for seven.

After 15 overs in reply, New Zealand had raced to 103 for no wicket. Mark Greatbatch hit three sixes and nine fours in making 68 from 60 balls and New Zealand cruised to victory by seven wickets in the 35th over.

After a week of competition, England and New Zealand were together at the top of the league table and England, indeed, had supplanted Australia as favourites.

The next day, two matches revealed the peculiarities of the rain rule. In Adelaide, on an ideal morning for seam and swing bowling, Pakistan were put in by England and shot out in the 41st over for 74, with Derek Pringle taking three for eight. Only three batsmen got to double figures. England had to start their innings before the interval and had lost Gooch, caught behind, in making 17 runs from six overs when they took lunch.

Rain delayed the restart until five o'clock, leaving time for ten more overs. With the rain rule taking off Pakistan's least productive overs to set the target, England's target became 64 from 16 overs. So, having lost 34 overs, the target was reduced by just 10 runs – scant reward for the prodigious efforts of the bowlers. In the event, after two more overs the rain returned to spare embarrassment either to England or the architects of the rule.

Afterwards, Pakistan's stand-in captain Javed Miandad criticised the pitch, adding: "I'm sure England will qualify for the semi-finals. For the rest of us it is a very open battle."

In Brisbane, meanwhile, Australia batted first against India. An innings of 90 in 109 balls by Dean Jones – who started with a four and a six – took them to 237 for nine. At 45 for one in the 17th over of India's reply, a squall of rain

'It seems strange that you can bowl a side out for 74 and then be chasing 63 in 15 overs. It takes some understanding. But you will never get an ideal rule – and it didn't matter here because the rain beat us anyway.'

GRAHAM GOOCH
after England's rained-off game against Pakistan

drove the players off for a quarter of an hour. Three overs were docked but only two runs were taken from the target.

Mohammed Azharuddin had come in at the early fall of Srikkanth's wicket and he played an innings to match that of Jones – 93 from 103 balls – before being run out from midwicket by Border. With Tom Moody taking the vital wickets of Ravi Shastri and Tendulkar, it came down to the wire.

Border admitted later that he had mis-planned his bowling in leaving the last over for Moody to bowl. Thirteen runs were needed from it, with three wickets in hand. Kiran More hit the first two balls for fours, but was bowled next ball. Prabhakar managed one run and was run out off the penultimate ball; four were needed off the last ball. Javagal Srinath skied to long on, where Steve Waugh dropped the catch. As the batsmen hared back for the third run which would tie the match, Waugh's throw winged in to run out Raju, and Australia had won by one run.

South Africa had moved down New Zealand's North Island to play Sri Lanka, in Wellington, where they again found themselves bogged down on a slow pitch, and were all out on the last ball for 195. Allan Donald took two early wickets, but Mahanama and Ranatunga steered Sri Lanka into a winning position. Seven were needed from the last over. A boundary from the fifth ball gave Sri Lanka an unexpected victory by three wickets with one ball to spare.

A rainy day in Napier had New Zealand and Zimbabwe dodging in and out of the pavilion. Batting first, the New Zealanders repeatedly had their allocation of overs re-set but, between the showers, Andy Waller saw his record fastest fifty bettered by one ball by Martin Crowe. Off 20 overs and five balls, New Zealand made 162 for three with Crowe 74 not out from only 74 balls.

The target for Zimbabwe was set as 154 from 18 overs. On a damp afternoon, the New Zealand medium-pacers held sway. Larsen and Harris each took three wickets as Zimbabwe made 105 for seven.

It had been meant to be the final in 1987, but at last the first World Cup meeting between India and Pakistan took place in Sydney on March 4. Almost inevitably, it was a testy occasion. At the centre of India's innings was an impressive 54 not out by Tendulkar. Mushtaq Ahmed took three important wickets, but Kapil Dev's rapid 35 took the score up to 216 for seven.

In reply, Pakistan were tied down by the Indian medium-pacers. Javed Miandad's frustration boiled over when India wicketkeeper Kiran More – an old antagonist – made a vociferous appeal for a legside catch which English umpire David Shepherd turned down. When, next ball, More made an ugly leap to catch a fielder's return, Miandad erupted into a bizarre pantomime, leaping up and down on the spot in imitation and shouting at his opponent.

The umpires lectured both Miandad and India captain Mohammed Azharuddin but, as match referee Ted Wykes observed later: "The major problem is that what they said wasn't in English." Despite Miandad's antics, and an innings of 62 by opener Aamir Sohail, the Indians bowled

'He (Javed Miandad) is very difficult. He is always like this and it is not necessary. This should not have happened but the umpires handled it well and I just told Kiran to stay away from him."

MOHAMMED AZHARUDDIN
on Javed Miandad's bust-up with Kiran More

Pakistan out in the 49th over for 173 to win by 43 runs.

Of all the matches in this rebirth of South Africa, the most symbolic was their encounter with the West Indies in Christchurch, though both teams tried to play down the political significance. West Indies captain Richie Richardson said diplomatically: "I have been playing cricket for a good many years with South Africans now without meeting one I didn't like. I hope it stays that way."

In cricketing terms, the match was important enough anyway, with West Indies looking for their third win and South Africa only their second. Richardson put South Africa in on a grey morning, and on a pitch with some life Malcolm Marshall and Curtly Ambrose were a handful. Peter Kirsten was the backbone of an innings of 200 for eight, although a strained calf muscle meant he had to bat half of his innings with a runner.

If this match was billed as a clash of the world's fastest bowlers, eyes were now on Donald, but it was his opening partner, the apparently less threatening Meyrick Pringle, who caused the chaos. In 11 balls he removed Lara, Richardson, Hooper and Arthurton with only 19 runs on the board in the eighth over. Worse still, Desmond Haynes had had to retire with a blow on the finger, but he returned to add 51 with Logie for the fifth wicket. It was Kuiper who accounted for both of them – Haynes for 30 and Logie for 69. There was no coming back from 70 for six. The West Indies were bowled out in the 39th over for 136 and South Africa had won by 64 runs.

Five minutes after that last wicket had fallen in Christchurch, the first ball was bowled in Sydney in the day/night match between Australia and England in front of a rumbustious 39,000 crowd. This perennial needle match had assumed added significance in light of Australia's

plight, and in the pre-match war of words, Dean Jones had proclaimed bullishly: "England have had three easy games so far. They will meet a much stronger side on Thursday." Graham Gooch had been rather more circumspect; on being on being asked if he thought this was the biggest match of the World Cup, his deadpan response was: "I wouldn't mind playing in the Final."

The Australians sent in Tom Moody to capitalise on the extra fielding restrictions of the first 15 overs, and he responded with a half-century. Jones helped him bring up the hundred at the halfway point of the innings. Enter the inspirational Botham. In seven balls he removed Border, Healy, Peter Taylor and Craig McDermott without conceding a run. Australia were dismissed for 171. With the start that Gooch and Botham gave England, there was never any doubt that they were going to overcome that.

Neville Oliver: "*Here comes Whitney to start a new over. He bowls to Botham, who deflects the ball down towards fine leg and that roar is for Ian Botham's 50. Applause from the Australian players and a capacity crowd here at the Sydney Cricket Ground for another great deed by Ian Botham. He took four wickets. He's followed it up with 51 not out and has set England well and truly on the road to victory. They are none for 102. It's been Beefy's day.*"

Botham made 53, Gooch 58 and England won with nine overs to spare by eight wickets. Manager Mickey Stewart was quick to praise his side: "It was a stage game, a genuinely big game, and I wondered how our players would react. But they have all done well."

Each team had now played four of their eight games. New Zealand had a 100 per cent record and eight points, England had only dropped a point in their abandoned match with Pakistan, Sri Lanka lay third with two wins and

'The Pakistan team's preparation has suffered. The injury to Waqar Younis is probably the biggest blow to us. I think with his presence, our pace attack is very formidable. We could defend any total. There's no one else we can replace him with. No one of his calibre. But nevertheless we have to go on.'

IMRAN KHAN
before the World Cup. Waqar's new-ball partner Wasim Akram (right) took up the challenge, becoming the tournament's top wicket-taker, Pakistan's most economical bowler, and Man of the Match in the World Cup Final

Left: Graham Gooch top-scores with 58 in England's victory over Australia. His brilliant batting and tough captaincy took his team to their third World Cup Final. Gooch played in all three

a no-result game, West Indies and South Africa were tied with two wins, India and Pakistan were a point below them, while Australia had only the pointless Zimbabwe below them. Allan Border, staring humiliation in the face, could only say: "We need England and New Zealand to keep winning and then a few other results to go our way. We have got to win the rest of our games."

On a showery Saturday at Hamilton, Zimbabwe tried to improve their position, but fell foul of the by now notorious rain rule. In an innings shortened by rain to 32 overs, India made 203, featuring 81 from 77 balls from Tendulkar. In reply Zimbabwe were looking very good at 104 for one early in the 20th over. Then the rain set in again in earnest. The calculations started by taking the score for India's most productive 19 overs and then decided that Zimbabwe had fallen 55 runs short of that.

Australia had finer weather for their game in Adelaide against Sri Lanka, who were put in to bat. Only Aravinda

de Silva looked like dominating the Australian bowlers, and his 62 contained only two boundaries. A target of 190 was put into perspective by the opening stand of 120 by Moody and Marsh, and Australia gratefully recorded their second win by seven wickets with six overs to spare.

Back on the slow Auckland pitch next day, New Zealand again opened the bowling with Dipak Patel, this time against the West Indies. His ten overs cost only 19 runs and brought him the wicket of Carl Hooper. Lara's 52 was the only substantial contribution in a total of 203 for seven.

Martin Crowe had come to terms with the needs of the first 15 overs and Mark Greatbatch's orders were to use them. He hit three sixes, seven fours, made 63 from 77 balls, and even stirred Ambrose into an exchange of words with his impudence. The West Indian fast bowlers did strike back, but by then Crowe was at the helm of his ship and commanding the innings home with 12 fours in his 81 not out. Yet another win for New Zealand, by five wickets.

On Sunday March 8 in Brisbane, South Africa made 211 for seven in their 50 overs against Pakistan. Imran, now trusting his damaged shoulder enough, had bowled his quota of ten overs economically and picked up the useful wickets of Hudson and Kuiper. Pakistan were without Rameez Raja and Javed Miandad, but had reached 74 for two in the 22nd over when the game was interrupted by rain.

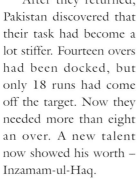

After they returned, Pakistan discovered that their task had become a lot stiffer. Fourteen overs had been docked, but only 18 runs had come off the target. Now they needed more than eight an over. A new talent now showed his worth – Inzamam-ul-Haq.

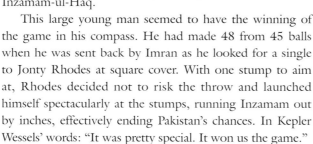

This large young man seemed to have the winning of the game in his compass. He had made 48 from 45 balls when he was sent back by Imran as he looked for a single to Jonty Rhodes at square cover. With one stump to aim at, Rhodes decided not to risk the throw and launched himself spectacularly at the stumps, running Inzamam out by inches, effectively ending Pakistan's chances. In Kepler Wessels' words: "It was pretty special. It won us the game."

Imran Khan begged to differ. In his eyes, what actually won South Africa the game was the rain rule. He said angrily: "It is a ridiculous rule because the team batting second has no chance. You might as well toss a coin." The 21-run win gave South Africa real hopes of a semi-final place, while fortune seemed to be scowling on Pakistan.

England's first major setback came in the old gold-mining town of Ballarat – they were forced to moved out of their hotel because the beds were too small. The next day dawned blisteringly hot, and a large proportion of Melbourne's considerable Sri Lankan community took the sixty-mile trip to see if their team could beat the new tournament favourites.

Ian Botham, Graeme Hick and Neil Fairbrother made telling contributions with the bat, and Alec Stewart and Chris Lewis drove home the point, Stewart's 59 coming

from 36 balls and Lewis's 20 from only six. Seventy-three runs came off the last five overs; 280 for six was their total.

The biggest damage suffered by England in the field was the early withdrawal of Graham Gooch with a torn hamstring. By that time, Lewis was already making inroads on the Sri Lankan batting, reducing them to 60 for four and finishing with four for 30. They were all out in 44 overs for 174.

Gooch's injury was a serious blow: his firm, confident leadership had been a major factor in England's success, and his majestic form with the bat had helped to cover up for the absence of Allan Lamb, who had not yet started a game due to his own hamstring trouble. "I am not going to take any chances," Gooch said. "With one batsman struggling already, we can't afford to lose another."

With rain around in Wellington next day, India wisely decided to bat first against the West Indies. It was more like the West Indies of old, as the fast bowlers dismissed India inside the distance for 197. But, as the rain clouds gathered, there was a real fear that they might end up with another impossible target set by the infamous rule.

Their first target was to get to 103 in 15 overs and after 11 they had reached 81 for one, with Brian Lara going well in company with Phil Simmons. But then the rain did arrive. Four overs were lost – just two runs off the target. Still they kept up the assault, afraid of the effect of another shower on the calculations. But after a mad few overs, in which Lara, Simmons, Richardson and Logie had all fallen, the skies cleared enough for sanity to prevail and – by five wickets – the West Indies became the first side batting second to triumph over the iniquities of that rule.

At the same time, in Canberra, South Africa continued their progress towards a semi-final place with ruthless suppression of their African neighbours, Zimbabwe. A 112-run partnership between Wessels and Kirsten helped them to a seven-wicket with nearly five overs in hand.

At the other end of Australia, under the floodlights of Perth, the hosts met Pakistan in an ill-tempered affair between two sides near the bottom of the table. Imran came out for the toss wearing a T-shirt with an angry tiger on it, explaining: "The tiger is always most dangerous when cornered." And so it proved – eventually.

Given a good start by Aamir Sohail's 76, the Pakistan innings fell away from 193 for three to 220 for nine at the end. Aqib Javed promptly put the skids under Australia, Marsh and Jones rallied them, and then the leg spin of Mushtaq Ahmed sparked an even more gory collapse – the last eight wickets going down for 56. Pakistan won by 48 runs and Allan Border said frankly: "I don't think we can get through now. In fact, the way we are playing, it might be a travesty if we did."

On a cold, blustery day in Dunedin, India's cricketers must have been only too well aware of the proximity of Antarctica as they played the rampant New Zealanders. Patel's early overs were once again significant, with the removal of Srikkanth for nought with his third ball, while the other Indian opener, Jadeja, had to retire with a pulled hamstring. But Azharuddin and Tendulkar provided much-needed warmth to the cockles of their supporters' hearts with a stand of 127 in 20 overs, Azharuddin making 55 and Tendulkar 84. It enabled Kapil Dev to lay about him towards the end, and 230 for six gave India a good chance.

That was reckoning without Greatbatch's now familiar onslaught at the start of New Zealand's innings. He hit three sixes, gained another with the aid of four overthrows, and stayed for 76 balls to crash his way to 73.

By the time he fell to the left-arm spinner, Raju, it was 118 for two and Andrew Jones now guided the innings home by four wickets with nearly four overs in hand.

New Zealand had now won six games in a row, and Martin Crowe said: "We're enjoying it. We're in the dressing room and we're close, we're talking away, we're analysing our opposition a lot and we're revelling in the fact that our own teammates are doing well." Indian manager Abbas Ali Baig paid tribute to Crowe's tactics, saying: "We were a little surprised when Patel opened the bowling against us. We fancy ourselves as good players of spin and we had a plan to get at him, but when Srikkanth got out, it failed."

While players went off to try to get warm in Dunedin, it was a hot night in Melbourne, where England and South Africa were playing each other for the first time for 27 years. Alec Stewart, leading England in the absence of the hamstrung Gooch, put South Africa in. It took the off-spin of Graeme Hick, who had had to take over when Dermot Reeve was injured, to break an opening stand of 151 between Wessels and Hudson for 85 and 79 respectively. After a start like that, South Africa would have hoped for more than their 236 for four.

Stewart gave England a great start, but at 62 for one after 12 overs the rain started. The hold-up was three-quarters of an hour and all the while the batsmen knew that the rule would be making their job harder. The new target was 226 from a total of 41 overs; nine overs fewer to score only 11 runs fewer. In the second over of their return, McMillan bowled Botham for 22. He then had Robin Smith caught behind second ball and Snell had Hick caught behind for one. Three wickets had fallen in six balls.

Alec Stewart made 77 from 88 balls before being run out by Rhodes, but Dermot Reeve and Neil Fairbrother maintained the momentum. Still 67 runs were needed

Left: Arjuna Ranatunga averaged over 50 with the bat but his team fell away after starting the tournament with a record run-spree

from the last ten overs. Lewis made 33 from 22 balls and when he was run out, ten were needed off the last two overs. Nine came from the next nine balls. Jonathan Agnew described the tense climax for the BBC:

"One required from three balls. Derek Pringle on strike and a cluster of South Africa fieldsmen now as Snell bowls to Pringle, with one required to win. It's a full toss! Pringle hits it in the air. It's caught! Ho ho! Caught by Kuiper at midwicket. It was a full toss and surely on any other day Pringle could have hit that wherever he wanted on this MCG. Instead he hit it straight to Adrian Kuiper, who took a good catch above his head on the rebound."

The new batsman was Phillip DeFreitas. *"DeFreitas has a hamstring strain. He has a groin strain. One off two. In comes Snell. One run required. DeFreitas faces. He hammers that through the off side. It's there! They take the single. Jonty Rhodes fields the ball and England are home with one ball to spare. They've won a thrilling match by three wickets."*

It was a result to confirm England's position in the semi-finals, and Kepler Wessels said magnanimously: "We were definitely beaten by a better team, because the rain was in our favour. England are the strongest team here."

If that was a hot night, it was hotter still at Berri, South Australia, next day when the West Indies took on Sri Lanka. More heat was applied by Phil Simmons with a whirlwind of a century. Coming in at six for one, he bludgeoned 110 from 125 balls, being dropped no fewer than three times. A total of 268 for eight was too much for Sri Lanka, who faded to 177 for nine. The 91-run win had kept the West Indies' semi-final hopes alive.

Australia's form and not-so-distant history warned them to take Zimbabwe seriously when they met at Hobart. Showers reduced the Australian innings to 46 overs, but in that time, Boon, Jones and the Waugh twins

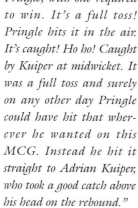

all contributed substantially to a score of 265 for six – a total that Zimbabwe, their earlier steam apparently spent, could not approach. They were all out for 137.

Sunday March 15 saw three matches spread over nearly 4,000 miles. The day's action started in Wellington. New Zealand had been the surprise package to date. Now they were out for revenge. England had beaten them in the series just before this tournament. Today they would play for the leadership of the table.

England's casualty list was becoming a problem, with Gooch and Fairbrother out of action and others carrying injuries. They were put in to bat and treated to the Patel-opening-bowler routine. He got a valuable wicket, too: Ian Botham, bowled for eight. Hick joined Stewart in a stand of 70 in 14 overs, but then it became a story familiar to New Zealand's opponents in this competition. After Stewart had become Patel's second victim for 41 and Hick had gone for 56, the strangulation set in and in their frustration, the batsmen found ways to get out. Their 50-over score was only 200 for eight.

Mark Greatbatch again started with some blistering hitting in his 35. Andrew Jones followed with 78 and Martin Crowe finished it with 73 not out from just 81 balls. New Zealand won by seven wickets with nine overs to spare and could not conceal their glee at their revenge.

Facing South Africa in Adelaide, India knew that their chance of reaching the semi-finals had gone. It was an unappetising day for cricket, too, cold and wet, and a late start reduced the game to 30 overs a side. But India's pride was still intact. Put in to bat, they reached 180 for six thanks to another brilliant innings from Azharuddin – 79 from 77 balls, with Kapil Dev in even more devastating style with his 42 from 29 balls.

Andrew Hudson and Peter Kirsten launched South

Left: Smile, you're on *Candid Camera*! Brian McMillan of South Africa takes out England opener Ian Botham's stumpcam

Africa's reply with a stand of 128 – Kirsten's 84 from 86 balls. A brief flurry of tumbling wickets took South Africa into the last over, but they confirmed a semi-final berth with a six-wicket victory. Their manager Alan Jordaan said happily: "I don't think our boys will be in bed before nine tonight."

That left one semi-final place to fill. Given Pakistan's early form and problems, they were unlikely contenders. But in their penultimate league match in Perth they kept the outside chance alive. Sri Lanka were restricted to 212 for six, and Javed Miandad and Salim Malik scored half-centuries to give Pakistan victory by four wickets.

Now that last semi-final place rested between three countries, all playing their final league match on March 18. Leading contenders were the West Indies. A simple win against Australia would give them the place. Australia could do it on net run-rate by winning that match, providing New Zealand beat Pakistan as expected. Pakistan had the most tenuous chance. They needed to beat New Zealand and then pray for Australia to beat the West Indies later that evening.

A side show to the day was England's first ever meeting with Zimbabwe in the New South Wales/Victoria border town of Albury Wodonga. As might have been expected, England dismissed them well inside the distance for 134 and Graham Gooch went out to play himself back after his hamstring injury. Christopher Martin-Jenkins and Vic Marks watched what happened next.

Christopher Martin-Jenkins: *"Eddo Brandes, the big man, to bowl the first over. Graham Gooch to face and Gooch would love to bat right through, wouldn't he?"*

Vic Marks: *"That's right. He has missed the last couple of days, and he wants to test out his hamstring."*

Christopher Martin-Jenkins: *"Two slips and a gully as Brandes comes in from the far end – and beats Gooch for pace. He's lbw first ball of the innings! And he looked very out. A ball of full length hit him on the back pad."*

It was the start of a débâcle for England, for whom Zimbabwe were to become something of a bogey team. Brandes finished with four for 21, the veteran off-spinner

John Traicos bowled his ten overs for 16, England became strokeless and Zimbabwe were able to return home with a notable scalp – England, beaten by nine runs in the last over.

The more significant action, though, was in Christchurch. Pakistan had put New Zealand in to bat and, after suffering a couple of obligatory lusty blows from Greatbatch, seen Aqib Javed and Wasim Akram reduce them to 39 for three. The introduction of young Mushtaq Ahmed's leg spin tied the rest of the innings in knots. The bemused Greatbatch fell to him, sweeping, for 42 and Mushtaq's ten overs cost 18. Wasim Akram finished it off with four for 32 and New Zealand were all out for 166.

New Zealand had given a first outing for the tournament to their fastest bowler, Danny Morrison, and he did give them a distinct hope by reducing Pakistan to nine for two, but Ramiz Raja was not to be denied. He was 119 not out when Pakistan won by seven wickets.

Now the Pakistanis must huddle round the television to watch the day/night game in Melbourne. Their win had denied Australia a semi-final. Would Australia do the job they needed in beating the West Indies?

Winning the toss, Border decided to bat, and Moody and Boon gave him the start he needed of 107 for the first wicket. Boon continued to his hundred, but the total of 216 was disappointing. The West Indies had a semi-final place beckoning.

It became a mirage. Two wickets for McDermott in the seventh over had them 27 for two. Four wickets for Mike Whitney prevented anyone staying with Lara, who was eventually run out for 70 and the West Indies were all out in the 43rd over 57 runs short.

Back in New Zealand's South Island, Pakistan's cricketers knew that they had scraped into the semi-finals. They would play New Zealand, the top team, in Auckland, while England would meet South Africa in Sydney.

· FIRST ROUND ·

No qualifying groups – each country played all the others once before the top four in the table played off in the semi-finals

FEBRUARY 22 AT AUCKLAND
New Zealand 248 for 6 (M D Crowe 100*, K R Rutherford 57) **beat Australia 211** (D C Boon 100, Larsen 3-30) **by 37 runs**

FEBRUARY 22 AT PERTH (DAY/NIGHT)
England 236 for 9 (R A Smith 91, G A Gooch 51) **beat India 227** (R J Shastri 57, Reeve 3-38) **by nine runs**

FEBRUARY 23 AT NEW PLYMOUTH
Sri Lanka 313 for 7 (A Ranatunga 88, M Samaresekera 75, R S Mahanama 59, Brandes 3-70) **beat Zimbabwe 312 for 4** (A Flower 115*, A C Waller 83*) **by three wkts**

FEBRUARY 23 AT MELBOURNE
West Indies 221 for 0 (D L Haynes 93*, B C Lara ret ht 88) **beat Pakistan 220 for 2** (Ramiz Raja 102*, Javed Miandad 57*) **by 10 wickets**

FEBRUARY 25 AT HAMILTON
New Zealand 210 for 4 (K R Rutherford 65*, J G Wright 57) **beat Sri Lanka 206 for 9** (R S Mahanama 80, Watson 3-37, Harris 3-43) **by six wickets**

FEBRUARY 26 AT SYDNEY (DAY/NIGHT)
South Africa 171 for 1 (K C Wessels 81*) **beat Australia 170 for 9** (Donald 3-34) **by nine wickets**

FEBRUARY 27 AT HOBART
Pakistan 254 for 4 (Aamir Sohail 114, Javed Miandad 89, Butchart 3-57) **beat Zimbabwe 201 for 7** (Wasim Akram 3-21) **by 53 runs**

FEBRUARY 27 AT MELBOURNE (DAY/NIGHT)
England 160 for 4 (G A Gooch 65, G A Hick 54) **beat West Indies 157** (K L T Arthurton 54, Lewis 3-30, DeFreitas 3-34) **by six wickets**

FEBRUARY 28 AT MACKAY
India 1 for 0 v Sri Lanka: No result

FEBRUARY 29 AT AUCKLAND
New Zealand 191 for 3 (M Greatbatch 68, R Latham 60) **beat South Africa 190 for 7** (P Kirsten 90) **by seven wkts**

FEBRUARY 29 AT BRISBANE
West Indies 264 for 8 (B C Lara 72, C L Hooper 63, R B Richardson 56, Brandes 3-45) **beat Zimbabwe 189 for 7** (A H Shah 60*, D L Houghton 55) **by 75 runs**

MARCH 1 AT BRISBANE
Australia 237 for 9 (D Jones 90, Kapil Dev 3-41, Prabhakar 3-41) **beat India 234** (M Azharuddin 93) **by one run**

MARCH 1 AT ADELAIDE
Pakistan 74 (Pringle 3-8), **England 24 for 1: No result**

QUALIFYING TABLE

	P	W	L	NR	Pts	Nrr*
New Zealand	8	7	1	0	14	0.59
England	8	5	2	1	11	0.47
South Africa	8	5	3	0	10	0.13
Pakistan	8	4	3	1	9	0.16
Australia	8	4	4	0	8	0.20
West Indies	8	4	4	0	8	0.07
India	8	2	5	1	5	0.14
Sri Lanka	8	2	5	1	5	0.68
Zimbabwe	8	1	7	0	2	1.14

*Net run rate: The formula for Nrr was runs scored per over minus runs conceded per over. Figures in shortened matches were revised and those in 'no-result' fixtures discounted.

MARCH 2 AT WELLINGTON
Sri Lanka 198 for 7 (R S Mahanama 68, A Ranatunga 64, Donald 3-42) **beat South Africa 195** (Anurasiri 3-41) **by three wickets**

MARCH 3 AT NAPIER
New Zealand 162 for 3 (M Crowe 74*, A Jones 57) **beat Zimbabwe 105 for 7** (Harris 3-15, Larsen 3-16) **by 48 runs**

MARCH 4 AT SYDNEY (DAY/NIGHT)
India 216 for 7 (S R Tendulkar 54*) **beat Pakistan 173** (Aamir Sohail 62) **by 43 runs**

MARCH 5 AT CHRISTCHURCH
South Africa 200 for 8 (P N Kirsten 56) **beat West Indies 136** (A L Logie 61, Pringle 4-11) **by 64 runs**

AT SYDNEY (DAY/NIGHT)
England 173 for 2 (G A Gooch 58, I T Botham 53) **beat Australia 171** (T M Moody 51, Botham 4-31) **by eight wkts**

MARCH 7 AT HAMILTON
India 203 for 7 (S R Tendulkar 81, Traicos 3-35, Burmester 3-36) **beat Zimbabwe 104 for 1 by 55 runs**

MARCH 7 AT ADELAIDE
Australia 190 for 3 (G R Marsh 60) **beat Sri Lanka 189 for 9** (P A de Silva 62) **by seven wickets**

MARCH 8 AT AUCKLAND
New Zealand 206 for 5 (M D Crowe 81, M J Greatbatch 63) **beat West Indies 203 for 7** (B C Lara 52) **by five wickets**

MARCH 8 AT BRISBANE
South Africa 211 for 7 (A C Hudson 54) **beat Pakistan 173 for 8** (Kuiper 3-40) **by 20 runs**

MARCH 9 AT BALLARAT
England 280 for 6 (N H Fairbrother 63, A J Stewart 59) **beat Sri Lanka 174** (Lewis 4-30) **by 106 runs**

MARCH 10 AT WELLINGTON
West Indies 195 for 5 (K L T Arthurton 58*) **beat India 197** (M Azharuddin 61, Cummins 4-33) **by five wickets**

MARCH 10 AT CANBERRA
Sth Africa 164 for 3 (K Wessels 70, P Kirsten 62*) **beat Zimbabwe 163** (McMillan 3-30, Kirsten 3-31) **by seven wkts**

MARCH 11 AT PERTH (DAY/NIGHT)
Pakistan 220 for 9 (Aamir Sohail 76, S R Waugh 3-36) **beat Australia 172** (Aqib 3-21, Mushtaq 3-41) **by 48 runs**

MARCH 12 AT DUNEDIN
New Zealand 231 for 6 (M Greatbatch 73, A Jones 67*) **beat India 230 for 6** (S Tendulkar 84, Harris 3-55) **by four wkts**

MARCH 12 AT MELBOURNE
England 226 for 7 (A J Stewart 77, N H Fairbrother 75*, Snell 3-42) **beat South Africa 236 for 4** (K C Wessels 85, A C Hudson 79) **by three wickets**

MARCH 13 AT BERRI
West Indies 268 for 8 (P V Simmons 110, Haturusinghe 4-57) **beat Sri Lanka 177 for 9 by 91 runs**

MARCH 14 AT HOBART
Australia 265 for 6 (M E Waugh 66*, S R Waugh 55, D M Jones 54) **beat Zimbabwe 137 by 128 runs**

MARCH 15 AT WELLINGTON
New Zealand 201 for 3 (A H Jones 78, M D Crowe 73*) **beat England 200 for 8** (G A Hick 56) **by seven wickets**

MARCH 15 AT ADELAIDE
South Africa 181 for 4 (P N Kirsten 84, A C Hudson 53) **beat India 180 for 6** (M Azharuddin 79) **by six wickets**

MARCH 15 AT PERTH
Pakistan 216 for 6 (Javed Miandad 57, Salim Malik 51) **beat Sri Lanka 212 for 6 by four wickets**

MARCH 18 AT CHRISTCHURCH
Pakistan 167 for 3 (Ramiz Raja 119*, Morrison 3-42) **beat New Zealand 166** (Wasim Akram 4-32) **by seven wkts**

MARCH 18 AT ALBURY
Zimbabwe 134 (Botham 3-23, Illingworth 3-33) **beat England 125** (Brandes 4-21) **by nine runs**

MARCH 18 AT MELBOURNE (DAY/NIGHT)
Australia 216 for 6 (D C Boon 100, Cummins 3-38) **beat West Indies 159** (B C Lara 70, Whitney 4-34) **by 57 runs**

1992

THE AUCKLAND
·SEMI-FINAL·

On March 21, New Zealand played Pakistan, the only team to have beaten them in the tournament so far, in the first semi-final in Auckland. This time there was no batting collapse as New Zealand won the toss and chose to bat. The openers were both out with the score 39, but that brought in Martin Crowe – tactically and with his own bat the star of the World Cup so far.

When Andrew Jones was out, Crowe was joined by Ken Rutherford in a stand of 107 that seemed to be taking the game away from Pakistan. But a double blow befell them with the dismissal of Rutherford. As he top-edged a pull at Wasim Akram to be caught behind for 50, the batsmen ran and Crowe tweaked a hamstring. Batting with a

runner, Crowe was able to watch himself being run out in a mix-up between two others for 91, made from only 83 balls. A total of 262, though, was surely enough.

It certainly appeared so in the 35th over, when Pakistan's fourth wicket fell at 140. A reasonable start, with Ramiz Raja and Imran Khan each making 44, was slipping away. But now came Inzamam-ul-Haq, who had shown us a few glimpses already of what destruction he could wreak with the bat. None more than today. With Javed Miandad happy to play second fiddle, he reached his fifty in only 31 balls and when he was run out by a direct throw from Chris Harris, he had made 60 from 37 balls with a six and seven fours.

At 227 for five, the target was in reach. Watson bowled Wasim Akram, but that brought in hard-hitting wicket-keeper Moin Khan. In the commentary box, New Zealander Bryan Waddle watched the home team's last throw of the dice: *"Nine runs, eight balls. Miandad 57, Moin Khan 10, as*

Right: Martin Crowe, the top batsman in the tournament, on his way to yet another big score. But this time it was all in vain. Opposite, top: Chris Harris collides with Wasim Akram as he attempts to run him out, but the batsman survived. Opposite, bottom: Mushtaq Ahmed and Moin Khan celebrate as Andrew Jones is lbw

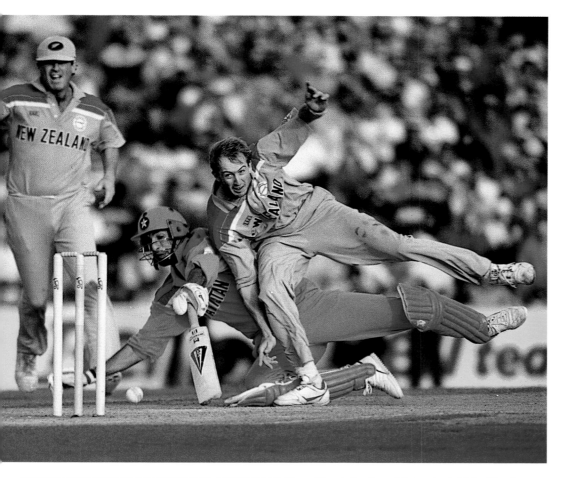

Harris bowls to Moin. And Moin hits down to cover, over the head – and six runs! He hits it into the stand! And that has pretty well sealed it for Pakistan now. That six from Moin, back over extra cover, over the head of Greatbatch, has taken their score to 260 for six.

"Three runs required to win. And it's almost certain now Pakistan will be in the final at the Melbourne Cricket Ground."

The next ball it *was* certain, as Moin crashed another four, finishing with 20 made from 11 balls. New Zealanders who had been encouraged by their team's apparently unstoppable progress to believe that their name was on the Cup were inconsolable.

· SEMI-FINAL ·
AUCKLAND • 21 MARCH

NEW ZEALAND
won the toss

M J Greatbatch b Aqib Javed	17
J G Wright c Ramiz Raja b Mushtaq Ahmed	13
A H Jones lbw b Mushtaq Ahmed	21
*M D Crowe run out	91
K R Rutherford c Moin Khan b Wasim Akram	50
C Z Harris st Moin Khan b Iqbal Sikandar	13
†I D S Smith not out	18
D N Patel lbw b Wasim Akram	8
G R Larsen not out	8
Extras (B 4, l-b 7, w 8, n-b 4)	23
Total (50 Overs, for 7 wickets)	**262**

Did not bat: D K Morrison and W Watson

Fall of wickets: 1/35 2/39 3/87 4/194 5/214 6/221 7/244

Bowling: Wasim Akram 10-0-40-2; Aqib Javed 10-2-45-1; Mushtaq Ahmed 10-0-40-2; Imran Khan 10-0-59-0; Iqbal Sikandar 9-0-56-1; Aamir Sohail 1-0-11-0.

PAKISTAN

Aamir Sohail c Jones b Patel	14
Ramiz Raja c Morrison b Watson	44
*Imran Khan c Larsen b Harris	44
Javed Miandad not out	57
Salim Malik c sub (R T Latham) b Larsen	1
Inzamam-ul-Haq run out	60
Wasim Akram b Watson	9
†Moin Khan not out	20
Extras (B 4, l-b 10, w 1)	15
Total (49 Overs, for 6 wickets)	**264**

Did not bat: Iqbal Sikandar, Mushtaq Ahmed and Aqib Javed

Fall of wickets: 1/30 2/84 3/134 4/140 5/227 6/238

Bowling: Patel 10-1-50-1; Morrison 9-0-55-0; Watson 10-2-39-2; Larsen 10-1-34-1; Harris 10-0-72-1.

Umpires: S A Bucknor and D R Shepherd

Man of the Match: Inzamam-ul-Haq

PAKISTAN
won by four wickets

The month a nation came alive

NEW ZEALAND'S 1992 ROLLER-COASTER

It was a stirring World Cup campaign – but if the selectors had had their way,
the captain would have been sacked before it even began

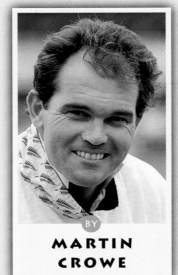

BY

MARTIN CROWE

For over 18 months we had planned our 1992 World Cup campaign. There were inevitable hiccups after Ian Smith and I started thinking about it during the 1990 England tour. Key players like Hadlee, Bracewell, Snedden and brother Jeff were no longer available, but a great bonus occurred when Warren Lees was made coach.

Our plans were based around the likely conditions, for as co-hosts we were set to play all the round-robin games at home. We had not lost a Test series in New Zealand for 13 years, because we dealt with the low bounce and uncertain weather better than visitors. One of the concepts was to make our bowling light and feathery, with a set of surprises, so that the batsmen had to make the pace themselves.

Another was to field like demons, backing up the 'dibbly-dobbly' bowling by keeping pressure on the batsmen, denying them the chance to rotate the strike. Several matches were set down for Eden Park, a rectangular-shaped rugby field with some short boundaries that needed special protection.

An idea I had seen used by a New Zealand team against Australia was our main surprise. The use of Howarth's spin to open the bowling in a one-day game at Eden Park amazed the Australians of the time. It stuck in my mind but it took some courage and support from Lees before we went ahead and opened the bowling with Dipak Patel, the off-spinner, in the first game. The most scaring task was setting the field with only two men allowed outside the 30-metre circle.

'Our selectors lost their nerve. After all our planning, they asked me to resign as captain and play purely as a batsman. I refused'

By this time we were under fire from a number of directions. The media were unhappy with our lead-up performance against England. It was our first series loss at home in a decade and we failed to impress in the one-day matches against a confident touring party.

Our selectors lost their nerve. Twenty-four hours before announcing the World Cup squad, they asked me to resign as captain and play purely as a batsman – a condition I was not prepared to accept, given all the preparation and planning. Once the squad of 14 was announced, the selectors had no further involvement, thankfully, for they were not welcome in the dressing room. In their final selection our best one-day bowler, Chris Pringle, was left out. He had shown his mettle 'at the death' against Australia in Hobart the previous year and we were to miss his coolness under fire.

The crux was the first match against Australia at Eden Park. Our total of 248 was built around a vital partnership I shared with Ken Rutherford, but a matching century from David Boon meant we had to attack and deceive the incoming batsmen at the other end. We used one- and two-over spells with our slower-than-slow 'medium-pacers' and eventually we won by 37 runs, an upset result against the playing-through champions who had also dominated us in trans-Tasman clashes.

We won seven matches in a row, a feat never previously accomplished in this competition. The plan had worked to perfection. In addition to the success of Dipak Patel, whose slow bowling was also the most economical in the series, we had Chris Harris taking most wickets and Willie Watson deceiving with his clever changes of pace. The fielding was the best of the Cup, with Larsen, Harris and Latham only fractionally ahead of their colleagues. These three bowlers were interchanged with regularity so the opposition batsmen could never get used to them.

The loss of John Wright with injury gave Mark Greatbatch his chance and he seized it avidly. His blockbuster approach at the top of the order shattered the world's best fast bowlers. He hit 14 sixes, many with daring strokes like his charge of the fearsome Malcolm Marshall to lift him over extra cover into the top tier some 120 metres away. He hit the South African pacemen on to the roof of the number four stand, and swatted Curtly Ambrose into the main stand for a six over third man.

The opening win over Australia was followed by an even more astonishing victory over South Africa a week later. The greatest feature was the way 33,000 Kiwis exploded like never before. At Napier the weather was dubious and we just managed to squeeze in an official match in the minimum 15 overs. Back at Eden Park, the West Indies made 204 and Greatbatch set us up with his three spectacular sixes. I managed to steer us home with an innings I rated as perhaps my best ever to that time, for it was made against immense pressure from the West Indian pace quartet in more ways than one.

Our visits to Dunedin and Wellington were made on a high, for we had by now already qualified for the semi-finals with five wins. Successive victories over India and England saw Andrew Jones come into his own, and the last match of the round robin in Christchurch was against Pakistan. Here we faltered, for the Pakistanis had to win everything to make the last four and they had been very lucky to escape a defeat in Adelaide when rain intervened. For our part, we had to deal with the unusual situation of having to play Australia in Sydney if we won! Instead we lost and lined up for the semi-final on our home turf.

Crowe limps on for a lap of honour after New Zealand's semi-final defeat

Throughout New Zealand the sporting nation was inspired. We were mobbed and cheered, in stark contrast to the gloomy mutterings only a month before. The World Cup was a reality, welcome news to sports-lovers who were still coming to terms with the loss of the Rugby World Cup.

The scene was set at Eden Park, with Pakistan confident after beating over us in Christchurch. We wanted to field first but were obliged to bat after winning the toss because of weather warnings and the ridiculous rain rule in place for the tournament. We made 261 on a slow pitch with a brilliant all-round display, which should have been sufficient.

Two things stood in New Zealand's path to the World Cup Final. While on 81, I pulled by left hamstring severely, denying me the chance to field and continue my surprise tactics. The unpredictability of the Pakistanis meant that at any moment their brilliance could emerge.

It came apart at Eden Park only in the last 14 overs. A stunned crowd watched our reorganised attack thrashed by an unknown 23-year-old, Inzamam-ul-Haq. Sixty runs from only 37 deliveries – and then when he was run out, the little wicketkeeper Moin Khan made 20 from 11 balls. All this while the wily Javed Miandad, who had played in every World Cup, manipulated and managed the counter-attack as only he could.

They had achieved the impossible, 122 from 14 overs, as at the very last hurdle our game plan faded away. Perhaps we didn't rotate our bowlers enough, perhaps our field placings didn't take account of the peculiar shape of the ground, perhaps we thought we had it in the bag? I sat on the edge of my chair, leg braced and bound, and I wept.

The dressing room scene was indescribable. The tension, the anticipation, the bathos were all exposed as we realised we had to thank our fervent supporters. We had to tour the ground and acknowledge the support of a nation whose hearts we had won. It was a choking, breath-taking experience. It was unforgettable, and it was devastating. It was cricket in the broadest canvas.

1992

THE SYDNEY
·SEMI-FINAL·

The second semi-final was a day/night match at Sydney – a chance for those with enough stamina to attend both games. Surprisingly sent in to bat by Hansie Cronje despite the threat of rain, England lost Gooch early on and, after a few belligerent blows, Botham for a swift 21. It was 39 for two in the eighth over.

Now came Graeme Hick with an innings of devastating power. Alec Stewart was caught behind for 33 when the score was 110, but Hick went on to make 83 from 90 balls and the only answer the South Africans had was to slow their over-rate so that, when time ran out, they had only bowled 45. Under the rules prevailing then, it just became a 45-over match and in that time England had made 252 for six.

South Africa were not daunted by needing over five-and-a-half an over. Hudson went for 46, Kuiper for 36, and Cronje was caught from a skier off Gladstone Small for 26, but Jonty Rhodes kept them in the hunt, picking his gaps and scampering hard. His lofted catch to the cover boundary off Small ended a 39-ball innings of 43. It was 206 for six in the 40th over.

Brian McMillan and Dave Richardson had already showed what useful runs they could score, and they took it to 231 for six in the 43rd over. Twenty-two were needed from the last 13 balls.

Then it rained. It was not heavy and the South African batsmen were happy to continue but, on the umpires' offer, Gooch opted to come off. Play was held up for 12 minutes. There seemed to be time, had common sense prevailed, for the match to be finished. But the rules had to be stuck to and that time had been lost. The scoreboard flashed up that the new target was 22 from seven balls! As the players came back, worse was to follow. The radio commentary summed

> 'I can tell you that as a lover of this game, I almost feel disgusted to have to broadcast this. What an absolute joke.'
> NEVILLE OLIVER

Right: Graeme Hick scored a powerful 83 in 90 balls. South Africa's only response was to slow the over-rate. Opposite: The Sydney scoreboard tells the farcical story after the rain rule's intervention

up the disbelief of those watching everywhere:

Peter Roebuck: *"They must be delaying the start for an announcement or for someone to investigate something."*

Neville Oliver: *"It's an either/or. I notice the cluster of officials down in front of the members is still in the same position. Now Allan Lamb believes that he knows the rules – and now we've got one ball to be bowled! I can tell you that as a lover of this game, I almost feel disgusted to have to broadcast this. What an absolute joke."*

Peter Roebuck: *"This is a farce. You might as well bowl it under-arm. People are throwing bottles on the field and they're quite right too, I'm afraid. This time I don't blame them."*

Neville Oliver: *"This is a disgrace. The umpires are stood around. Well, that makes a farce of the World Cup. I really believe that. That is a joke. Look at the refuse coming out on to the ground. Here comes the last delivery. Lewis walks in at half power and it's just pushed away, gently out towards midwicket. A run will be scored and the game is over.*

"Well, you couldn't imagine a worse ending than that. England have won the game by 20 runs and a contest that promised so much has finished up like a bomb that didn't go off. It's a dreadful way for this game to finish."

The recriminations and rowdy press conferences went late into the night as the rain regulation had provided its most high-profile example of its absurdity.

But, whatever the circumstances, England were to meet Pakistan at the Melbourne Cricket Ground on March 25.

· SEMI-FINAL ·
SYDNEY • 22 MARCH

ENGLAND

*G A Gooch c Richardson b Donald	2
I T Botham b Pringle	21
†A J Stewart c Richardson b McMillan	33
G A Hick c Rhodes b Snell	83
N H Fairbrother b Pringle	28
A J Lamb c Richardson b Donald	19
C C Lewis not out	18
D A Reeve not out	25
Extras (B 1, l-b 7, w 9, n-b 6)	23
Total *(45 Overs, for 6 wickets)*	**252**

Did not bat: P A J DeFreitas, R K Illingworth and G C Small

Fall of wickets: 1/20 2/39 3/110 4/183 5/187 6/221

Bowling: Donald 10-0-69-2; Pringle 9-2-36-2; Snell 8-0-52-1; McMillan 9-0-47-1; Kuiper 5-0-26-0; Cronje 4-0-14-0.

SOUTH AFRICA
won the toss

*K C Wessels c Lewis b Botham	17
A C Hudson lbw b Illingworth	46
P N Kirsten b DeFreitas	11
A P Kuiper b Illingworth	36
W J Cronje c Hick b Small	24
J N Rhodes c Lewis b Small	43
B M McMillan not out	21
†D J Richardson not out	13
Extras (L-b 17, w 4)	21
Total *(43 overs, for 6 wickets)*	**232**

Did not bat: R P Snell, M W Pringle and A A Donald

Fall of wickets: 1/26 2/61 3/90 4/131 5/176 6/206

Bowling: Botham 10-0-52-1; Lewis 5-0-38-0; DeFreitas 8-1-28-1; Illingworth 10-1-46-2; Small 10-1-51-2.

Umpires: B L Aldridge and S G Randell

Man of the Match: Graeme Hick

ENGLAND
won by 19 runs

1992

MELBOURNE
·THE FINAL·

With the new Great Southern Stand towering over the game, 87,000 were crammed into the world's largest cricket ground, Australians facing a crisis of conscience over whether to support Pakistan or the Poms. Imran Khan sported his celebrated tiger T-shirt as he tossed with Graham Gooch and it brought him luck. He chose to bat.

It was not an electric start. Both openers fell to Derek Pringle with only 24 scored. Now Imran and Javed Miandad established a solid, if far from rapid, third-wicket stand. At 34 overs they had reached 113 for two, but then they began to accelerate. When Miandad went for 58 and Imran for 72, there was just a short time for the end-of-innings onslaught for Imzamam-ul-Haq – 42 off 34 balls – and Wasim Akram – 33 off 19. The 50-over total was 249 for six.

England made a poor start. By the end of the seventh over they had lost Ian Botham for nought and Alec Stewart for seven and it was 21 for two. Gooch and Graeme Hick

Imran Khan (left) and Javed Miandad (opposite) were the only men to play in the first five World Cup competitions. Their partnership of 139 ensured that they finally went home winners

'LISTEN, JUST BE AS IF YOU WERE A CORNERED TIGER '

Imran Khan on the 1992 World Cup Final

'We had watched the South African game very closely and assessed the England attack. We realised that DeFreitas and Pringle used the new ball very well when it had seam and shine on it. The reason I was at number three was to see off that shine, because we had these big hitters at the back who would then go and hit out.

"So that's why we started a little slowly. But it worked out to plan, because our target was between 230 and 250. When Wasim got those two wickets in a row, when he got Chris Lewis out, I thought it would be difficult for England to get back into the game from there.

"I didn't think we had lost the tournament at any stage, even though it seemed like it at times. The hardest thing for a captain is when the team is doing badly. There was a time when morale was very low, after the Brisbane match against South Africa, where I thought we would have won the game, but then rain came in and took away the target from us. That was rock bottom.

"It's quite a young team. We've got a core of four or five players who are experienced – Javed and me, Ramiz, Salim and Wasim – but the rest are very young. And rather than have team meetings and tell the boys they had done something wrong, I just told them: 'Listen, just be as if you were a cornered tiger – you've got nowhere to go. Just go and fight.' And it worked. It was certainly the most fulfilling, satisfying cricketing moment of my life."

'WE PEAKED TOO EARLY'

Graham Gooch on the 1992 World Cup Final

'I thought that, for that World Cup, we had one of the best one-day sides England have every put together. We started off the tournament as a tight-knit unit and played really well, beating Australia comfortably in Sydney. And our run went well up to the Final.

"We had had a couple of off matches just before the semi-final but, as far as I'm concerned, the outcome against South Africa was no false result because when Dermot Reeve and Graeme Hick were batting really well, South Africa slowed the over-rate down and we missed out on five overs. So when the time ran out at the end of their innings, that was their fault.

"In the Final we just played a bit under par on the day. We had played Pakistan earlier on and bowled them out for 74 before the game was abandoned due to rain. If they had lost that game, they wouldn't even have made the semi-finals. We peaked a bit early in the competition, whereas Pakistan had started off awfully and were peaking at the right time, and that was the difference on the day.

"I played in three World Cups and England reached the Final in each one. That's not a bad record, but I would have liked one winner's medal."

Gooch (second right) congratulates Derek Pringle as Ramiz Raja walks; but that brought Javed in to join Imran. Top: The tiger T-shirt

put on another 38, but into the attack came Mushtaq Ahmed and in successive overs he had Hick lbw to the googly for 17 and Gooch caught sweeping for 29. Alarm bells were ringing in the England camp at 69 for four in the 21st over.

Now Neil Fairbrother and Allan Lamb began to push the score on at the right rate, adding 72. So Imran brought back Wasim Akram, who did the job for him. In successive balls he bowled both Lamb for 31 and the new batsman, Chris Lewis.

It was 141 for six in the 35th over and Pakistan's name was all but on the trophy. With the demise of Fairbrother in the 43rd over for 62, made from 70 balls, England's last realistic chance had gone – though they took the game into the last over.

Peter Baxter: *"And Imran marches back. Turns now, to run in to bowl to Illingworth. Illingworth takes two paces down the pitch – he's hit it high – he's going to be caught. Yes! The catch is taken there by Ramiz and Illingworth is out. Pakistan have won the World Cup!*

"England are all out for 227 in the last over of their innings. And Pakistan have won the Final by 22 runs.

"Tremendous scenes. A large Pakistani flag has come out to greet them, plus a smaller one. They're embracing each other. The two English batsmen walk off rather sadly ahead of the Pakistan team towards the dressing room.

"Pakistan are delighted. They have paced themselves ideally. They started this tournament as though they hadn't a hope of getting into the semi-finals and now they have won the Cup for the first time."

The green and white banners waved exultantly. A side that had seemed to all intents out of the competition a couple of weeks before had carried off the crystal globe that was the fifth World Cup.

Imran Khan triumphed after coming out of retirement for his fifth shot at the World Cup

· THE FINAL ·
MELBOURNE • 25 MARCH

PAKISTAN
won the toss

Aamir Sohail c Stewart b Pringle	4
Ramiz Raja lbw b Pringle	8
*Imran Khan c Illingworth b Botham	72
Javed Miandad c Botham b Ilingworth	58
Inzamam-ul-Haq b Pringle	42
Wasim Akram run out	33
Salim Malik not out	0
Extras (L-b 19, w 6, n-b 7)	32
Total (50 Overs, for 6 wickets)	**249**

Did not bat: Ijaz Ahmed, †Moin Khan, Mushtaq Ahmed and Aqib Javed

Fall of wickets: 1/20 2/24 3/163 4/197 5/249 6/249

Bowling: Pringle 10-2-22-3; Lewis 10-2-52-0; Botham 7-0-42-1; DeFreitas 10-1-42-0; Illingworth 10-0-50-1; Reeve 3-0-22-0.

ENGLAND

*G A Gooch c Aqib Javed b Mushtaq Ahmed	29
I T Botham c Moin Khan b Wasim Akram	0
†A J Stewart c Moin Khan b Aqib Javed	7
G A Hick lbw b Mushtaq Ahmed	17
N H Fairbrother c Moin Khan b Aqib Javed	62
A J Lamb b Wasim Akram	31
C C Lewis b Wasim Akram	0
D A Reeve c Ramiz Raja b Mushtaq Ahmed	15
D R Pringle not out	18
P A J DeFreitas run out	10
R K Illingworth c Ramiz Raja b Imran Khan	14
Extras (L-b 5, w 13, n-b 6)	24
Total (49.2 overs)	**227**

Fall of wickets: 1/6 2/21 3/59 4/69 5/141 6/141 7/180 8/183 9/208 10/227

Bowling: Wasim Akram 10-0-49-3; Aqib Javed 10-2-27-2; Mushtaq Ahmed 10-1-41-3; Ijaz Ahmed 3-0-13-0; Imran Khan 6.2-0-43-1; Aamir Sohail 10-0-49-0

Umpires: B L Aldridge and S A Bucknor

Man of the Match: Wasim Akram

PAKISTAN
won by 22 runs

· 1992 STATISTICS ·

Highest totals

313 for 7   Sri Lanka against Zimbabwe
312 for 4   Zimbabwe against Sri Lanka
280 for 6   England against Sri Lanka
268 for 8   West Indies against Sri Lanka
265 for 6   Australia against Zimbabwe

Lowest totals (complete innings, excludes innings reduced by rain)

74   Pakistan against England
125   England against Zimbabwe
134   Zimbabwe against England
136   West Indies against South Africa
157   West Indies against England

Highest winning margins

10 wickets   West Indies against Pakistan
9 wickets   South Africa against Australia
8 wickets   England against Australia
7 wickets   New Zealand against South Africa
7 wickets   Australia against Sri Lanka
7 wickets   South Africa against Zimbabwe
7 wickets   New Zealand against England
7 wickets   Pakistan against New Zealand
128 runs   Australia against Zimbabwe
106 runs   England against Sri Lanka
91 runs   West Indies against Sri Lanka
75 runs   West Indies against Zimbabwe
64 runs   South Africa against West Indies

Lowest winning margins

1 run   Australia against India
9 runs   England against India
9 runs   Zimbabwe against England
19 runs   England against South Africa
20 runs   South Africa against Pakistan

Highest match aggregates

625 for 11   Sri Lanka v Zimbabwe
526 for 13   Pakistan v New Zealand
484 for 12   England v South Africa
476 for 16   England v Pakistan
471 for 19   Australia v India

Wins by non-Test teams

Zimbabwe beat England by 9 runs

Centuries

119 n.o.   Ramiz Raja, Pakistan v New Zealand
115 n.o.   A Flower, Zimbabwe v Sri Lanka
114   Aamir Sohail, Pakistan v Zimbabwe
110   P V Simmons, West Indies v Sri Lanka
102 n.o.   Ramiz Raja, Pakistan v West Indies
100 n.o.   M D Crowe, New Zealand v Australia
100   D C Boon, Australia v New Zealand
100   D C Boon, Australia v West Indies

Highest score for each position

1   A Flower, 115 n.o., Zimbabwe v Sri Lanka
2   Ramiz Raja, 119 n.o., Pakistan v West Indies
3   P V Simmons, 110 West Indies v Sri Lanka
4   M D Crowe, 100 n.o., New Zealand v Australia
5   A Ranatunga, 88 n.o., Sri Lanka v Zimbabwe
6   A C Waller 83 n.o., Zimbabwe v Sri Lanka
7   A H Shah, 60 n.o., Zimbabwe v West Indies
8   B M McMillan 33, South Africa v Pakistan
9   G R Larsen, 37, New Zealand v Pakistan
10   W K M Benjamin 24 n.o., West Indies
         v Sri Lanka
11   G P Wickremasinghe 21 n.o., Sri Lanka
         v West Indies

Most runs

456   at 114   M D Crowe, New Zealand
437   at 62.42   Javed Miandad, Pakistan
410   at 68.33   P N Kirsten, South Africa
368   at 52.57   D C Boon, Australia
349   at 58.16   Ramiz Raja, Pakistan

Most wickets

18   at 18.77   Wasim Akram, Pakistan
16   at 19.12   I T Botham, England
16   at 19.43   Mushtaq Ahmed, Pakistan
16   at 21.37   C Z Harris, New Zealand
14   at 25.28   E A Brandes, Zimbabwe

Most wickets in a match

4-11   M W Pringle, South Africa v West Indies
4-21   E A Brandes, Zimbabwe v England
4-31   I T Botham, England v Australia
4-33   A C Cummins, West Indies v India
4-34   M R Whitney, Australia v West Indies
4-57   U C Hathurusinghe, Sri Lanka v West Indies
4-32   Wasim Akram, Pakistan v New Zealand

Most dismissals by a wicketkeeper

15   (14ct, 1st)   D J Richardson, South Africa
14   (11ct, 3st)   Moin Khan, Pakistan
14   (11ct, 3st)   D Williams, West Indies
9   (8ct,1st)   A J Stewart, England
9   (9ct)   I A Healy, Australia

Most catches by an outfielder

7   K C Wessels, South Africa
6   N H Fairbrother, England
5   A R Border, Australia
5   G A Hick, England
5   D A Reeve, England
5   P A J DeFreitas, England
5   G R Larsen, New Zealand
5   C L Cairns, New Zealand

Australia *batting*

	M	I	NO	Runs	HS	Avge	100	50	Ct	St
D.C.Boon	8	8	1	368	100	52.57	2	-	-	-
D.M.Jones	8	8	1	276	90	39.42	-	2	2	-
M.E.Waugh	5	5	1	145	66*	36.25	-	1	4	-
G.R.Marsh	5	5	0	151	60	30.20	-	1	-	-
S.R.Waugh	8	7	0	187	55	26.71	-	1	2	-
T.M.Moody	8	8	0	202	57	25.25	-	2	2	-
M.R.Whitney	7	3	2	22	9*	22.00	-	-	-	-
I.A.Healy	7	6	2	51	16	12.75	-	-	9	-
A.R.Border	8	7	0	60	22	8.57	-	-	5	-
M.A.Taylor	2	2	0	13	13	6.50	-	-	-	-
B.A.Reid	6	4	2	9	5*	4.50	-	-	-	-
P.L.Taylor	7	6	2	17	10*	4.25	-	-	1	-
C.J.McDermott	8	5	0	9	6	1.80	-	-	2	-
M.G.Hughes	1	1	1	0	0*	-	-	-	-	-

Australia *bowling*

	O	M	R	W	Avge	Best	5w	Econ
M.R.Whitney	66	12	215	9	23.88	4-34	-	3.25
C.J.McDermott	73	5	246	8	30.75	2-29	-	3.36
A.R.Border	14	0	53	1	53.00	1-40	-	3.78
B.A.Reid	54.4	3	209	3	69.66	1-17	-	3.82
P.L.Taylor	37.4	1	147	5	29.40	2-14	-	3.90
S.R.Waugh	60.4	1	277	8	34.62	3-36	-	4.56
T.M.Moody	49	2	225	7	32.14	3-56	-	4.59
M.G.Hughes	9	1	49	1	49.00	1-49	-	5.44
M.E.Waugh	5	0	40	0	-	-	-	8.00

England *batting*

	M	I	NO	Runs	HS	Avge	100	50	Ct	St
N.H.Fairbrother	9	7	2	285	75*	57.00	-	3	6	-
D.A.Reeve	9	5	3	79	25*	39.50	-	-	5	-
A.J.Stewart	10	8	1	259	77	37.00	-	2	8	1
G.A.Hick	10	9	1	264	83	33.00	-	3	5	-
R.A.Smith	8	8	2	193	91	32.16	-	1	3	-
G.A.Gooch	8	8	0	216	65	27.00	-	3	1	-
I.T.Botham	10	10	1	192	53	21.33	-	1	4	-
C.C.Lewis	9	6	2	81	33	20.25	-	-	4	-
A.J.Lamb	4	4	0	79	31	19.75	-	-	1	-
R.K.Illingworth	6	3	1	27	14	13.50	-	-	3	-
D.R.Pringle	8	5	2	30	18*	10.00	-	-	2	-
G.C.Small	5	1	0	5	5	5.00	-	-	-	-
P.A.J.DeFreitas	10	5	1	16	10	4.00	-	-	5	-
P.C.R.Tufnell	4	2	2	3	3*	-	-	-	-	-

England *bowling*

	O	M	R	W	Avge	Best	5w	Econ
D.R.Pringle	66.4	15	218	7	31.14	3-8	-	3.27
I.T.Botham	89	7	306	16	19.12	4-31	-	3.43
G.C.Small	35	3	127	5	25.40	2-29	-	3.62
D.A.Reeve	34.4	4	126	8	15.75	3-38	-	3.63
P.A.J.DeFreitas	85.3	12	319	11	29.00	3-34	-	3.73
C.C.Lewis	50.4	5	214	7	30.57	4-30	-	4.22
R.K.Illingworth	58.1	2	250	8	31.25	3-33	-	4.29
P.C.R.Tufnell	28	2	133	3	44.33	2-36	-	4.75
G.A.Hick	14.2	0	70	2	35.00	2-44	-	4.88

**Neil Fairbrother topped the England
batting averages and took six catches**

India *batting*

	M	I	NO	Runs	HS	Avge	100	50	Ct	St
M.Azharuddin	8	7	0	332	93	47.42	-	4	1	-
S.R.Tendulkar	8	7	1	283	84	47.16	-	3	2	-
R.J.Shastri	2	2	0	82	57	41.00	-	1	1	-
S.Banerjee	3	2	1	36	25*	36.00	-	-	2	-
J.Srinath	8	6	5	34	11	34.00	-	-	-	-
S.V.Manjrekar	6	6	0	154	47	25.66	-	-	3	-
A.Jadeja	6	5	1	93	46	23.25	-	-	2	-
Kapil Dev	8	8	1	161	42	23.00	-	-	-	-
K.Srikkanth	8	8	1	117	40	16.71	-	-	4	-
P.K.Amre	4	3	1	27	22	13.50	-	-	-	-
K.S.More	8	6	2	41	15*	10.25	-	-	6	1
V.G.Kambli	5	4	0	29	24	7.25	-	-	-	-
M.Prabhakar	8	4	1	11	8	3.66	-	-	1	-
S.L.V.Raju	6	2	0	1	1	0.50	-	-	1	-

India *bowling*

	O	M	R	W	Avge	Best	5w	Econ
M.Prabhakar	57.1	5	245	12	20.41	3-41	-	4.28
S.L.V.Raju	48.1	3	208	5	41.60	2-38	-	4.31
Kapil Dev	58	2	251	9	27.88	3-41	-	4.32
S.R.Tendulkar	41	0	180	2	90.00	1-35	-	4.39
J.Srinath	53.1	3	249	8	31.12	2-23	-	4.68
A.Jadeja	7.3	0	39	0	-	-	-	5.20
S.Banerjee	13	1	85	1	85.00	1-45	-	6.53
K.Srikkanth	2.1	0	15	0	-	-	-	6.92
R.J.Shastri	4	0	28	1	28.00	1-28	-	7.00

New Zealand *batting*

	M	I	NO	Runs	HS	Avge	100	50	Ct	St
M.D.Crowe	9	9	5	456	100*	114.00	1	4	3	-
A.H.Jones	9	9	2	322	78	46.00	-	3	2	-
G.R.Larsen	9	2	1	45	37	45.00	-	-	5	-
M.J.Greatbatch	7	7	0	313	73	44.71	-	3	4	-
K.R.Rutherford	9	7	2	212	65*	42.40	-	3	3	-
R.T.Latham	7	7	0	136	60	19.42	-	1	3	-
J.G.Wright	4	4	0	71	57	17.75	-	1	1	-
I.D.S.Smith	9	5	1	61	19	15.25	-	-	5	-
D.N.Patel	9	3	1	25	10*	12.50	-	-	2	-
D.K.Morrison	5	1	0	12	12	12.00	-	-	1	-
C.Z.Harris	9	6	1	44	14	8.80	-	-	4	-
C.L.Cairns	5	3	3	21	16*	-	-	-	5	-
W.Watson	8	1	1	5	5*	-	-	-	1	-

New Zealand *bowling*

	O	M	R	W	Avge	Best	5w	Econ
D.N.Patel	79	8	245	8	30.62	2-26	-	3.10
G.R.Larsen	76	7	262	9	29.11	3-16	-	3.44
W.Watson	79	11	301	12	25.08	3-37	-	3.81
A.H.Jones	12	0	52	2	26.00	2-42	-	4.33
D.K.Morrison	40	1	180	5	36.00	3-42	-	4.50
C.Z.Harris	72.1	4	342	16	21.37	3-15	-	4.73
M.J.Greatbatch	1	0	5	0	-	-	-	5.00
R.T.Latham	23	0	136	1	136.00	1-35	-	5.91
M.D.Crowe	1	0	6	0	-	-	-	6.00
C.L.Cairns	25	1	161	2	80.50	2-43	-	6.44
K.R.Rutherford	1.4	0	11	0	-	-	-	6.60

Pakistan *batting*

	M	I	NO	Runs	HS	Avge	100	50	Ct	St
Javed Miandad	9	9	2	437	89	62.42	-	5	1	-
Ramiz Raja	8	8	2	349	119*	58.16	2	-	4	-
Aamir Sohail	10	10	0	326	114	32.60	1	2	3	-
Imran Khan	8	6	0	185	72	30.83	-	1	1	-
Inzamam-ul-Haq	10	10	0	225	60	22.50	-	1	4	-
Salim Malik	10	9	3	116	51	19.33	-	1	3	-
Moin Khan	10	5	2	44	20*	14.66	-	-	11	3
Wasim Haider	3	2	0	26	13	13.00	-	-	-	-
Wasim Akram	10	8	2	62	33	10.33	-	-	1	-
Mushtaq Ahmed	9	4	1	27	17	9.00	-	-	2	-
Zahid Fazal	2	2	0	13	11	6.50	-	-	1	-
Ijaz Ahmed	7	4	1	14	8*	4.66	-	-	4	-
Aqib Javed	10	2	2	2	1*	-	-	-	2	-
Iqbal Sikander	4	1	1	1	1*	-	-	-	-	-

Pakistan *bowling*

	O	M	R	W	Avge	Best	5w	Econ
Wasim Akram	89.4	3	338	18	18.77	4-32	-	3.76
Aqib Javed	84.5	11	328	11	29.81	3-21	-	3.86
Mushtaq Ahmed	78	3	311	16	19.43	3-41	-	3.98
Ijaz Ahmed	36	1	149	1	149.00	1-28	-	4.13
Wasim Haider	19	1	79	1	79.00	1-36	-	4.15
Imran Khan	60.2	2	251	7	35.85	2-32	-	4.16
Iqbal Sikander	35	2	147	3	49.00	1-30	-	4.20
Salim Malik	4	0	18	0	-	-	-	4.50
Aamir Sohail	40	2	184	4	46.00	2-26	-	4.60

South Africa *batting*

	M	I	NO	Runs	HS	Avge	100	50	Ct	St
P.N.Kirsten	8	8	2	410	90	68.33	-	4	2	-
B.M.McMillan	9	5	3	125	33*	62.50	-	-	4	-
K.C.Wessels	9	9	2	313	85	44.71	-	3	7	-
A.C.Hudson	8	8	0	296	79	37.00	-	3	-	-
W.J.Cronje	8	6	3	102	47*	34.00	-	-	3	-
D.J.Richardson	9	5	2	66	28	22.00	-	-	14	1
J.N.Rhodes	9	8	1	132	43	18.85	-	-	4	-
M.W.Rushmere	3	3	0	49	35	16.33	-	-	1	-
A.P.Kuiper	9	8	1	113	36	16.14	-	-	3	-
R.P.Snell	9	4	2	24	11*	12.00	-	-	-	-
O.Henry	1	1	0	11	11	11.00	-	-	-	-
A.A.Donald	9	1	0	3	3	3.00	-	-	1	-
M.W.Pringle	7	1	1	5	5*	-	-	-	1	-
T.Bosch	1	0	0	0	0	-	-	-	-	-

South Africa *bowling*

	O	M	R	W	Avge	Best	5w	Econ
O.Henry	10	0	31	1	31.00	1-31	-	3.10
M.W.Pringle	57	6	236	8	29.50	4-11	-	4.14
B.M.McMillan	73	7	306	11	27.81	3-30	-	4.19
A.A.Donald	78	5	329	13	25.30	3-34	-	4.21
W.J.Cronje	20	1	85	2	42.50	2-17	-	4.25
R.P.Snell	72.5	10	310	8	38.75	3-42	-	4.25
P.N.Kirsten	18	1	87	5	17.40	3-31	-	4.83
A.P.Kuiper	41	0	235	9	26.11	3-40	-	5.73
T.Bosch	2.3	0	19	0	-	-	-	7.60

Sri Lanka *batting*

	M	I	NO	Runs	HS	Avge	100	50	Ct	St
A.Ranatunga	8	7	2	262	88*	52.40	-	2	1	-
M.A.R.Samarasekera	6	6	0	219	75	36.50	-	1	-	-
R.S.Mahanama	8	7	0	247	81	35.28	-	3	3	-
P.A.de Silva	8	7	0	175	62	25.00	-	1	1	-
G.F.Labrooy	1	1	0	19	19	19.00	-	-	-	-
R.S.Kalpage	7	6	2	67	14	16.75	-	-	3	-
S.T.Jayasuriya	6	5	0	74	32	14.80	-	-	4	-
H.P.Tillekeratne	8	7	1	80	25*	13.33	-	-	6	1
A.P.Gurusinha	8	7	0	73	37	10.42	-	-	2	-
S.D.Anurasiri	5	4	2	20	11	10.00	-	-	1	-
U.C.Hathurusinghe	4	3	0	26	16	8.66	-	-	1	-
C.P.H.Ramanayake	8	6	2	25	12	6.25	-	-	4	-
G.P.Wickremasinghe	8	3	3	30	21*	-	-	-	2	-
K.Wijegunawardene	3	0	0	0	0	-	-	-	-	-

Sri Lanka *bowling*

	O	M	R	W	Avge	Best	5w	Econ
S.D.Anurasiri	50	3	184	5	36.80	3-41	-	3.68
C.P.H.Ramanayake	64.4	6	265	5	53.00	2-37	-	4.09
G.P.Wickremasinghe	60.1	5	276	7	39.42	2-29	-	4.58
R.S.Kalpage	50	0	241	4	60.25	2-33	-	4.82
K.I.W.Wijegunawardene	17	1	88	0	-	-	-	5.17
A.Ranatunga	18	0	94	3	31.33	2-26	-	5.22
A.P.Gurusinha	48	0	256	6	42.66	2-67	-	5.33
U.C.Hathurusinghe	17	0	97	5	19.40	4-57	-	5.70
P.A.de Silva	1	0	6	0	-	-	-	6.00
G.F.Labrooy	10	1	68	1	68.00	1-68	-	6.80
S.T.Jayasuriya	6	0	44	0	-	-	-	7.33

West Indies *batting*

	M	I	NO	Runs	HS	Avge	100	50	Ct	St
B.C.Lara	8	8	1	333	88*	47.57	-	4	2	-
D.L.Haynes	7	7	1	251	93*	41.83	-	1	4	-
K.L.T.Arthurton	8	7	1	233	58*	38.83	-	2	1	-
P.V.Simmons	4	4	0	153	110	38.25	1	-	1	-
W.K.M.Benjamin	8	6	4	54	24*	27.00	-	-	4	-
C.L.Hooper	8	7	1	120	63	20.00	-	1	4	-
R.B.Richardson	8	8	1	132	56	18.85	-	1	3	-
A.L.Logie	8	7	0	101	61	14.42	-	1	3	-
D.Williams	8	6	2	52	32*	13.00	-	-	11	3
C.E.L.Ambrose	7	4	1	33	15*	11.00	-	-	1	-
A.C.Cummins	6	2	1	11	6	11.00	-	-	-	-
M.D.Marshall	5	4	1	16	6	4.00	-	-	-	-
R.A.Harper	2	1	0	3	3	3.00	-	-	1	-
B.P.Patterson	1	0	0	0	0	-	-	-	1	-

West Indies *bowling*

	O	M	R	W	Avge	Best	5w	Econ
B.P.Patterson	10	0	25	1	25.00	1-25	-	2.50
C.E.L.Ambrose	68	6	235	7	33.57	2-24	-	3.45
W.K.M.Benjamin	79	8	297	10	29.70	3-27	-	3.75
C.L.Hooper	80	2	312	8	39.00	2-19	-	3.90
M.D.Marshall	43	3	174	2	87.00	2-26	-	4.04
A.C.Cummins	59	1	246	12	20.50	4-33	-	4.16
R.A.Harper	14	0	63	2	31.50	1-30	-	4.50
P.V.Simmons	20	1	91	3	30.33	2-40	-	4.55
K.L.T.Arthurton	15	0	70	2	35.00	2-40	-	4.66

1996

THE WILLS WORLD CUP

In India, Pakistan and Sri Lanka

A BOMB IN COLOMBO SET THE
TONE FOR A TOURNAMENT
PLAYED OUT IN AN
ATMOSPHERE OF SUSPICION
AND RECRIMINATION.
AS FOR THE CRICKET, IT WAS
POSITIVELY EXPLOSIVE

**Right: Coca-Cola win the sponsorship war as the Indian crowd hail
a boundary in the high-stakes match against Pakistan in Bangalore**

A WHIRLWIND OVERTURNS THE WORLD ORDER

No one had ever seen anything like it. Sri Lanka's openers came in blasting. Then the middle order came in blasting. And if it got beyond them, the tail end came in blasting. But surely their luck could not last all the way to the Final. Or could it…?

'The Australian Cricket Board had received a fax threatening that the team would be greeted by a suicide bomber in the baggage hall at Colombo airport'

Right: The spectacular laser show at the opening ceremony at Eden Gardens, Calcutta

In 1993 an acrimonious ICC meeting was held at Lord's. There had been an understanding that the next World Cup would be in England, but South Africa's return re-opened the debate. Bizarrely, that enabled India, Pakistan and Sri Lanka to put in a joint bid. This provoked scenes of discord in the Lord's corridors and an impasse was only breached by the withdrawal of England, who were now inked in to host the World Cup of 1999.

But that was the least of the political problems. A bomb, thought to be placed by the Tamil Tigers, killed 100 people in Colombo on January 31 1996. It made Australia reluctant to play their first World Cup match there 18 days later. The Australians had recently been host to Sri Lanka in an ugly series during which Muttiah Muralitharan was no-balled for throwing. The Australian Cricket Board had received a fax threatening that the team would be met by a suicide bomber in the baggage hall at Colombo airport.

The Australians' decision not to go to Sri Lanka sparked sub-continental wrath of almost hysterical proportions –

some of it fuelled, no doubt, by the accusations of bribery attempts made by some Australian players against Salim Malik of Pakistan. The condemnation was rather more muted when the West Indies, too, stated their unwillingness to play in Sri Lanka.

Diplomacy and arguments went on up to the opening ceremony, but to no avail. Australia and the West Indies would forfeit their matches against Sri Lanka, with all four points to Sri Lanka.

The fact that they could afford to do that demonstrated the strange format of this tournament. The organisers had won the support of the ICC associate members by including three ICC Trophy qualifiers. With 12 teams, the competition reverted to the group system, but with a quarter-final round – which rather devalued the group stage, as a team had only to finish fourth in a group of six to go through.

Group A, based in India and Sri Lanka, was Australia, India, Sri Lanka, West Indies, Zimbabwe (now a full member of ICC) and Kenya. Group B, based in Pakistan with a few games in India, was England, New Zealand,

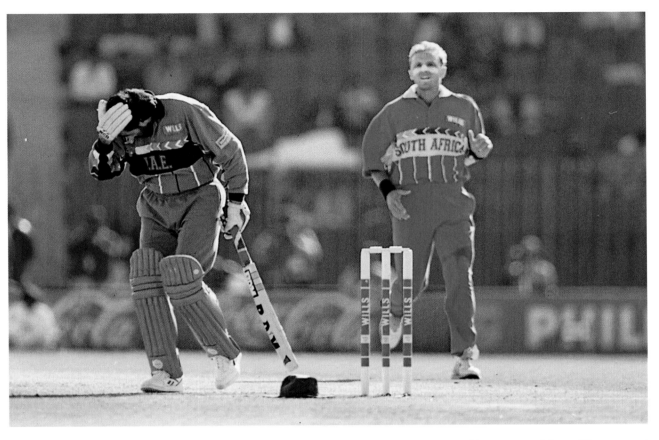

Left: Sultan Zarawani of the UAE learns the hard way you don't bat against Allan Donald without a helmet. Below: Even the scoreboard got England all mixed up at Ahmedabad, where 'Michel Artherton' ran Hick out while acting as his runner (bottom)

Pakistan, South Africa, Holland and the United Arab Emirates.

The problems of organisation were highlighted before dawn on the morning after the opening ceremony as six teams began wearying journeys to far-flung destinations. England and New Zealand flew to Delhi, then had a day's wait for an evening flight to the venue for their first game – Ahmedabad.

England had just lost a one-day series 6-1 in South Africa. Now, on Valentine's Day, Mike Atherton put New Zealand in and ran into a new name: Nathan Astle, who had been reeling off big one-day scores in other parts. He was dropped on one and made 101 from 132 balls, with two sixes. Darren Gough suffered most, his ten overs costing 63 runs. However, 239 for six should not prove insurmountable.

Dion Nash's removal of Atherton in the second over

> 'The United Arab Emirates made their World Cup debut, captained by Sultan Zarawani, of whom one observer said: "His leg spin is less impressive than his Lamborghini".'

was a blow restored by a 99-run stand between Stewart and Hick. Hick had to finish his innings with a runner, and was inevitably run out, for 85. As the rate mounted and wickets fell regularly, England saw the spectre of defeat looming again. At the end, with nine wickets down, they were 11 runs short.

Two days later, over the border in Rawalpindi, the United Arab Emirates made their World Cup debut, captained by Sultan Zarawani, of whom one observer said: "His leg spin is less impressive than his Lamborghini." Zarawani duly 'top scored' among the UAE bowlers, going for 69 runs as Gary Kirsten hammered a World Cup record of 188, hitting four sixes and 13 fours from his 159 balls.

UAE could never hope to get near a score like 321 for two, though they died bravely. None was braver – or perhaps

> 'There must be better pairs of hands in school cricket than this bunch of Englishmen.'
>
> THE INDIAN EXPRESS reporting on an England warm-up game

1. MICHEL ART HERTON
2. ALEC STEWART
3. GRAEME HICK
4. GRAHAM THORPE
5. NEIL.H.FAIR BROTHER
6. RUSSEL
7. CRAIG WHITE
8. DOMINIC CORK
9. DARREN GOUGH
10. RICHARD ILLINGWORTH
11. PETER JAMES MARTN

Bring on the pantomime horses!

THE 1996 OPENING CEREMONY

As BBC Radio's cricket producer, Peter Baxter has witnessed every World Cup opening ceremony. Lucky chap!

It would be hard to imagine a more over-the-top opening ceremony than the 1996 extravaganza in Calcutta. The first three World Cups in England had been much more low-key. Publicity shots were taken – who can now suppress a chuckle at the splendid fashion statements in that array of flared trousers? – and in 1983 the teams went to Buckingham Palace. But that was the extent of it.

The 1987 opening ceremony was in front of India's Prime Minister, Rajiv Gandhi, in New Delhi's Nehru stadium. When the teams had trooped past, the tournament was declared open with a release of balloons.

That, at least, was the plan. Keen eyes would have spotted that, moments before the balloons were supposed to soar into the Indian skies, they were lurking sullenly on the floor of the cage in which they were theoretically restrained. When the cage door was flung open with enormous panache, they refused to budge until enticed out by attendants, after which they slunk around the stadium.

This presented another problem, as the culmination of these wild celebrations was to be a friendly match between the host countries, India and Pakistan – and an army of pyjama-clad stewards reminiscent of the Keystone Cops had to gather the recalcitrant balloons before any cricket could be played.

The Australasian World Cup of 1992 had a splendid setting for its

BY
PETER BAXTER

'When the cage door was flung open with enormous panache, the balloons sullenly refused to budge'

publicity launch, with the teams photographed on *H.M.A.S. Canberra* on Sydney Harbour. But the opening ceremony before the first match in Auckland lacked that panache. A procession of flat lorries toured the ground, each with a rather wobbly polystyrene set of giant bat, ball and stumps in the colour of the country it represented and a former player waving from the truck. Some eyebrows were raised at the choice of Tony Greig, breaking off from his duties in the Channel Nine television box, to represent England again.

So in 1996, the most commercially motivated World Cup thus far, an Italian director was engaged to mount a laser display as a centre piece in Eden Gardens, Calcutta. Twelve teams paraded, girls danced, a lady sang – even before the final rites; the actor Saeed Jaffrey was splendidly imperturbable in the face of potential chaos and 100,000 enjoyed the laser show. Or they would have done if the wind had not billowed the curtains on which it was to be projected. This breeze apparently came as an enormous surprise, as no one had made any provision for holding the curtains down.

However, when the Italian director had torn his flowing hair out and the bemused players had gone to their official banquet, the laser show was repeated – this time with a couple of boy scouts holding down each curtain. And very good it was, too.

more foolhardy – than the Sultan, who came in to bat against Allan Donald in a sun hat. Donald could hardly believe his eyes, and Zarawani was duly hit on the head for his cheek. The newcomers made 152 for eight and Zarawani said that in future he would wear a helmet "to stop Mother worrying".

New Zealand moved south to Baroda to meet Group

B's other minnows, Holland. Following his century against England, Astle was run out for nought, but 307 for eight precluded an upset. Aussie Peter Cantrell and Glamorgan's Roland Lefebvre made 45s in Holland's 180 for seven.

Group A launched with a day/night game in the southern Indian city of Hyderabad, where Zimbabwe, after deciding to bat first, struggled against the West Indies. Curtly Ambrose took three, Ian Bishop bowled ten overs for 18 runs and they made 151 for nine. Sherwin Campbell, Richie Richardson and Brian Lara made sure they got there in the 30th over.

Next day, Sri Lanka's cricketers went through the ritual of turning up at the R. Premadasa Stadium in Colombo to be awarded the match against Australia, an outcome that took the gloss off their big occasion.

The only genuine minnows in the group, Kenya, played India at Cuttack in their first proper one-day international. They did well, too, in making 199 for six, with Steve Tikolo scoring 65. But an opening stand of 163 between Jadeja and Tendulkar put it in perspective, Tendulkar being 127 not out when India won by seven wickets with eight overs to spare.

To reach the next stage, the senior teams in Group B just had to ensure victory against the two associate members. England's encounters with these took place in Pakistan's North West Frontier city of Peshawar – a 27-hour journey from Ahmedabad.

England met the UAE in front of a sparse crowd in which gun-carrying troops outnumbered spectators. They bowled them out for 136, but Craig White strained an intercostal muscle – ending his World Cup. Neil Smith had a mixed day, too. The Warwickshire all-rounder took three for 29, then opened the innings – but was violently sick on the pitch when he had scored 27. He retired ill, and received little sympathy from his captain, Mike Atheron, who observed: "It's part of playing cricket out here." With Thorpe 44 not out, England cruised in in the 35th over by eight wickets.

They found Holland a tougher nut to crack. Graeme Hick's unbeaten hundred and Graham Thorpe's 89 took them to 279 for four. Dominic Cork shot out the oldest man in the World Cup, 47-year-old opener Nolan Clarke,

for a duck – but then the Cup's youngest man, 18-year-old Bas Zuiderent, helped add 114 for the fifth wicket to raise the possibility of an embarrassment. Peter Martin made sure there was none, dismissing Klass van Noortwijk for 64 and Zuiderent for 54, and Holland ended at 230 for six.

In Faisalabad, South Africa gave New Zealand an object lesson in tight fielding and kept them to 177 for nine, which was passed in the 38th over thanks to Hansie Cronje's 78.

At last, on February 21, Sri Lanka staged its first game, at the Sinhalese Sports Club in Colombo. Zimbabwe got a huge welcome for what might be a crucial game for them both. After making 228 for six, with Alistair Campbell 75, Zimbabwe were the first team to encounter Sri Lanka's incendiary approach to the first 15 overs, when all but two fielders had to be in the 30-yard circle. They scorched to 90 for two in that time, Asanka Gurusinha making 87 and Aravinda de Silva 91 as Sri Lanka won by six wickets with 13 overs to spare.

At the princely city of Gwalior that evening, the floodlights shone on an equally princely victory by India over the West Indies – watched on TV by 240 million people. First Manoj Prabhakar, Javagal Srinath and Anil Kumble bowled the West Indies out for 173. Then Sachin Tendulkar's 70 secured the win by five wickets with ten overs in hand.

In the Indian east coast town of Vishakhapatnam, Kenya won many admirers with their spirited resistance to Australia. This match featured three sets of brothers – Kenya's being Maurice and Edward Odumbe, and Steve and David Tikolo. But it was the Waugh twins who stole the headlines with a third-wicket stand of 207 – the first double-century partnership in World Cup history. Mark made 130 from 128 balls; Steve 82 from 88; and Australia racked up 304 for seven. Yet Kenya were undaunted. After 15 overs Australia had been 52

Above: Gary Kirsten set a World Cup record with his 188 not out against the UAE. Left: Graeme Hick laid into the other Group B minnows with 104 not out against Holland

'I was determined to make runs. The crowds here have been starved of good cricket and we must thank Zimbabwe for coming and playing in such a good spirit.'

ARAVINDA DE SILVA
after scoring 91 in Colombo

for two; by that stage Kenya had rushed to 74 for two. Maurice Odumbe made 50 and Kennedy Otieno, who had to retire briefly with cramp, 85. They finished on 207 for seven, 97 short. Australia's day was spoilt when Craig McDermott's calf injury took him out of the attack and the tournament.

Two days later Sri Lanka claimed two more points for the forfeited game with the West Indies – a costly 'victory'. Ana Punchihewa, president of the Sri Lankan Board of Control, said: "We have lost 80 per cent of what we expected to make. That money might have helped us to develop cricket here for the next five years."

The third host nation had also been inactive so far: Pakistan would not play until the end of the Muslim holy month of Ramadan. Their opponents at Gujranwala were the UAE, who did not give them too searching a test. In a match reduced by rain to 33 overs a side, they made 109 for nine, gave Mushtaq Ahmed three wickets and then saw Pakistan reach the target in 18 overs.

At the halfway stage of their match at Rawalpindi next day, England believed they had a good chance of avenging the previous month's indignities at the hands of South Africa. They had restricted them to 230 all out in their 50 overs. Atherton promptly went for a duck in Shaun Pollock's first over and, though Graham Thorpe made 46, England were all out in the 45th over as much as 78 runs short.

With manager Ray Illingworth complaining about the lack of practice facilities wherever they went, this was starting to look like a doomed tournament for England – a feeling compounded at the post-match press conference when Mike Atherton called a Pakistani journalist "a buffoon". One local newspaper, *The News*, acidly reported that "England, the mother country of the game, came up with a kind of display yesterday that could lead to calls for them to go through the ICC qualification competition in

future." Atherton's South African counterpart Hansie Cronje rubbed salt into England's persecution complex by saying that his team loved being in Pakistan, adding: "I have nothing but praise for the way we have been looked after."

Pakistan made up for lost time with their second match in three days, and booked their quarter-final place by overwhelming Holland in Lahore. The lighting pylons which would illuminate the Final there in three weeks were no more than a few feet high so far, but everyone seemed remarkably cheerful about it

Zimbabwe could have been embarrassed in Patna, when Kenya reduced them to 45 for three. But rain spared their blushes, as, under the rules, a new match had to be started next day – and in this one Kenya batted first and were dismissed by the Strang brothers for 134. The leg spin of Paul accounted for five for 21 and the medium pace of Bryan two for 24. Zimbabwe lost five wickets in reaching their target. People were finding that it did not pay to take Kenya too lightly.

Bombay staged its first day/night international that day when India met Australia. There had already been chaotic scenes when tickets went on sale, with the police making *lathi* charges to disperse the crowd. The match did not disappoint.

Mark Waugh became the first man to make successive World Cup centuries, hitting three sixes and eight fours before he was run out for 126 from 135 balls. But then Australia folded. The last seven wickets crashed for 26, and the last over was a connoisseur's delight, with two wickets for Prasad and two runouts. They were all out at the end for 258.

India had pulled themselves back into the match, but seemed to be sliding out of it again when Damien Fleming removed Ajay Jadeja and Mohammed Azharuddin inside the 15 overs. Now Tendulkar declared this his show and really started the crowd's firecrackers exploding with 90

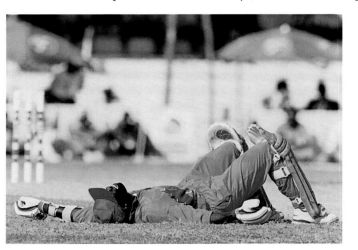

Right: Kennedy Otieno of Kenya suffers an attack of cramp against Australia, when within sight of becoming the third player from a non-Test country to score a World Cup century. After going off to recover, he was out three runs later for 85

'I have found the public here very friendly, but the Pakistan press is hostile to us and I can only think that dates back to previous English teams. I don't court popularity and if crowds take against me, then it is part of my nature to be spurred to extra effort. Having said that, after what has happened this weekend I shall have to be more careful.'

MIKE ATHERTON
after he was pilloried in Pakistan for calling a local journalist a buffoon

from 84 balls. But Mark Waugh, bowling his off spin, had him stumped off a wide, to ensure himself the Man of the Match award. Despite Sanjay Manjrekar's 62, India's last wicket fell in the 48th over with 17 needed.

Leap year day may only come every four years, but the sort of result that this February 29 produced is rarer still. In Pune, Kenya came up against their idols. Kenya captain Maurice Odumbe said: "West Indies are our favourite cricketers. It's an honour to play them. We try to play like them, aggressive and entertaining. The boys will learn a lot." He also hoped to get Brian Lara's autograph, because the last time he had asked, several years previously in Swansea, Lara had refused...

Kenya, put in to bat, were dismissed for 166 – which owed a lot to 35 extras, including a disgraceful 27 in wides and no-balls. Even so, 166 seemed a formality. But the medium-paced opening bowlers, Martin Suji and Rajab Ali, sent back Richardson, Campbell and Lara in quick succession and suddenly it was 33 for three. Two runs later, Keith Arthurton was run out. Now Odumbe came on with his off-breaks and captured the wickets of Shivnarine Chanderpaul, Jimmy Adams and Roger Harper and it was 78 for seven.

Early risers in the Caribbean were waking to a horror story. And when they heard on the BBC World Service that Rajib Ali had bowled Cameron Cuffy, they knew it was not fiction. The West Indies were bowled out for 93, their lowest World Cup score. They had lost to lowly Kenya by 73 runs. And with their forfeited game against Sri Lanka, they could no longer be sure of making the quarter-finals.

Odumbe acknowledged that his team, in humbling the former World Champions, had created history. Richardson, knowing this might spell the end of his captaincy, said: "It was a really bad performance. I've never felt this bad in all my life."

In Group B, New Zealand ended their sojourn in Faisalabad by beating the UAE by 109 runs with Roger Twose, New Zealand's adopted Devonian, making 92.

The match in Karachi on February 29 was likely to settle the leadership of Group B. Pakistan's total of 242 depended hugely on Aamir Sohail's 111, but South Africa capitalised on the first 15 overs, imaking 105 for two in that time, and won by five wickets.

At Nagpur, Australia bowled Zimbabwe out for 154. Mark Waugh had to make do with 76 not out in the eight-wicket win.

There was a more significant match in Delhi next day, when Group A's two host countries met. Sri Lanka put India in. They started slowly – only 47 in 15 overs – but then Tendulkar cut loose, making 137 in as many balls. With Azharuddin 72 not out, 271 for three seemed a comfortable enough score to defend.

Enter the human whirlwind, Sanath Jayasuriya. Sri Lanka passed 50 in the fifth over and their 15-over score was 117 for one. The ball was flying to all parts of the Ferosz Shah Kotla ground. Kumble ended Jayasuriya's assault at 79, made off 76 balls, but Arjuna Ranatunga and Hashan Tillekeratne picked up the charge and Sri Lanka won by six wickets with eight balls to spare. This had been a performance to make the cricket world take note of their potential for the first time.

Of less import – but certainly important to the contestants – was the game between Holland and the United Arab Emirates. Although the UAE were the ICC Trophy Champions, the evidence to date suggested Holland were the more likely winners. But in the event they could not defend their score of 216 for nine. Saleem Raza, a native of Lahore, with 84 from 64 balls, brought UAE victory by seven wickets.

In Karachi, England looked set for their first victory over a Test country with an opening stand against Pakistan of 147, of which Robin Smith made 75. But with Mushtaq taking three wickets, the innings ended at 249 for nine. Revelling in the

Left: Ian Healy enjoys a quiet half-hour by the hotel pool in Vishakhapatnam, where the Australian team were guarded by 634 police officers plus eight armed platoons, an anti-sabotage squad and sniffer dogs

'To us this was like winning the World Cup itself. The turning point was when we got Brian Lara, because it has been said over and over again that once you get Lara, the West Indies are a little bit shaky. When the last wicket fell, everybody was excited about it. We've created history here. I can't believe it. I'll just have to wait and wake up in the morning before it hits me.'

MAURICE ODUMBE
Kenya captain

· GROUP A ·

FEBRUARY 16 AT HYDERABAD (DAY/NIGHT)
West Indies 155 for 4 (Strang 4-40) **beat Zimbabwe** 151 for 9 (Ambrose 3-28) **by six wickets**

FEBRUARY 17 AT R PREMADASA STADIUM, COLOMBO
Sri Lanka awarded match by default after **Australia** failed to turn up

FEBRUARY 18 AT CUTTACK
India 203 for 3 (S R Tendulkar 127*, A Jadeja 53) **beat Kenya** 199 for 6 (S Tikolo 65, Kumble 3-28) **by seven wkts**

FEBRUARY 21 AT SINHALESE SPORTS CLUB, COLOMBO
Sri Lanka 229 for 4 (P A de Silva 91, A P Gurusinha 87, Streak 3-60) **beat Zimbabwe** 228 for 6 (A D R Campbell 75) **by six wickets**

FEBRUARY 21 AT GWALIOR (D/N)
India 174 for 5 (S R Tendulkar 70) **beat West Indies** 173 (Prabhakar 3-39) **by five wickets**

FEBRUARY 23 AT VISHAKHAPATNAM
Australia 304 for 7 (M E Waugh 130, S R Waugh 82, Rajab Ali 3-45) **beat Kenya** 207 for 7 (K Otieno 85, M Odumbe 50) **by 97 runs**

FEBRUARY 25 AT R PREMADASA STADIUM, COLOMBO
Sri Lanka awarded match by default after **West Indies** failed to turn up

FEBRUARY 26 AT PATNA
Zimbabwe 45-3 v **Kenya** – no result

FEBRUARY 27 AT PATNA
Zimbabwe 137 for 5 (Rajab Ali 3-22) **bt Kenya** 134 (Strang 5-21) **by five wkts**

FEBRUARY 27 AT BOMBAY (D/N)
Australia 258 (M E Waugh 126, M A Taylor 59) **beat India** 242 (S R Tendulkar 90, S V Manjrekar 62, Fleming 5-36) **by 16 runs**

FEBRUARY 29 AT PUNE
Kenya 166 (Harper 3-15, Walsh 3-46) **beat West Indies** 93 (M Odumbe 3-15, Rajab Ali 3-17) **by 73 runs**

MARCH 1 AT NAGPUR
Australia 158 for 2 (M E Waugh 76*) **beat Zimbabwe** 154 (A C Waller 67, Warne 4-34) **by eight wickets**

MARCH 2 AT DELHI
Sri Lanka 272 for 4 (S T Jayasuriya 79, H P Tillekeratne 70*) **beat India** 271 for 3 (S R Tendulkar 137, M Azharuddin 72*) **by six wickets**

MARCH 4 AT JAIPUR
West Indies 232 for 6 (R B Richardson 93*, B C Lara 60, M E Waugh 3-38) **beat Australia** 229 for 6 (R T Ponting 102, S R Waugh 57) **by four wickets**

MARCH 6 AT KANPUR
India 247 for 5 (V G Kambli 106, N S Sidhu 80) **beat Zimbabwe** 207 (Raju 3-30) **by 40 runs**

MARCH 6 AT KANDY
Sri Lanka 398 for 5 (P A de Silva 145, A Gurusinha 84, A Ranatunga 75*) **beat Kenya** 254-7 (S Tikolo 96) **by 144 runs**

GROUP A FINAL TABLE

	P	W	L	Pts	*Run rate
Sri Lanka	5	5	0	10	1.60
Australia	5	3	2	6	0.90
India	5	3	2	6	0.45
West Indies	5	2	3	4	-0.13
Zimbabwe	5	1	4	2	-0.93
Kenya	5	1	4	2	-1.00

*Run-rate is a net value. Teams on equal points were separated by the winner of their head-to-head game

adoration of a noisy crowd, Pakistan's batsmen soon showed the paucity of that score. Aamir Sohail, Saeed Anwar, Ijaz Ahmed and Inzamam-ul-Haq all got substantial scores, but the biggest cheer was for the ageless Javed Miandad. In front of his home-town crowd, he was also creating history, having come out of a two-year retirement to become the only man to appear in all six World Cups. He was there with 11 when Pakistan won by seven wickets.

With that defeat, England knew that, as the fourth qualifier from Group B, they would play their quarter-final in Faisalabad against Sri Lanka. Feeling that Sri Lanka's position was a little false, this seemed to be their preferred option, anyway.

Back in India, the West Indies needed to beat Australia to get into the quarter-finals. Still smarting from the humiliation of Pune, Curtly Ambrose and Courtney Walsh made life tough for the Australian openers. But Ricky Ponting came in to make a century, setting the West Indies 230 to win.

The early loss of the openers brought together Brian Lara and Richie Richardson. Richardson had borne the brunt of the abuse from the Caribbean following the Kenyan defeat, but now he proudly led his side to victory. With Lara making 60, they enjoyed a stand of 87 and Richardson was 93 when they won with seven balls to go.

The West Indies would be fourth qualifiers, provided Kenya did not win their last game. The prize was to go to Karachi to meet the winners of Group A, confirmed as being South Africa next day, when Andrew Hudson made 161 in a remarkable 132 balls as they ran up 328 for three to beat the orange shirts of Holland.

The second place in Group B was decided in Lahore in a head-to-head between Pakistan and New Zealand. It should have been played under lights, but it surprised nobody who had paid earlier visits to the ground that these were not yet ready ... although mischievous stories emerging from India that Calcutta was preparing to take over the Final were guaranteed to hasten completion. The winners would go to Bangalore to take on India at home; the losers to Madras to face Australia. It was an intriguing option. There were even suggestions that one or other side might prefer to throw the game.

Pakistan certainly did not bat as if that was in their minds. Aamir Sohail's 50 ended in the 15th over and Saeed Anwar made 62, while the closing acceleration came from Salim Malik, whose 55 not out ensured that as many as 83 came from the last ten overs.

'Seeing Kenya beat the West Indies was the happiest moment of my life. I've been trying to convince the boys that there was not as much difference between them and the Test players as they think. The difference is not in ability, but experience.'

HANUMANT SINGH
Kenya coach and former Indian Test player

England's Darren Gough is blasted out by Wasim Akram in Karachi

A score of 281 for five would be daunting to overhaul, but New Zealand remained in the hunt. Their captain and wicketkeeper, the personable Lee Germon, took the responsibility, coming in at number three and making 41, but they were always just a wicket or two down on being in a challenging position and were all out in the 48th over, 46 runs short. Each country knew it must now meet its own neighbour in the next round.

Group A finished its business on the same day, with India playing Zimbabwe in Kanpur, and Sri Lanka back in their own island for the visit of Kenya. India were given a little early shock at 32 for three with the considerable talents of Tendulkar, Manjrekar and Azharuddin back in the pavilion, but Navjot Sidhu and Vinod Kambli saved embarrassment. They added 142, Sidhu making 80 and Kambli 106.

For a time Zimbabwe seemed to have that within their compass, for a late inclusion in the quarter-finals, but the slow left-armer Raju snuffed out their ambition. Zimbabwe were all out 40 runs adrift.

If Sri Lanka's assault on India's bowlers had raised a few eyebrows, their demolition of Kenya's in the hill city of Kandy was amazing. They set a new record for any one-day international with a total of 398 for five, having reached 123 in the first 15 overs. Aravinda de Silva made 145 in only 115 balls and Ranatunga's 75 not out came from an explosive 40 balls. Even in the face of this, Kenya's batsmen continued to impress. Steve Tikolo's 96 contained eight fours and four sixes and took only 95 balls. They still lost by 144 runs, leaving no doubt which team had been the surprise stars of the group stage.

· GROUP B ·

FEBRUARY 14 AT AHMEDABAD
New Zealand 239 for 6 (N J Astle 101) **beat England** 228 for 9 (G A Hick 85, Nash 3-26) **by 11 runs**

FEBRUARY 15/16 AT RAWALPINDI
South Africa 321 for 2 (G Kirsten 188*, W J Cronje 57) **beat UAE** 152 for 8 (McMillan 3-11, Donald 3-21) **by 169 runs**

FEBRUARY 17 AT BARODA
New Zealand 307 for 8 (C M Spearman 68, S P Fleming 66, A C Parore 55, C Cairns 52, Lubbers 3-48) **beat Holland** 188 for 7 (Harris 3-24) **by 119 runs**

FEBRUARY 18 AT PESHAWAR
England 140 for 2 **beat UAE** 136 (Smith 3-29) **by eight wickets**

FEBRUARY 20 AT FAISALABAD
South Africa 178 for 5 (W J Cronje 78) **beat New Zealand** 177 for 9 (Donald 3-34) **by five wickets**

FEBRUARY 22 AT PESHAWAR
England 279 for 4 (G A Hick 104*, G P Thorpe 89) **beat Holland** 230 for 6 (K J van Noortwijk 64, B Zuiderent 54, DeFreitas 3-31) **by 49 runs**

FEBRUARY 24 AT GUJRANWALA
Pakistan 112 for 1 (Ijaz Ahmed sen 50*) **beat UAE** 109 for 9 (Mushtaq Ahmed 3-16) **by nine wickets**

FEBRUARY 25 AT RAWALPINDI
South Africa 230 (Martin 3-33) **beat England** 152 **by 78 runs**

FEBRUARY 26 AT LAHORE
Pakistan 151 for 2 (Saeed Anwar 83*) **beat Holland** 145 for 7 (G Aponso 58, Waqar Younis 4-26) **by eight wkts**

FEBRUARY 27 AT FAISALABAD
New Zealand 276 for 8 (R G Twose 92, C M Spearman 78, Azhar Saeed 3-45) **beat UAE** 167 for 9 (Thomson 3-20) **by 109 runs**

FEBRUARY 29 AT KARACHI
South Africa 243 for 5 (D J Cullinan 65, Waqar Younis 3-50) **beat Pakistan** 242 for 6 (Aamir Sohail 111) **by five wkts**

MARCH 1 AT LAHORE
UAE 220 for 3 (Saleem Raza 84) **beat Holland** 216 for 9 (Dukanwala 5-29) **by seven wkts**

MARCH 3 AT KARACHI
Pakistan 250 for 3 (Saeed Anwar 71, Ijaz Ahmed sen, 70) **beat England** 249 for 9 (R A Smith 75, M A Atherton 66, G P Thorpe 52*, Mushtaq Ahmed 3-53) **by seven wkts**

MARCH 5 AT RAWALPINDI
South Africa 328 for 3 (A C Hudson 161, G Kirsten 83) **beat Holland** 168 for 8 **by 160 runs**

MARCH 6 AT LAHORE
Pakistan 281 for 5 (Saeed Anwar 62, Salim Malik 55*, Aamir Sohail 50) **beat New Zealand** 235 **by 46 runs**

Teams were in two groups of six from which eight sides went to the knockout stages. In the first 15 overs of an innings a maximum of two fielders were allowed outside the circle.

GROUP B FINAL TABLE

	P	W	L	Pts	*Run rate
South Africa	5	5	0	10	2.04
Pakistan	5	4	1	8	0.96
New Zealand	5	3	2	6	0.55
England	5	2	3	4	0.08
UAE	5	1	4	2	-1.83
Holland	5	0	5	0	-1.92

*Run-rate is a net value. Teams on equal points were separated by the winner of their head-to-head game

1996 · QUARTER-FINALS ·
THE
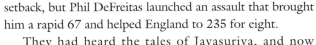

The first quarter-final was at Faisalabad on March 9. England, despite their disappointing showing so far, were confident that their elusive form was there. But Atherton and Hick had gone by the end of the 15 overs, when they were 59 for two, but a bigger blow was just round the corner. In the BBC commentary box, Jonathan Agnew watched as Dharmasena came in to bowl:

"Sixty-six for two and he's bowling now to Robin Smith, who's on 25. And this first ball is tucked away towards short fine leg. They're taking a quick single. The throw comes in. Ooh, it hits the stumps! A good throw and Ian Robinson calling for the replay. Well, he looked well in from here, but a fine throw and the off stump, as we look at it, leaning back at the moment. Robin Smith looks confident. He's having a chat with Graham Thorpe as they watch the replay. He's been given out! Gosh!"

Peter Roebuck: *"Well I'm very, very surprised by that."*

Jonathan Agnew: *"I'm amazed by it. But it's 66 for three."*

The loss of Thorpe in the 24th over for 14 was a big setback, but Phil DeFreitas launched an assault that brought him a rapid 67 and helped England to 235 for eight.

They had heard the tales of Jayasuriya, and now England found themselves on the receiving end.

Peter Baxter: *"Now in comes De Freitas again to bowl to Jayasuriya – and he hits it many a mile up in the air! I'm not sure it's not coming into our commentary box. But it doesn't. It demolishes the VIP stand down below us. Six runs again. Umpire Mahboob Shah stretches his hands skywards. He's just brought up the 100. One hundred and one for one in the 12th over, 72 now to Jayasuriya. The last 50 has come off 23 balls."*

Jayasuriya was out in the next over – the 13th – but he had already made 82 from 44 balls, hitting three sixes and 13 fours. The game was as good as won, and it was indeed in the 41st over by five wickets. England, who had been complaining about the convoluted arrangements for getting to the Calcutta semi-final, were on their way home having failed for the first time to get a World Cup semi.

Michael Atherton's parting shot on Jayasuriya was: "I wouldn't say it was one of the great one-day innings." Most observers begged to disagree.

The Iqbal Stadium in Faisalabad, never full, as indeed Pakistani grounds in this tournament tended not to be, had virtually emptied rather than watch Jayasuriya's pyrotechnics. The rival attraction was happening a thousand miles to the south-east and beamed to their televisions. All over the sub-continent, home to a fifth of the world's population, countless millions of pairs of eyes were glued to events in Bangalore.

This was more than a game of cricket. It was India v Pakistan. Their first meeting on Indian soil since 1987. While the teams were squaring up on the field of play, their armies were still sniping at each other across the border. Security at the stadium would include 3,000 policemen, three rapid action forces and a bomb squad, with another 100 troops deployed to guard the Pakistan team's hotel.

Yet Pakistan captain Wasim Akram claimed it was an advantage to be playing in India. "The Indian team were full of tension when we saw

It's high fives for Romesh Kaluwitharana and Sanath Jayasuriya as England's top scorer Phillip DeFreitas is out lbw – a vital break for Sri Lanka

them yesterday. Our boys were laughing and joking. If we were playing in Pakistan the roles would be reversed and the pressure would be on us, so it is preferable for us to play the game here. We get along fine with their players. It is politics that builds this game into something more than cricket."

Wasim was less happy about his own fitness, and eventually had to withdraw before the start of play with ruptured side muscles. Even so, Waqar Younis and Aqib Javed curbed the early Indian scoring rate and the third seamer, Ata-ur-Rehman, bowled the biggest danger man, Sachin Tendulkar, for 31 when the score had reached 90. Even the hard-hitting Navjot Sidhu's 93 never quite broke the shackles, before he was bowled by Mushtaq Ahmed.

It was Ajay Jadeja, coming in at six, who provided the rocket power at the end of the innings, hitting 45 from 25 balls. With the aid of Anil Kumble and Javagal Srinath, he managed to boost the score to an impressive 287 for eight. With Pakistan having failed to complete their overs in the time limit – though they had to bowl the last over – their reply was reduced to 49 overs in which to chase that target.

That slight reduction scarcely seemed to matter as Aamir Sohail, the stand-in captain, and Saeed Anwar set off in pursuit. By the time Sohail was bowled by Prasad in the 15th over, the score was 113 for two. In retrospect, that was the crest of Pakistan's wave. Prasad also removed Ijaz Ahmed and Inzamam-ul-Haq, and then the spinners made further inroads. The end of Pakistan's reign was effectively sealed by the run-out of Javed Miandad for 38. At the finish they were 248 for nine and India had won by 39 runs.

The emotions were extreme. During the match, Pakistan players had been bombarded with fruit and bottles, and the game was stopped several times while match referee Raman Subba Row called in the police. Now, a full stadium rejoiced in Bangalore and that joy spread to the streets around India.

In Pakistan there was stunned amazement and then anger and recrimination. Wasim Akram had deliberately thrown the match by withdrawing, was one wild suggestion. The whole team were in a plot. Javed Miandad announced his retirement, complaining that his abilities could have been better used. The team, returning to Pakistan, had to be guarded in a hotel for their own protection. There were

Saeed Anwar hits out as Pakistan's openers put on 84 against India

demonstrations and several destroyed television sets and even a report that one grief-stricken fan had killed himself.

Wasim Akram, whose house was pelted with stones, eggs and tomatoes, said: "I do not deserve this. I have received death threats and my family is getting abusive phone calls. I have always played my best for Pakistan. I am ready to swear over the holy Koran that I do not get involved in betting and that I am clean."

With the West Indies having scraped into the quarter-finals to face the unbeaten South Africans, they were hardly favourites for a place in the semi-finals. The West Indies decided to bat in Karachi and at 42 for one Brian Lara was unleashed on the South African attack.

He made 111 in 94 balls, putting on 138 with Shivnarine Chanderpaul, who made 56. Lara hit 16 fours, no less than five of them in one over from Pat Symcox, though Symcox did get his revenge – and after he dismissed Lara, caught off a top-edged sweep, the later batsmen could not capitalise in the closing overs. The hapless Keith Arthurton was out for one. Nevertheless, 264 for eight was a useful total.

At 118 for one from 25 overs, South Africa seemed to

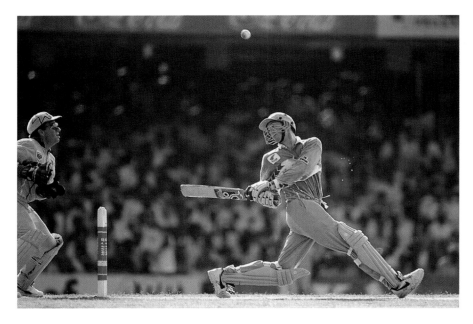

Above: Chris Harris of New Zealand thumped five sixes in his 130 but ended on the losing side against Australia.

Right: Roger Harper and Richie Richardson dance for joy as Harper has Steve Palframan caught and bowled – his third wicket in the over

have the game at their mercy. The breakthrough came not from a blast of Walsh, Ambrose or Bishop, but the slow left arm of Jimmy Adams, who removed Hudson for 54 and Cullinan for 69, and then Cronje for 40.

The veteran off-spinner, Roger Harper, rolled easily in now – and with his first ball had Jonty Rhodes caught on the boundary. With his second he had Brian McMillan lbw, and in that same over he took a diving return catch to remove Steve Palframan. At 198 for seven it was really over, though Symcox did lay about him mightily for his 24. South Africa were all out in the last over for 245 – 19 runs behind.

A hot evening in Madras found the unfancied New Zealanders putting up an impressive show against Australia. Damien Fleming, Paul Reiffel and Glenn McGrath each took an early wicket, but Lee Germon was joined by Chris Harris in a fourth-wicket stand of 168, Germon's 89 coming from 96 balls. Harris continued after his captain's departure, fighting a lone crusade, until the 49th over, when Warne had him caught, going for his fifth six, for 130 off 124 balls. New Zealand had certainly set Australia a competitive target in making 286 for nine, and memories of the underdogs surprising them four years before must have returned to some Australians.

A further aide-memoire would have been the sight of Dipak Patel opening the bowling, a ploy that worked to the extent of having Taylor caught behind for ten. Mark Waugh, though, had no such memories and, with help from Ponting, then a few lusty blows from Warne and brother Steve, he stroked his way to his record third century of the tournament. At his departure for 110, 74 runs were still needed, but Steve Waugh and Stuart Law saw Australia home with more than two overs to spare.

· QUARTER-FINALS ·

MARCH 9 AT FAISALABAD
Sri Lanka 236 for 5 (S T Jayasuriya 82) **beat England** 235 for 8 (P A J DeFreitas 67) **by five wickets**

MARCH 9 AT BANGALORE (DAY/NIGHT)
India 287 for 8 (N S Sidhu 93) **beat Pakistan** 248 for 9 (Aamir Sohail 55, Prasad 3-45, Kumble 3-48) **by 39 runs**

MARCH 11 AT KARACHI
West Indies 264 for 8 (B C Lara 111, S,Chanderpaul 56) **beat South Africa** 245 (D J Cullinan 69, A C Hudson 54, Harper 4-47, Adams 3-53) **by 19 runs**

MARCH 11 AT MADRAS (DAY/NIGHT)
Australia 289 for 4 (M E Waugh 110, S R Waugh 59 not out) **beat New Zealand** 286 for 9 (C Z Harris 130, L K Germon 89) **by six wickets**

THE CALCUTTA
·SEMI-FINAL·

Above: Crowds outside Eden Gardens, Calcutta. Left: Sanath Jayasuriya walks off and Sri Lanka are two wickets down in the first over

As the Australians began the wearying journey to northern India for their semi-final against the West Indies, the two remaining host countries were assembled in Calcutta for the first semi under the lights of the huge 110,000-capacity Eden Gardens stadium. The groundsman's big concern was … rats. Rats had burrowed under the square, chewed up the wire to the stump camera, and might interrupt play. But he was happier with the wicket, admitting frankly: "We have watered the wicket a lot in the past few days to remove the bounce. It will be a pitch factory-made for the Indian batsmen and spinners."

Put in to bat by India, Sri Lanka found themselves in early trouble. With just four balls bowled, Sanath Jayasuriya and Romesh Kaluwitharana were both out, caught at third man off the kind of all-or-nothing shots that had made their opening partnership the sensation of the tournament. But Aravinda de Silva, coming in at one for two, continued his side's usual policy of all-out attack in the first 15 overs. Off 47 balls he made 66. The first 15 overs may have cost them four wickets, but they had 86 runs on the board and Mahanama, Ranatunga and Tillekeratne kept the momentum up to a total of 251 for eight – just about a par score.

India, too, suffered an early setback, with the departure of Sidhu, but Tendulkar showed his flair, adding 90 with Manjrekar. They took the score to 98 in the 23rd over when the first seeds of a crisis were sown.

Simon Mann: *"Here's Jayasuriya. Bowls to Tendulkar. Flat delivery. Tendulkar – he's stumped, is he? Here's a third-umpire decision. A lovely bit of work by Kaluwitharana. The ball was down the leg side. Tendulkar looked to turn it away and it looked as if he lifted his foot there. He's out! Tendulkar has gone. Gone for 65. It was very tight indeed. It's 98 for two in the 23rd over and now we have a game."*

Next over Azharuddin was bowled, and Manjrekar followed for 25 three overs later. Srinath was run out in a mix-up with Kambli at 110, and Jayasuriya bowled Jadeja at 115. The crowd, faced with this débâcle, were now in a state of stunned silence . When two more wickets fell at 120, their sullen quiet erupted in rage.

Jonathan Agnew: *"Debris is now being chucked on regularly from all over the ground, I'm afraid. Bottles of water are being hurled on."*

Simon Mann: *"But the crowd realise that India have lost this match and Sri Lanka are going to go through to the Final. It's 120 for eight in the 35th over. The Sri Lankan fielders are all gathered round at one end of the pitch. The batsmen are standing there as well, looking back towards the pavilion, wondering what to do. And Clive Lloyd, the match referee, has come out."*

Agnew: *"Well, what do the umpires do? It's a hopeless situation. There are bottles now coming on from all quarters of the ground. And I think they are taking the players off. It's about all they can do. Clive Lloyd, the match referee, is going out. I'm pretty sure he will suggest that they come off.*

"The batsmen are standing there looking rather confused, but quite what will happen if the match is abandoned – well, it will have to be given to Sri Lanka, I guess. And in fact I think

'It was very scary out there. I guess the safest place was on the square while it was going on, because there was just a barrage of missiles. One glass bottle came out of the members' stand, straight over the sight screen. It was unbelievable.'

IAN ROBINSON
Standby umpire

India leave the stage in a hail of bottles

THE 1996 WORLD CUP SEMI-FINAL • INDIA v SRI LANKA

As the World Cup exploded, the BBC Cricket Correspondent was huddling in a dugout.
But at least he was in a safer situation than the team from Radio Pakistan…

It had not been an easy build-up to the match. The organisers had decided in their wisdom that every journalist should go for re-accreditation to a small potting shed in Calcutta. Having queued there all morning, I set off for Eden Gardens. There was much to do – locating a commentary point, building a commentary box, setting up the circuit to London – and by the time Radio Pakistan breezed in and attempted to commandeer my position, I was in no mood even to negotiate.

"Go outside and broadcast from amongst the crowd," I urged. "You'll be perfectly safe. After all, there's hardly going to be a riot tomorrow night!"

I must admit to feeling a twinge of guilt when, 24 hours later and in the midst of the mass riot that caused the match to be abandoned, I glanced out at Radio Pakistan. They did look rather vulnerable, huddled together as, all around them, rocks and water bottles rained down from the terraces.

Large bonfires burned uncontrollably and deafening thunder flashes exploded on the outfield. Sri Lanka's fielders gathered safely out of range on the pitch as the match referee, Clive Lloyd, emerged from the dressing rooms to make an unsuccessful call for calm. It was an appalling spectacle.

My main recollection of that evening is the stifling heat and humidity. It was overpowering. We sat and commentated in shorts and T-shirts but our discomfort was not eased by the total lack, anywhere on the ground, of bottled water. We assumed that the 100,000 spectators had bought it all up and it was only when Christopher Martin-Jenkins

JONATHAN AGNEW

'Go outside and broadcast from amongst the crowd,' I urged. 'You'll be perfectly safe. After all, there's hardly going to be a riot tomorrow night!'

– an unlikely rioter – revealed that the authorities had seized the bottle of water he had brought with him from the hotel that we realised something was up.

The moment India's cause was lost, a full-scale riot began with a hail of bottles. Funnily enough, we did not feel the least bit threatened. Peering out from our dugout, we could see the riot police moving in and then, as the bonfires still raged, we observed the most bizarre ceremony in which Aravinda de Silva was hurriedly handed the Man of the Match award.

As the smoke slowly cleared away, Simon Mann and I sat in eerie silence. It was his first visit to Calcutta. "How on earth do we get back to the hotel?" he asked.

"Easy!" I replied. "We'll walk."

And sure enough, when we set off across the maidan – the parkland between Eden Gardens and the Grand Hotel – there was not even the slightest trace of the mayhem that had reigned only half an hour earlier. In the pitch darkness, we carried our cases full of expensive broadcasting equipment feeling perfectly safe. The locals waved, as usual, and went about their business. Calcutta's cricket-crazy population had registered its protest and that, as far as it was concerned, was the end of the matter.

However, it had been a thoroughly selfish act and one which showed no respect whatsoever to Sri Lanka's team. It would not be long before Arjuna Ranatunga's men were to have the last laugh.

• *Jonathan Agnew is the BBC's Cricket Correspondent and a commentator on radio's Test Match Special*

Supporters hoped India's batting would set Eden Gardens alight. When it failed, they did it for themselves

'The barbarians have captured the nation. India has succeeded in establishing that it deserves to be excommunicated from the world of cricket.'
CALCUTTA TELEGRAPH

that is what is going to happen. They are being led off now by Clive Lloyd. The crowd are booing and shouting, but quite frankly they have brought this on themselves. The Sri Lankans are coming off. Gurusinha has his arms outstretched. They've won. And this match has been abandoned."

And that was the outcome. The match was awarded to Si Lanka by default. It was a huge embarrassment for the secretary of the World Cup organising committee, whose home town this was, and afterwards Clive Lloyd summed up the feelings of all involved: "It was a sad day for cricket and for the people of Calcutta. It is very disappointing to see a crowd behave in this way. I

am also disappointed that there were not more police mingling with the crowd, because I had specifically requested it before the game began.

"The safety of the players is paramount and I had no choice but to call it off."

The next morning, the headline in the *Calcutta Telegraph* summed it up: "Nation Hangs Its Head In Shame".

· SEMI-FINAL ·
CALCUTTA · 13 MARCH

SRI LANKA

S T Jayasuriya c Prasad b Srinath	1
†R S Kaluwitharana c Manjreka b Srinath	0
A P Gurusinha c Kumble b Srinath	1
P A de Silva b Kumble	66
R S Mahanama retired hurt	58
*A Ranatunga lbw b Tendulkar	35
H P Tillekeratne c Tendulkar b Prasad	32
H D P K Dharmasena b Tendulkar	9
W P U J C Vaas run out	23
G P Wickremasinghe not out	4
M Muralitharan not out	5
Extras (B 1, l-b 10, w 4, n-b 2)	17

Total (50 Overs, for 8 wickets) **251**

Fall of wickets: 1/1 2/1 3/35 4/85 5/168 6/206 7/236 8/244

Bowling: Srinath 7-1-34-3; Kumble 10-0-51-1; Prasad 8-0-50-1; Kapoor 10-0-40-0; Jadeja 5-0-31-0; Tendulkar 10-1-34-2.

INDIA
won the toss

S R Tendulkar st Kaluwitharana b Jayasuriya	65
N S Sidhu c Jayasuriya b Vaas	3
S V Manjreka b Jayasuriya	25
*M Azharuddin c and b Dharmasena	0
V G Kambli not out	10
J Srinath run out	6
A Jadeja b Jayasuriya	0
†N R Mongia c Jayasuriya b de Silva	1
A R Kapoor c De Silva b Muralitharan	0
A Kumble not out	0
Extras (L-b 5, w 5)	10

Total (34.1 Overs, for 8 wickets) **120**

Did not bat: B K V Prasad

Fall of wickets: 1/25 2/93 3/165 4/173 5/178 6/183 7/187 8/194 9/202

Bowling: Wickremasinghe 5-0-24-0; Vaas 6-1-23-1; Muralitharan 7.1-0-29-1; Dharmasena 7-0-24-1; Jayasuriya 7-1-12-3; de Silva 2-0-3-1.

Umpires: R S Dunne and C J Mitchley

Man of the Match: Aravinda de Silva

SRI LANKA
won by default after crowd riot

1996 THE MOHALI ·SEMI-FINAL·

Sri Lanka's opponents would be decided next day in the unlikely venue of Mohali, a suburb of Chandigarh, coincidentally home of the Indian Cricket Board president. A well-appointed bowl of a ground, it did have the drawback of having the floodlights – though plentiful – mounted on low pylons because of its proximity to an air base.

Australia chose to bat and very soon it seemed that their World Cup must be over, as Curtly Ambrose and Ian Bishop reduced them to 15 for four, with Mark Waugh's magical run ended by Ambrose in the worst possible way – out second ball, lbw for a duck. At the end of the 15 overs the Aussies were still reeling on 29 for four.

Before this match, neither Stuart Law nor Michael Bevan had managed a half-century, but now they stayed together for 32 overs, gradually coming out of grim defence to carry the game to the opposition and put on 138 for the fifth

wicket. Harper eventually claimed Bevan for 69, and Law was run out for 72. With Healy's 31, Australia passed 200 – but not by much. 207 for eight would be hard to defend.

Nothing in the early stages of the West Indian innings gave Australia much cause for hope. Warne did make an early appearance to have Courtney Browne caught and bowled, but after 15 overs the West Indies were cruising at 60 for one.

Chanderpaul was playing a sheet anchor role, while the runs flowed from the other end. Lara made 45 of their 68-run partnership and when he was bowled by Steve Waugh, in came Richie Richardson.

There was no halt to the West Indian progress. At 41 overs they had reached 165 for two, needing only 43 more for a place in the Final. Australian commentator Jim Maxwell watched what happened next:

"McGrath bowls and Chanderpaul drives at this. He's caught at mid-on! He has holed out to Fleming. So a fairly exhausted Shivnarine Chanderpaul, going for a heave down the ground, didn't quite get hold of it – and the Australians have picked up a wicket. It does give them some glimmer of hope, I suppose, with Chanderpaul out, and he has made a splendid contribution here. His 80 looks to have set up a position in the Final for the West Indies. It's three for 165 in the 42nd over."

It still looked straightforward enough for the West Indies, but there was evidently some concern in their camp about the run rate, so the big-hitting Roger Harper was sent in ahead of time. When McGrath had him lbw for two, Ottis Gibson came in with the same mission and he was caught behind for one. Adams came in at number seven, as Richardson watched this carnage from the other end – but Adams, too, fell to Warne, lbw for two. Could the West Indies possibly throw this away? They now needed 25 from

'One highly unusual thing occurred out on the field afterwards. As the teams shook hands… Curtly spoke! It was something like: "Well played, don't waste it now, mon." A simple 'thanks' was all we could muster in reply, more due to shock than anything.'

STEVE WAUGH
in his World Cup Diary

their last three overs with four wickets standing.

Peter Baxter: *"Arthurton it is, facing Fleming now. He steps away and heaves at that one – and he's caught behind! Healy takes the catch, and one does rather feel that the West Indies are going to go out of this tournament unless someone can keep a very cool head. It's 187 for seven."*

Bryan Davies: *"I'm witnessing some of the most ridiculous strokeplay I've ever seen in a cricket match."*

Arthurton's duck completed a disastrous tournament for him, having mustered just two runs in five innings. And only seven runs had been added to the total when I described the next wicket to fall.

"Fourteen runs needed for the West Indies to go into the Final. In comes Warne. Bowls to Bishop. He's hit on the pad – and he's out! Umpire Venkat almost apologetically raises the finger. The eighth West Indian wicket goes down."

Four runs later, Jim Maxwell took up the commentary. *"Ten needed. Away goes Fleming, he bowls to Richardson. Richardson swings at this, it's going out towards midwicket. It's a tremendous hit and it goes across the boundary for four. Six runs required now from five balls.*

"Fleming runs in and bowls to Richardson. Richardson swings at this, miscues, it goes out – Healy has a throw at the stumps. A replay! There will be a run-out here, I think. Healy has thrown the stumps down. Ambrose was struggling to make his ground, and umpire Venkat has gone for the replay. We've got to look for the lights – they are somewhere above us. He got the red light! He's out. So Ambrose has been run out.

"That makes it even more desperate, because it's nine for 202. Six to win. Last man in. Four balls left. It's come down to this. Courtney Walsh can put his name in lights here and blast a six.

"Fleming runs in to bowl to Walsh. Walsh swings at this. He's bowled him! Australia have won. Oh, what a victory this is. What an amazing win. They're all coming out of the dressing room, all the Australians. And Australia dramatically proceed to the Final against Sri Lanka."

It had been a staggering turnaround, but Australia would meet Sri Lanka in Lahore for the Final on March 17.

· SEMI-FINAL ·
MOHALI • 14 MARCH

AUSTRALIA
won the toss

M E Waugh lbw b Ambrose	0
*M A Taylor b Bishop	1
R T Ponting lbw b Ambrose	0
S R Waugh b Bishop	3
S G Law run out	72
M G Bevan c Richardson b Harper	69
†I A Healy run out	31
P R Reiffel run out	7
S K Warne not out	6
Extras (L-b 11, w 5, n-b 2)	18
Total (50 Overs, for 8 wickets)	**207**

Did not bat: D W Fleming and G D McGrath

Fall of wickets: 1/0 2/7 3/8 4/15 5/153 6/171 7/186 8/207

Bowling: Ambrose 10-1-26-2; Bishop 10-1-35-2; Walsh 10-1-33-0; Gibson 2-0-13-0; Harper 9-0-47-1; Adams 9-0-42-0.

WEST INDIES

S Chanderpaul c Fleming b McGrath	80
†C O Browne c and b Warne	10
B C Lara b S R Waugh	45
*R B Richardson not out	49
R A Harper lbw b McGrath	2
O D Gibson c Healy b Warne	1
J C Adams lbw b Warne	2
K L T Arthurton c Healy b Fleming	0
I R Bishop lbw b Warne	3
C E L Ambrose run out	2
C A Walsh b Fleming	0
Extras (L-b 4, w 2, n-b 2)	8
Total (49.3 overs)	**202**

Fall of wickets: 1/25 2/93 3/165 4/173 5/178 6/183 7/187 8/194 9/202.

Bowling: McGrath 10-2-30-2; Fleming 8.3-0-48-2; Warne 9-0-36-4; M E Waugh 4-0-16-0; S R Waugh 7-0-30-1; Reiffel 5-0-13-0; Bevan 4-1-12-0; Law 2-0-13-0.

Umpires: B C Cooray and S Venkataraghavan

Man of the Match: Shane Warne

AUSTRALIA
won by five runs

1996

·THE FINAL·

So Australia were to play the team they had refused to meet in Colombo a month earlier. Both captains tried to play down the animosity that had arisen during Sri Lanka's recent tour of Australia. Mark Taylor said: "I think the Final will be tense because it is the Final. But I don't foresee any problems with Sri Lanka. The last time we played them in a Test, we got on well with their players."

Arjuna Ranatunga said: "We should not treat this game as revenge, or we will be putting pressure on ourselves. I just want to forget that tour. Night after night the manager and I were up until one in the morning talking about our problems. In a way, though, it toughened us up, made us more worldly. There is a culture of respect in our country and if teams ever abused us, we would give them back a smile. Now we give them back a little more." And no one was more competitive than the 'pocket Napoleon' Ranatunga himself…

For Australia, this was their third final, while before 1996

> 'The boys had worked really hard, right through the tournament, and I think it was my duty this time for the seniors to perform. Because it was an important game, the Final. And I think the seniors took their responsibility on their shoulders and performed very well. The boys deserved a good win. It's a very very special occasion and I needed to concentrate a lot. I preserved everything for this occasion.'
> ARAVINDA DE SILVA

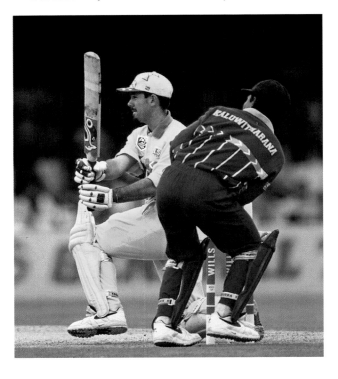

Right: Ricky Ponting made 45 for Australia. Far right: Aravinda de Silva becomes the third man to score a century in a World Cup Final

We let ourselves get distracted

THE 1996 WORLD CUP FINAL • AUSTRALIA v SRI LANKA

*The Australia wicketkeeper remembers the exhilaration of a miraculous victory –
followed by the hollow thud of defeat*

**IAN
HEALY**

*'Aravinda accumulates runs
very quickly. Then he
releases the dynamite, and
it can really give you
some damage. And that's
what he did that night'*

In retrospect, I think the semi-final against the West Indies was our Final. Even when they were 165 for two, needing only 43 to win in nine overs, we had never given it up, because we felt that you might as well go hard until they beat you. We may have resigned ourselves that we weren't going to be in the Final, but we thought that we might as well have a crack and see what happened.

The West Indies seemed to get a little bit bogged down and bored with the way they were batting. One or two wickets fell, Shane Warne came back on and created a bit of havoc. It just seemed to keep happening. Then for us to beat them by just five runs … I suppose it was one of the most memorable wins I've ever been involved with. After that, the atmosphere of exhilaration in the dressing room was second to none that I've ever experienced.

Then we had to get to Lahore and start all over again. Maybe there was a little bit of a let-down from such a good semi, but there were also so many distractions. The hotel was full of people. You couldn't go near the foyer for all the fans everywhere. Our practice was too drawn-out the day before by the shortage of net facilities. There was rain around and rumours that there might be a delayed start. Then, during the game there were the distractions of the lights going out. But when those sort of things distract you, it suggests you may not be in the right frame of mind. You should be good enough to cope with all that.

We had played Sri Lanka in Australia during our previous season and had beaten them comfortably. Their tactics of the whirlwind start hadn't worked there. So we knew their game pretty well and obviously we had heard how that tactic had been working on the sub-continent. So we half expected that one of the openers would get away and then, of course, they had a stacked batting line-up if they could have a player as good as Mahanama batting at seven.

We started pretty well. We were heading for 300, but then we hit a sort of a wall when their spinners got to work. We got nowhere and that's where we lost the game. We under-achieved in the field, maybe because we felt let down that our total wasn't enough for us to cruise and be confident, and maybe even because we were tired from the semi-final.

Even when we got the Sri Lankan openers out cheaply, Gurusinha came in and played a solid innings so that Aravinda could open his shoulders. De Silva is as good as anyone around. He can hit the ball powerfully on both sides of the wicket and straight down the wicket. Short balls or full balls, he can jump on them and he can play spin as well as he can the quicks. He accumulates runs very quickly, so even if you think you're containing him, you look up at the scoreboard and he's 40 off 45 balls without having done much. Then he releases the dynamite and it can really give you some damage.

And that's what he did that night. He started out consolidating and then he fired up on us and he really enjoyed himself, I think. It was a great innings. They were better than us on the night.

• *Ian Healy is Australia's record-breaking Test wicketkeeper*

This was beyond our wildest ambitions

THE 1996 WORLD CUP FINAL • AUSTRALIA v SRI LANKA

*The Sri Lanka captain confesses that even he did not expect his 'family'
to win the 1996 World Cup*

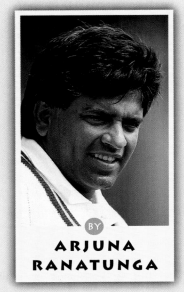

ARJUNA RANATUNGA

It was one of my ambitions to get Sri Lanka into a World Cup semi-final. I don't think we ever thought that we could win a World Cup. From the time of our victory against India in Delhi, though, I thought we had a decent chance. While I had been very happy to take the points for the games forfeited by Australia and West Indies, because it guaranteed us a place in the quarter-finals, I was very disappointed for the Sri Lankan public. They had been really looking forward to seeing the top cricketers from those countries playing there.

The quarter-final against England at Faisalabad was the most worrying game in prospect for me. England had had a really bad run, but in one-day cricket you can just have a bad day and you are out of the competition, as happened to South Africa.

But we made it to the semi-final and the Calcutta crowd must have been 110,000 – and out of that there seemed to be only about ten supporting Sri Lanka. So it was a bit of a surprise that we could hear them shouting for us in that huge crowd. It was wonderful to hear own language from those ten guys. We had achieved our first goal in getting to the semi-finals. Now we would just go out and give 100 per cent.

Although we had a terrible start, we kept playing in our same style. If we had changed that, we would have been just an ordinary side. We had to keep playing the way we were used to. While I don't condone what happened at the end of that semi-final, the trouble that came from the crowd was just their big disappointment. They thought they had a great chance to win the World Cup, with Sachin and Azhar playing so

'The most important factor in our success was the way the team was like a family. They all helped each other'

well. They weren't giving us a hard time and it didn't take anything away from our joy at reaching the Final.

The next evening, the panel on TV were selecting the Most Valued Player of the tournament and it came down to a choice between Sachin Tendulkar and Sanath Jayasuriya. I was watching in the hotel as they all went for Sanath. I thought I wouldn't disturb him with a call, but I went along to his room and found the whole team in there, celebrating his success.

We were just delighted to be in the Final – the Australians were probably under more pressure as the favourites. We played our normal game and never thought of it as the Final, so that I hardly appreciated what we had done until I got back home.

Australia batted really well at the start, especially Mark Taylor, but then our spinners came into the action and Aravinda struck a couple of major blows. I think in that tournament Aravinda realised his full value for the first time. I had rated the top three batsmen in the world as Tendulkar, Lara and de Silva and now his talent really showed. The most important factor in our success, though, was the way the team was like a family. They all helped each other.

Somehow we were rather detached from all the presentations at the end. We had won the Cup and just wanted to go home. There, of course, cricket was the major talking point and now people knew about Sri Lanka. If we could achieve that for the country, I am very happy, and I am grateful that it happened when I was captain of the side.

• *Arjuna Ranatunga is the captain of Sri Lanka*

Aravinda de Silva (left) and Arjuna Ranatunga steered their team to a crushing victory with nearly five overs to spare

Sri Lanka had only ever won four World Cup matches. Somehow, the Lahore floodlights were ready in time and Ranatunga, after winning the toss, decided to defy history and put Australia in. No side had won the World Cup Final batting second.

It seemed a good move when Australia lost their most prolific batsman of the competition, Mark Waugh, for 12. Still, Ricky Ponting joined Mark Taylor in ensuring that they made the most of those first 15 overs, reaching 82 for one.

By then Ranatunga had abandoned his medium-pacers. The second wicket realised 101, but Aravinda de Silva's off-spin was their undoing. Taylor was caught on the sweep for 74 in the 27th over and then Ponting was bowled for 45. It was 156 for four when Shane Warne was deceived by Muttiah Muralitharan and stumped. The biter bit. Suddenly scoring runs seemed very hard work against four spinners. Stuart Law pulled a six, but 241 for seven was a let-down for Australia.

The restart was delayed after the Lahore electricity supply temporarily wilted under the demands of the Gaddafi Stadium's new lights, but soon the crowds could settle back to enjoy – they hoped – another extravagant Sri Lankan batting display. It seemed at first, though, that they might be disappointed, as Sri Lanka's devastating openers departed.

Jim Maxwell: *"Fleming bowls. Jayasuriya is cutting. Down to third man it goes. It'll be cut off by McGrath – throwing back. They're going for the second. Oh and there's an appeal! They're going for the replay. Gee, that was a challenging second run. A low, flat return coming in on the bounce from McGrath. I wonder how close this one will be. We're seeing endless slow-motion replays. He's been given out! The red light's gone up. Well, I think it's a bit stiff really. That was so close. It's one for 12 in the second over."*

Jonathan Agnew: *"Twenty-three for one. Fleming bowls to Kaluwitharana, who hits in the air. He's going to be caught at*

· THE FINAL ·
LAHORE · 17 MARCH

AUSTRALIA

*M A Taylor c Jayasuriya b de Silva	74
M E Waugh c Jayasuriya b Vaas	12
R T Ponting b de Silva	45
S R Waugh c de Silva b Dharmasena	13
S K Warne st Kaluwitharana b Muralitharan	2
S G Law c de Silva b Jayasuriya	22
M G Bevan not out	36
†I A Healy b de Silva	2
P R Reiffel not out	13
Extras (L-b 10, w 11, n-b 1)	22

Total *(50 Overs, for 7 wickets)* **241**

Did not bat: D W Fleming and G D McGrath

Fall of wickets: 1/36 2/137 3/152 4/156 5/170 6/202 7/205

Bowling: Wickremasinghe 7-0-38-0; Vaas 6-1-30-1; Muralitharan 10-0-31-1; Dharmasena 10-0-47-1; Jayasuriya 8-0-43-1; De Silva 9-0-42-3.

SRI LANKA
won the toss

S T Jayasuriya run out	9
†R S Kaluwitharana c Bevan b Fleming	6
A P Gurusinha b Reiffel	65
P A de Silva not out	107
*A Ranatunga not out	47
Extras (B 1, l-b 4, w 5, n-b 1)	11

Total *(46.2 overs, for 3 wickets)* **245**

Did not bat: R S Mahanama, H P Tillekeratne, H D P K Dharmasena, W P U J C Vaas, G P Wickremasinghe and M Muralitharan.

Fall of wickets: 1/12 2/23 3/148

Bowling: McGrath 8.2-1-28-0; Fleming 6-0-43-1; Warne 10-0-58-0; Reiffel 10-0-49-1; M E Waugh 6-0-35-0; S R Waugh 3-0-15-0; Bevan 3-0-12-0.

Umpires: S A Bucknor and D R Shepherd

Man of the Match: Aravinda de Silva

SRI LANKA
won by seven wickets

square leg. He is! Bevan takes it. A terrible start for Sri Lanka. Twenty-three for two in the sixth over. But coming out to bat now is Aravinda de Silva…"

And in Asanka Gurusinha, de Silva found the ideal foil. The pair gradually accelerated from what, by their standards, had been a sluggish start. Crucially, the Australians' catching was not in fine tune. Law put down Gurusinha when he had made 53, and other chances went begging. Warne, brought on to curb the rush, was treated with scant respect.

In the 31st over, Paul Reiffel did at last end the stand, which had put on 125, by bowling Gurusinha. But that just brought in Ranatunga. The pair played with a confidence in their own control of the game that never showed doubt that they would get there. De Silva became the third player to reach a World

Below: Ranatunga is interviewed by Ian Chappell after receiving the World Cup trophy from Pakistan's Prime Minister, Benazir Bhutto

Cup Final hundred, but it was his captain who had the honour of scoring the winning run.

Jonathan Agnew: *"Here's McGrath now. He bowls to Ranatunga. He nibbles that away through third man. He grabs a stump. The captain has scored the winning run for Sri Lanka, who have won the World Cup for the first time in their history. Chaotic scenes as the podium there – in two halves – is carried out into the middle. All the Sri Lankan team are out there now, embracing their captain, and Aravinda de Silva on 107 not out."*

And who could argue with the decision to make de Silva, scorer of that century and taker of three vital wickets, the Man of the Match? His colleague Sanath Jayasuriya was named Most Valued Player of the Tournament.

Thousands of people went on to the streets of Colombo, dancing and lighting firecrackers. Hundreds of vehicles drove around with yellow and orange national flags. The World Cup had come to Sri Lanka at last.

· 1996 STATISTICS ·

Teams were restricted to a maximum of two fielders outside the circle for the first 15 overs

Highest totals

398 for 5   Sri Lanka against Kenya
328 for 3   South Africa against Holland
321 for 2   South Africa against UAE
307 for 8   New Zealand against Holland
304 for 7   Australia against Kenya

Lowest totals
(completed innings only)

93   West Indies against Kenya
109 for 9   United Arab Emirates against Pakistan
120 for 8   India against Sri Lanka
134   Kenya against Zimbabwe
136   United Arab Emirates against England

Highest winning margins

9 wickets   Pakistan against United Arab Emirates
8 wickets   Australia against Zimbabwe
8 wickets   Pakistan against Holland
8 wickets   England against United Arab Emirates
169 runs   South Africa against United Arab Emirates
160 runs   South Africa against Holland
144 runs   Sri Lanka against Kenya
119 runs   New Zealand against Holland
109 runs   New Zealand against UAE

Highest match aggregates

652 for 12   Sri Lanka v Kenya
575 for 13   Australia v New Zealand
543 for 7   Sri Lanka v India
535 for 17   India v Pakistan
516 for 15   Pakistan v New Zealand

Wins by non-Test nations

Kenya beat West Indies by 73 runs
(United Arab Emirates beat Holland by 7 wickets)

Centuries

188 n.o. G Kirsten, South Africa
       v United Arab Emirates
161   A C Hudson, South Africa v Holland
145   P A de Silva, Sri Lanka v Kenya
137   S R Tendulkar, India v Sri Lanka
130   M E Waugh, Australia v Kenya
130   C Z Harris, New Zealand v Australia
127 n.o. S R Tendulkar, India v Kenya
126   M E Waugh, Australia v India
111   Aamir Sohail, Pakistan v South Africa
111   B C Lara, West Indies v South Africa
110   M E Waugh, Australia v New Zealand
107 n.o. P A de Silva, Sri Lanka v Australia (Final)
106   V G Kambli, India v Zimbabwe
104 n.o. G A Hick, England v Holland
102   R T Ponting, Australia v West Indies
101   N J Astle, New Zealand v England

Highest score for each position

1   M E Waugh 126, Australia v India
2   G Kirsten 188 n.o., South Africa
      v United Arab Emirates
3   B C Lara 111, West Indies v South Africa
4   P A de Silva 145, Sri Lanka v Kenya
5   C Z Harris 130, New Zealand v Australia
6   H P Tillekeratne 70 n.o., Sri Lanka v India
7   M G Bevan 36 n.o., Australia v Sri Lanka
8   D A Reeve 35, England v Sri Lanka
9   J A Samarasekera 47 n.o., United Arab Emirates
      v New Zealand
10   S Dukanwala 40 n.o., United Arab Emirates
      v South Africa
11   P S de Villiers 12, South Africa v England

Most runs

523   at 87.16   S R Tendulkar, India
484   at 80.66   M E Waugh, Australia
448   at 89.60   P A de Silva, Sri Lanka
391   at 78.20   G Kirsten, South Africa
329   at 82.25   Saeed Anwar, Pakistan

Most wickets

15   at 18.73   A Kumble, India
13   at 19.46   Waqar Younis, Pakistan
12   at 16.00   P A Strang, Zimbabwe
12   at 18.25   R A Harper, West Indies
12   at 18.41   D W Fleming, Australia
12   at 21.91   S K Warne, Australia

Most wickets in a match

5-21   P A Strang, Zimbabwe v Kenya
5-29   S Dukanwala, UAE v Holland
5-36   D W Fleming, Australia v India
4-26   Waqar Younis, Pakistan v Holland
4-34   S K Warne, Australia v Zimbabwe
4-36   S K Warne, Australia v West Indies
4-40   P A Strang, Zimbabwe v West Indies
4-47   R A Harper, West Indies v South Africa

Most dismissals by a wicketkeeper

12   (9ct, 3st)   I A Healy, Australia
9   (7ct, 2st)   Rashid Latif, Pakistan
8   (7ct, 1st)   R C Russell, England
8   (8ct)   S J Palframan, South Africa
7   (4ct, 3st)   N R Mongia, India

Most catches by an outfielder

8   A Kumble, India
5   G P Thorpe, England
5   C L Cairns, New Zealand
5   A D R Campbell, Zimbabwe
5   S T Jayasuriya, Sri Lanka

Australia *batting*

	M	I	NO	Runs	HS	Avge	100	50	Ct	St
M.E.Waugh	7	7	1	484	130	80.66	3	1	1	-
S.G.Law	7	6	2	204	72	51.00	-	1	-	-
S.R.Waugh	7	7	2	226	82	45.20	-	3	3	-
R.T.Ponting	7	7	0	229	102	32.71	1	-	1	-
M.G.Bevan	7	5	1	125	69	31.25	-	1	3	-
M.A.Taylor	7	7	0	193	74	27.57	-	2	1	-
P.R.Reiffel	5	4	3	27	13*	27.00	-	-	3	-
I.A.Healy	7	5	0	59	31	11.80	-	-	9	3
S.K.Warne	7	5	2	32	24	10.66	-	-	1	-
S.Lee	2	1	0	9	9	9.00	-	-	1	-
D.W.Fleming	6	1	0	0	0	0.00	-	-	2	-
G.D.McGrath	7	1	1	0	0*	-	-	-	1	-
C.J.McDermott	1	-	-	-	-	-	-	-	-	-

Australia *bowling*

	O	M	R	W	Avge	Best	5w	Econ
S.K.Warne	68.3	3	263	12	21.91	4-34	-	3.83
C.J.McDermott	3	0	12	1	12.00	1-12	-	4.00
G.D.McGrath	62.2	10	258	6	43.00	2-30	-	4.13
S.Lee	7	2	31	0	-	-	-	4.42
P.R.Reiffel	36	4	163	5	32.60	2-18	-	4.52
S.G.Law	5	0	23	0	-	-	-	4.60
M.E.Waugh	48	1	229	5	45.80	3-38	-	4.77
D.W.Fleming	45.2	3	221	12	18.41	5-36	-	14.87
M.G.Bevan	32	0	156	3	52.00	2-35	-	4.87
S.R.Waugh	31	2	157	5	31.40	2-22	-	5.06

England *batting*

	M	I	NO	Runs	HS	Avge	100	50	Ct	St
G.P.Thorpe	6	6	2	254	89	63.50	-	2	5	-
G.A.Hick	5	5	1	212	104*	53.00	1	1	1	-
R.A.Smith	2	2	0	100	75	50.00	-	1	1	-
P.A.J.DeFreitas	4	2	0	89	67	44.50	-	1	-	-
N.M.K.Smith	3	3	1	69	31	34.50	-	-	1	-
D.Gough	6	4	2	66	26*	33.00	-	-	1	-
N.H.Fairbrother	5	5	2	88	36	29.33	-	-	2	-
M.A.Atherton	6	6	0	119	66	19.83	-	1	-	-
D.A.Reeve	2	2	0	38	35	19.00	-	-	-	-
A.J.Stewart	5	5	0	86	34	17.20	-	-	-	-
C.White	2	1	0	13	13	13.00	-	-	-	-
D.G.Cork	5	3	0	36	19	12.00	-	-	2	-
R.C.Russell	6	4	0	27	12	6.75	-	-	7	1
P.J.Martin	5	4	2	6	3	3.00	-	-	-	-
R.K.Illingworth	4	2	2	4	3*	-	-	-	-	-

England *bowling*

	O	M	R	W	Avge	Best	5w	Econ
C.White	6.3	1	23	0	-	-	-	3.53
N.M.K.Smith	25.3	2	96	4	24.00	3-29	-	3.76
P.A.J.DeFreitas	33.1	6	140	6	23.33	3-31	-	4.22
R.K.Illingworth	40	4	174	4	43.50	1-25	-	4.35
D.G.Cork	48	2	216	8	27.00	2-33	-	4.50
P.J.Martin	44	2	198	6	33.00	3-33	-	4.50
D.Gough	51	4	238	4	59.50	2-48	-	4.66
D.A.Reeve	10.4	1	51	1	51.00	1-14	-	4.78
G.P.Thorpe	8	0	45	0	-	-	-	5.62
G.A.Hick	20	0	119	3	39.66	2-45	-	5.95

Kenya *batting*

	M	I	NO	Runs	HS	Avge	100	50	Ct	St
S.Tikolo	5	5	0	196	96	39.20	-	2	3	-
K.Otieno	5	5	0	147	85	29.40	-	1	1	-
L.Onyango	1	1	0	23	23	23.00	-	-	1	--
M.Odumbe	5	5	0	112	50	22.40	-	1	-	-
D.Chudasama	5	5	0	103	34	20.60	-	-	1	-
H.Modi	5	5	0	84	41	16.80	-	-	3	-
E.T.Odumbe	5	5	1	54	20	13.50	-	-	2	-
T.Odoyo	4	4	0	42	24	10.50	-	-	-	-
A.Y.Karim	5	3	1	19	11	9.50	-	-	-	-
M.Suji	5	4	2	18	15	9.00	-	-	3	-
I.Tariq Iqbal	2	2	0	17	16	8.50	-	-	2	-
D.Tikolo	3	2	2	36	25*	-	-	-	2	-
R.Ali	5	2	2	6	6*	-	-	-	1	-

Kenya *bowling*

	O	M	R	W	Avge	Best	5w	Econ
A.Y.Karim	48	4	171	4	42.75	1-19	-	3.56
M.Odumbe	42.5	6	187	6	31.16	3-15	-	4.36
R.Ali	36.2	3	176	9	19.55	3-17	-	4.84
M.Suji	40.2	3	213	4	53.25	2-55	-	5.28
E.T.Odumbe	14	0	87	2	43.50	2-34	-	6.21
T.Odoyo	16	0	102	0	-	-	-	6.37
D.Tikolo	8	0	55	0	-	-	-	-6.87
L.Onyango	4	0	31	0	-	-	-	7.75
S.Tikolo	10	0	83	1	83.00	1-26	-	8.30

India *batting*

	M	I	NO	Runs	HS	Avge	100	50	Ct	St
S.R.Tendulkar	7	7	1	523	137	87.16	2	3	2	-
V.G.Kambli	7	7	3	176	106	44.00	1	-	1	-
N.S.Sidhu	5	5	0	178	93	35.60	-	2	-	-
A.D.Jadeja	7	6	1	144	53	28.80	-	1	2	-
M.A.Azharuddin	7	6	1	143	72*	28.60	-	1	3	-
S.V.Manjrekar	5	5	0	141	62	28.20	-	1	2	-
N.R.Mongia	7	6	3	69	27	23.00	-	-	4	3
E.Gouka	3	2	1	19	19	19.00	-	-	-	-
A.R.Kumble	7	3	1	27	17	13.50	-	-	8	-
J.Srinath	7	3	1	25	12*	12.50	-	-	3	-
M.Prabhakar	4	3	0	11	7	3.66	-	-	2	-
B.K.V.Prasad	7	2	1	0	0*	0.00	-	-	1	-
A.R.Kapoor	2	1	0	0	0	0.00	-	-	-	-
S.L.V.Raju	4	1	1	3	3*	-	-	-	1	-
S.A.Ankola	1	-	-	-	-	-	-	-	-	--

India *bowling*

	O	M	R	W	Avge	Best	5w	Econ
S.L.V.Raju	40	4	158	8	19.75	3-30	-	3.95
A.R.Kumble	69.4	3	281	15	18.73	3-29	-	4.03
A.R.Kapoor	20	2	81	1	81.00	1-41	-	4.05
S.R.Tendulkar	36	1	148	2	74.00	2-34	-	4.11
J.Srinath	65.4	3	294	8	36.75	3-34	-	4.47
A.D.Jadeja	17	0	81	2	40.50	2-31	-	4.76
B.K.V.Prasad	65	1	312	8	39.00	3-45	-	4.80
M.Prabhakar	29	1	160	3	53.33	3-39	-	5.51
S.A.Ankola	5	0	28	0	-	-	-	5.60

Netherlands *batting*

	M	I	NO	Runs	HS	Avge	100	50	Ct	St
K.J.van Noortwijk	5	5	1	168	64	42.00	-	1	-	-
P.E.Cantrell	5	5	0	160	47	32.00	-	-	-	-
G.J.A.F.Aponso	5	4	0	120	58	30.00	-	1	-	-
R.P.Lefebvre	4	4	1	78	45	26.00	-	-	1	-
B.Zuiderent	5	5	1	91	54	22.75	-	1	5	-
T.B.M.de Leede	5	5	0	90	41	18.00	-	-	-	-
M.Schewe	5	4	1	49	20	16.33	-	-	2	1
N.E.Clarke	5	5	0	50	32	10.00	-	-	3	-
S.W.Lubbers	4	4	1	24	9	8.00	-	-	1	-
R.van Oosterom	2	2	2	7	5*	-	-	-	-	-
P.J.Bakker	5	1	1	0	0*	-	-	-	-	-
F.Jansen	2	-	-	-	-	-	-	-	1	-

Netherlands *bowling*

	O	M	R	W	Avge	Best	5w	Econ
R.P.Lefebvre	35	2	132	3	44.00	1-20	-	3.77
P.J.Bakker	43	2	215	3	71.66	2-51	-	5.00
S.W.Lubbers	36	0	187	5	37.40	3-48	-	5.19
P.E.Cantrell	31	0	170	3	56.66	1-18	-	5.48
G.J.A.F.Aponso	40.2	0	257	2	128.50	1-57	-	6.37
T.B.M.de Leede	27	0	179	0	-	-	-	6.62
F.Jansen	9	0	62	1	62.00	1-40	-	6.88
E.Gouka	3.4	0	51	1	51.00	1-32	-	13.90

New Zealand *batting*

	M	I	NO	Runs	HS	Avge	100	50	Ct	St
L.K.Germon	6	6	3	191	89	63.66	-	1	2	1
C.Z.Harris	4	4	0	156	130	39.00	1	-	1	-
S.A.Thomson	5	5	2	100	31*	33.33	-	-	3	-
S.P.Fleming	6	6	0	193	66	32.16	-	1	2	-
C.M.Spearman	6	6	0	192	78	32.00	-	2	1	-
R.G.Twose	6	6	0	175	92	29.16	-	1	1	-
C.L.Cairns	6	6	0	139	52	23.16	-	1	6	-
A.C.Parore	5	5	0	144	55	28.80	-	1	1	-
N.J.Astle	6	6	0	111	101	18.50	1	-	2	-
D.N.Patel	2	2	1	14	11	14.00	-	-	-	-
D.J.Nash	4	2	1	13	8	13.00	-	-	-	-
R.J.Kennedy	3	1	0	2	3	2.00	-	-	1	-
G.R.Larsen	2	1	0	1	1	1.00	-	-	1	-
D.K.Morrison	5	3	3	15	10*	-	-	-	1	-

New Zealand *bowling*

	O	M	R	W	Avge	Best	5w	Econ
S.P.Fleming	2	0	8	1	8.00	1-8	-	4.00
G.R.Larsen	18	2	73	3	24.33	2-32	-	4.05
C.Z.Harris	33	1	135	5	27.00	3-24	-	4.09
R.J.Kennedy	21	2	88	4	22.00	2-36	-	4.19
D.J.Nash	35	4	154	6	25.66	3-27	-	4.40
S.A.Thomson	42.3	2	197	5	39.40	3-20	-	4.63
C.L.Cairns	43.5	4	207	2	103.50	1-31	-	4.72
N.J.Astle	27	1	129	3	43.00	2-10	-	4.77
D.N.Patel	18	0	87	1	87.00	1-45	-	4.83
D.K.Morrison	29	1	147	3	49.00	1-37	-	5.06
R.G.Twose	13	0	79	0	-	-	-	6.07

Pakistan *batting*

	M	I	NO	Runs	HS	Avge	100	50	Ct	St
Saeed Anwar	6	6	2	329	83*	82.25	-	3	-	-
Salim Malik	6	3	1	133	55*	66.50	-	1	1	-
Inzamam-ul-Haq	6	5	2	145	53*	48.33	-	1	-	-
Aamir Sohail	6	6	0	272	111	45.33	1	2	1	-
Ijaz Ahmed	6	6	1	197	70	39.40	-	2	2	-
Javed Miandad	5	3	1	54	38	27.00	-	-	3	-
Rashid Latif	6	2	0	26	26	13.00	-	-	7	2
Mushtaq Ahmed	6	1	0	0	0	0.00	-	-	3	-
Ata-ur-Rehman	1	1	0	0	0	0.00	-	-	-	-
Wasim Akram	5	2	2	60	32*	-	-	-	1	-
Aaqib Javed	5	1	1	6	6*	-	-	-	-	-
Ramiz Raja	1	1	1	2	2*	-	-	-	-	-
Waqar Younis	6	1	1	4	4*	-	-	-	2	-
Saqlain Mushtaq	1	-	-	-	-	-	-	-	1	-

Pakistan *bowling*

	O	M	R	W	Avge	Best	5w	Econ
Saqlain Mushtaq	10	1	38	2	19.00	2-38	-	3.80
Ata-ur-Rehman	10	0	40	1	40.00	1-40	-	4.00
Wasim Akram	33.2	3	135	3	45.00	2-25	-	4.05
Mushtaq Ahmed	57	2	238	10	23.80	3-16	-	4.17
Aamir Sohail	46	1	200	4	50.00	2-48	-	4.34
Waqar Younis	54	5	253	13	19.46	4-26	-	4.68
Aaqib Javed	39.3	2	189	7	27.00	2-18	-	4.78
Salim Malik	21	1	107	3	35.66	2-41	-	5.09
Ijaz Ahmed	4	0	21	0	-	-	-	-5.25

South Africa *batting*

	M	I	NO	Runs	HS	Avge	100	50	Ct	St
G.Kirsten	6	6	1	391	188*	78.20	1	1	2	-
A.C.Hudson	4	4	0	275	161	68.75	1	1	2	-
D.J.Cullinan	6	6	2	255	69	63.75	-	2	3	-
W.J.Cronje	6	6	1	276	78	55.20	-	2	3	-
J.H.Kallis	5	4	2	63	26	31.50	-	-	1	-
J.N.Rhodes	4	3	0	59	37	19.66	-	-	1	-
S.M.Pollock	6	3	1	38	20*	19.00	-	-	2	-
S.J.Palframan	6	3	0	45	28	15.00	-	-	8	-
P.L.Symcox	4	2	0	25	24	12.50	-	-	-	-
P.S de Villiers	1	1	0	12	12	12.00	-	-	-	-
P.R.Adams	2	1	0	10	10	10.00	-	-	-	-
B.M.McMillan	6	4	1	20	11	6.66	-	-	4	-
C.R.Matthews	6	2	2	17	9*	-	-	-	1	-
A.A.Donald	4	-	-	-	-	-	-	-	-	-

South Africa *bowling*

	O	M	R	W	Avge	Best	5w	Econ
B.M.McMillan	43	5	127	6	21.16	3-11	-	2.95
G.Kirsten	3	1	9	0	-	-	-	3.00
D.J.Cullinan	2	0	7	0	-	-	-	3.50
A.A.Donald	34	0	126	8	15.75	3-21	-	3.70
P.L.Symcox	40	2	149	6	24.83	2-22	-	3.72
C.R.Matthews	59.3	2	226	7	32.28	2-30	-	3.79
P.S.de Villiers	7	1	27	2	13.50	2-27	-	3.85
W.J.Cronje	22	1	87	2	43.50	2-20	-	3.95
S.M.Pollock	53	4	218	6	36.33	2-16	-	4.11
J.H.Kallis	13	1	57	0	-	-	-	4.38
P.R.Adams	18	0	87	3	29.00	2-45	-	4.83

Sri Lanka *batting*

	M	I	NO	Runs	HS	Avge	100	50	Ct	St
A.Ranatunga	6	6	4	241	75*	120.50	-	1	1	-
P.A.de Silva	6	6	1	448	145	89.60	2	2	4	-
H.P.Tillekeratne	6	5	3	128	70*	64.00	-	1	-	-
A.P.Gurusinha	6	6	0	307	87	51.16	-	3	1	-
S.T.Jayasuriya	6	6	0	221	82	36.83	-	2	5	-
W.P.U.C.J.Vaas	6	1	0	23	23	23.00	-	-	-	-
R.S.Kaluwitharana	6	6	0	73	33	12.16	-	-	3	2
H.D.Dharmasena	6	1	0	9	9	9.00	-	-	1	-
R.S.Mahanama	6	3	3	80	58*	-	-	1	-	-
M.Muralitharan	6	1	1	5	5*	-	-	-	2	-
G.P.Wickremasinghe	4	1	1	4	4*	-	-	-	-	-
K.R.Pushpakumara	2	-	-	-	-	-	-	-	-	-

Sri Lanka *bowling*

	O	M	R	W	Avge	Best	5w	Econ
M.Muralitharan	57.1	3	216	7	30.85	2-37	-	3.77
W.P.U.C.J.Vaas	49	6	193	6	32.16	2-30	-	3.93
H.P.Tillekeratne	1	0	4	0	-	-	-	4.00
H.D.Dharmasena	56	1	249	6	41.50	2-30	-	4.44
S.T.Jayasuriya	51	1	231	7	33.00	3-12	-	4.52
P.A.de Silva	17	0	87	4	21.75	3-42	-	5.11
G.P.Wickremasinghe	27	0	141	0	-	-	-	5.22
A.Ranatunga	11	0	68	2	34.00	2-31	-	6.18
K.R.Pushpakumara	15	0	99	1	99.00	1-53	-	6.60

United Arab Emirates *batting*

	M	I	NO	Runs	HS	Avge	100	50	Ct	St
S.Dukanwala	5	4	2	84	40*	42.00	-	-	2	-
Mohammad Ishaq	3	3	1	71	51*	35.50	-	1	1	-
Salim Raza	4	4	0	137	84	34.25	-	1	-	-
J.A.Samarasekera	5	4	1	90	47*	30.00	-	-	-	-
Arshad Laiq	4	4	1	66	43*	22.00	-	-	-	-
Mazhar Hussain	5	5	0	99	33	19.80	-	-	1	-
V.Mehra	4	4	1	44	29*	14.66	-	-	1	-
G.Mylvaganam	3	3	0	36	23	12.00	-	-	1	-
Azhar Saeed	5	5	0	58	32	11.60	-	-	2	-
Mohammad Aslam	4	4	0	38	23	9.50	-	-	-	-
Sultan Zarawani	5	4	0	16	13	4.00	-	-	1	-
Imtiaz Abbasi	5	4	3	4	2*	4.00	-	-	2	2
Shahzad Altaf	2	-	-	-	-	-	-	-	-	-
Saeed-al-Saffar	1	-	-	-	-	-	-	-	1	-

United Arab Emirates *bowling*

	O	M	R	W	Avge	Best	5w	Econ
Shazad Altaf	13 3	0	37	1	37.00	1-15	-	2.84
J.A.Samarasekera	34	4	156	3	52.00	1-17	-	4.58
S.Dukanwala	33	1	153	6	25.50	5-29	1	4.63
Salim Raza	22	1	108	1	108.00	1-48	-	4.90
Azhar Saeed	31	1	157	6	26.16	3-45	-	5.06
Sultan Zarawani	37	0	209	4	52.25	2-49	-	5.64
Arshad Laiq	19	0	117	1	117.00	1-25	-	6.15
Mazhar Hussain	8	0	60	0	-	-	-	7.50
Saeed-al-Saffar	3	0	25	0	-	-	-	8.33

West Indies *batting*

	M	I	NO	Runs	HS	Avge	100	50	Ct	St
R.B.Richardson	6	6	2	236	93*	59.00	-	1	1	-
B.C.Lara	6	6	1	269	111	53.80	1	1	2	-
S.Chanderpaul	6	6	0	211	80	35.16	-	2	1	-
J.C.Adams	4	4	2	41	17*	20.50	-	-	6	1
C.O.Browne	5	4	0	64	26	16.00	-	-	3	2
R.A.Harper	6	6	1	78	23	15.60	-	-	3	-
S.L.Campbell	4	4	0	57	47	14.25	-	-	-	-
I.R.Bishop	6	4	1	35	17	11.66	-	-	1	-
C.A.Walsh	6	3	1	13	9*	6.50	-	-	2	-
C.E.L.Ambrose	6	4	1	13	8	4.33	-	-	-	-
O.D.Gibson	3	2	0	7	6	3.50	-	-	1	-
R.I.C.Holder	2	2	0	5	5	2.50	-	-	-	-
C.E.Cuffy	1	1	0	1	1	1.00	-	-	1	-
K.L.T.Arthurton	5	5	0	2	1	0.40	-	-	1	-

West Indies *bowling*

	O	M	R	W	Avge	Best	5w	Econ
C.E.L.Ambrose	56.3	11	170	10	17.00	3-28	-	3.00
R.A.Harper	58	6	219	12	18.25	4-47	-	3.77
C.A.Walsh	55.3	9	210	7	30.00	3-46	-	3.78
C.E.Cuffy	8	0	31	1	31.00	1-31	-	3.87
I.R.Bishop	49	6	194	3	64.66	2-35	-	3.95
O.D.Gibson	19.4	1	90	1	90.00	1-27	-	4.57
J.C.Adams	22	0	110	3	36.66	3-53	-	5.00
K.L.T.Arthurton	20	0	108	1	108.00	1-29	-	5.40

Zimbabwe *batting*

	M	I	NO	Runs	HS	Avge	100	50	Ct	St
P.A.Strang	5	4	3	52	22*	52.00	-	-	1	-
A.C.Waller	5	5	0	159	67	31.80	-	1	-	-
C.N.Evans	5	5	2	92	39*	30.66	-	-	-	-
G.W.Flower	5	5	0	125	45	25.00	-	-	3	-
A.D.R.Campbell	5	5	0	114	75	22.80	-	1	5	-
H.H.Streak	5	5	1	80	30	20.00	-	-	1	-
G.J.Whittall	5	5	0	71	35	14.20	-	-	-	-
A.Flower	5	5	0	49	26	9.80	-	-	-	1
S.G.Davies	1	1	0	9	9	9.00	-	-	-	-
A.C.I.Lock	5	3	2	8	5	8.00	-	-	-	-
E.A.Brandes	2	1	0	7	7	7.00	-	-	-	-
S.G.Peall	4	2	0	9	9	4.50	-	-	1	-
B.C.Strang	3	2	0	3	3	1.50	-	-	2	-

Zimbabwe *bowling*

	O	M	R	W	Avge	Best	5w	Econ
B.C.Strang	18	1	66	3	22.00	2-24	-	3.66
H.H.Streak	44	8	175	4	43.75	3-60	-	3.97
A.D.R.Campbell	3	0	13	0	-	-	-	4.33
S.G.Peall	23	1	101	1	101.00	1-23	-	4.39
A.C.I.Lock	32	3	141	3	47.00	2-57	-	4.40
P.A.Strang	42.1	4	192	12	16.00	5-21	1	4.55
G.W.Flower	11	1	54	0	-	-	-	4.90
E.A.Brandes	15	0	77	0	-	-	-	5.13
G.J.Whittall	14	0	79	0	-	-	-	5.64

1999 – A WORLD CUP TO SAVOUR

It's coming home, it's coming home, it's coming, cricket's coming home. But will it inspire England the way Euro 96 did? Cricket's biggest tournament will have plenty of new angles, new faces – and new teams

The World Cup is cricket's shop window, the summit meeting of the world's cricketing nations. It is the only one-day competition that, once finished, we can remember who the winners were a week later. Who can forget how Sri Lanka magically won the trophy last time, defeating Australia and spawning unprecedented celebrations in Colombo.

The World Cup is the key to cricket's popularity as a global game. It has to succeed – though inevitably a big factor this year will be one of the capricious English weather … and the Welsh, Scottish and Dutch weather; don't forget there are fixtures there in 1999. With 12 teams playing 42 matches, the seventh World Cup is the biggest ever – and there is a lot at stake.

Two teams in particular can't afford a bad show. In England and the West Indies, young sportsmen are increasingly seduced by other sports. In the Caribbean, US cable TV dominates; youngsters' heroes are more likely to hurl a big ball through a hoop than crack a boundary at the Kensington Oval, Barbados. The West Indies, winners of the first two World Cups, need to thrive in 1999 to sustain interest in the one activity that binds the Caribbean islands.

England have never won the World Cup, though they have been finalists three times. In the UK, cricket is in danger of being subsumed by soccer. The hosting of the 1996 European Championship was a grand

BY
VIC MARKS

success and every youngster wants to be a Premiership footballer. And every youngster's dad wants his son to be a Premiership footballer as well, since they get paid such astronomical sums compared to our cricketers. So it's vital for English cricket that the imagination of the nation is captured by the quality and excitement of the play, preferably the play of the English team.

Mind you, there are plenty of incentives for the other teams to do well. South Africa often head those artificial league tables of one-day cricket, yet they tend to fall short in major finals. They have yet to appear in a World Cup final. Sri Lanka, proud winners last time, will want to prove that their success was no fluke. The fortunes of Pakistan cricket have been volatile, to say the least, since their 1992 victory. India, who stunned the West Indies in the 1983 Final, boast the best batsman in the world. The Australians, winners in 1987, can't bear losing at tiddlywinks. New Zealand and Zimbabwe, with their limited resources, always compete ferociously, while the minnows of 1999, Kenya, Bangladesh and Scotland, will be hell-bent on causing an upset or two.

Will the fickle white ball on moist early-summer pitches make it a tournament for bowlers, or will the pinch-hitting openers dominate as they did in 1996? These are all delicious imponderables, but we *can* say with some certainty that the following players will have a big role to play…

·AUSTRALIA·
PLAYERS TO WATCH

Michael Bevan

His Test career may have faltered – he's one of the few to be sorted out by English pacemen – but he's a brilliant improvisor with the bat and a pickpocket of a runner. Also a fine fielder, while occasionally his left-arm wrist spinners have turned one-day matches, though they are unlikely to be used much in England in May.

Adam Gilchrist

Must be a handy cricketer since he has ousted Ian Healy from the Australian one-day side. A no-nonsense, barnstorming left-hander, he is often used as an opening batsman, as the Australians seek to learn from the Sri Lankan approach. A real crowd-pleaser. Also a highly proficient wicketkeeper.

Shane Warne (below)

Warne has brought glamour, wit, subtlety and a whiff of scandal to Test cricket, and he's handy in the one-day game. If you're not sure which way the ball is going to bounce then it's harder to clobber it. Warne has also proved that he is an innovative captain, should his chance come in his second World Cup outing.

·ENGLAND·
PLAYERS TO WATCH

Alec Stewart

In Test cricket we agonise whether Stewart can fulfil the triple role of wicketkeeper, opener and captain. In one-dayers he just gets on with it. We know his worth in the first two roles; the World Cup will tell us much more about his tactical nous. Key responsibility: to launch the England innings with style and pace.

Nick Knight

A proven one-day opener who is adept at charging the new ball while still keeping an eagle eye on it and surprising international fast bowlers in the process. A never-say-die character and brilliant fieldsman anywhere.

Darren Gough (left)

Will be a vital bowler provided he has enough fuel left after a gruelling winter. Bowls at the crucial times in the innings: at the start, when the batsmen are swinging and an early wicket is needed to stem the tide; and at the end, when the batsmen are swinging and his in-swinging yorker is an invaluable weapon.

·INDIA·
PLAYERS TO WATCH

Mohammed Azharuddin

Now a veteran. No one has played more one-day internationals than Azhar, who first appeared on England's 1984/5 tour of India. Yet we never tire of watching this wristy genius at the crease, fallible yet utterly enchanting. And he's now a shrewd tactician.

Sachin Tendulkar (above)

Simply the best. In one-day cricket he usually opens now – why not let him bat 50 overs if he can? – and seems to score centuries at will. Offers a rare mix of technical expertise spiced with Eastern flair. Sir Don Bradman thinks he's the best of this era and he should know.

Javagal Srinath

Seems to have been around for decades yet is only 29. India's premier pace bowler and a vital figure given that this World Cup, contested in England in May with a fickle white ball, is likely to favour the seamers.

·NEW ZEALAND·
PLAYERS TO WATCH

Stephen Fleming (above)

Thrust into the captaincy of his country at the tender age of 23 in February 1997, Fleming is surviving – some achievement. A languid left-hander, will he turn up some surprise Kiwi tactics like Martin Crowe in the 1992 Cup? He may need to if New Zealand are to win.

Nathan Astle

Ideally suited to the one-day game, he is a free-scoring right-handed batsman, especially strong through the off side. And he bowls nagging dibbly-dobbly medium pacers which are better than they look, which is not hard.

Daniel Vettori

Tossed into Test cricket at 18 after two first-class appearances, Vettori could now have an impact in the one-day game. Shaggy-haired and bespectacled, he may look an unlikely cricketer, but he has a fine temperament as a left-arm spinner and an unflappable tail-end batsman.

·PAKISTAN·
PLAYERS TO WATCH

Wasim Akram

Played a key role as Imran's enforcer when Pakistan won the World Cup in Melbourne in 1992. A lot has happened to Wasim and Pakistan cricket since then, but if the force is with him he can still devastate in this form of cricket. And his knowledge of England after all those years at Old Trafford is extensive.

Inzamam-ul-Haq (above)

Ponderous, dozy and lazy batsman who can terrify any international bowler. It was his innings against New Zealand in Auckland in 1992 that catapulted his side into the Final when they seemed beaten. Not the quickest betwen the wickets but such a good timer of a cricket ball he rarely needs to run.

Saqlain Mushtaq

Cunning off-spinner who has in his armoury a mystery ball that looks like an off-break but which jags towards first slip. This can produce many stumpings in one-day cricket and keeps the batsmen guessing. Consistently niggardly in this form of cricket and well versed in English conditions after his years at The Oval.

·SOUTH AFRICA·
PLAYERS TO WATCH

Hansie Cronje

Leads the most consistent one-day side in the world, though they often falter in finals. Apart from his vast store of experience and acumen, Cronje is as an uninhibited hitter who is especially adept against the spinners, and a canny, innocuous looking medium-pacer.

Jacques Kallis (above)

All-rounders are a precious commodity in one-day cricket and Kallis is now one of the world's best. A stylish front-line batsman, his away-swingers improve each year and they can also surprise batsmen with pace. His experience of playing for Middlesex will prove handy.

Jonty Rhodes

Sets the tone for the South Africans in the field. His irrepressible athleticism is now legend in the cricket world. Crucially his batting has improved as he has grown older. Moreover he's at his most dangerous with the bat when his side are in a crisis.

·SRI LANKA·
PLAYERS TO WATCH

Arjuna Ranatunga

Napoleonic in gait and outlook. His team can be on the verge of a catastrophic defeat and it all still looks part of the Ranatunga master-plan. He's the only survivor of the 1983 World Cup; he lofted the 1996 Trophy to the skies and can still score canny runs down the order.

Sanath Jayasuriya

A key figure in Sri Lanka's success last time as a devastating opening batsman and niggardly left-arm spinner. All around the world, openers are now trying to copy the Jayasuriya method – smashing the ball here, there and everywhere during the first 15 overs.

Muttiah Muralitharan (above)

He's controversial because of his action – he has been no-balled on two tours of Australia – and almost unique in modern cricket: a finger spinner who terrifies the life out of opposition batsmen. He spins the ball on any surface and is a slippery fieldsman.

·WEST INDIES·
PLAYERS TO WATCH

Brian Lara

The West Indies can't succeed without their batting genius, but often they can't succeed with him. Stormy relationships between captain and Board, captain and players make West Indian cricket much more volatile – and more inconsistent – than in Clive Lloyd days.

Philo Wallace

Makes you turn up on time. He could pummel the ball way back over the bowler's head in the first over of a Test match, let alone a one-day international. This uncomplicated latecomer to international cricket brings a refreshing simplicity to the game. Marvellous to behold if he comes off.

Shivnarine Chanderpaul (below)

Somebody has got to do the unspectacular grafting in the West Indian side and Chanderpaul, something of a veteran now at the age of 24, is the most likely to do it. Conscientious, gifted left-hander who is also a superb fieldsman. If his leg breaks are used frequently in this World Cup, his team are struggling.

·ZIMBABWE·
PLAYERS TO WATCH

Alistair Campbell

Doughty captain and left-hander. His side lose more one-day matches than they win – except when playing England – but always compete fiercely and can never be taken for granted.

Andy Flower (right)

Campbell's predecessor as captain; a dangerous, yet conscientious player in any form of cricket. Zimbabwe's most-capped player. He recognised earlier than Stewart that he was not a superman. Now just keeps wicket and scores runs.

Heath Streak

Vigorous, no-nonsense pace bowler who has been vital to Zimbabwe's emergence in Test cricket. His one-day record is not so striking but English conditions should suit him.

- *Vic Marks played for England in the 1983 World Cup. He is The Observer's Cricket Correspondent and an expert summariser for Test Match Special*

A CUP WORTH A MILLION DOLLARS

Prize money of 1 million dollars (£613,000) will be up fo grabs in the 1999 World Cup, a bounty which will be distributed as follows:

Winning team $300,000 (£184,000);
Runner-up $150,000 (£92,000);
Losing semi-finalists $100,000 (£61,000).

The remaining fund will be split between fifth and sixth place, Super Six and group match winners and losers.

Right: The trophy they will all be vying for

...PLUS BANGLADESH, KENYA AND SCOTLAND

There are three non-Test teams in this year's World Cup: Kenya, Bangladesh and Scotland. They qualified by emerging as the top three at the 1997 ICC Trophy tournament, which was played in Kuala Lumpur, Malaysia – during the rainy season, for some reason.

Twenty-four teams competed, from as far afield as Argentina, Israel, USA and Namibia, with Kenya meeting Bangladesh in the final. Steve Tikolo was Man of the Match for his 147 in Kenya's 241 for seven, but rain gave Bangladesh a target of only 166 to win, which they did with two wickets in hand. In the rain-affected third-place play-off, Scotland made 187 for eight in 45 overs, then bowled out Ireland, coached by Mike Hendrick, for 141.

So the Scots, who have almost never beaten a county side in earlier adventures, will now take their chance against Warne, Tendulkar, Ambrose and Jayasuriya. If they manage to beat any of them, there really will be a few wee drams raised in the Highlands. The classy Kenyans, on the other hand, could well cause another World Cup upset or two…

WHICH SIX WILL TAKE THE SUPER HIGHWAY?

The 12 teams were seeded and divided into two groups – Group A: Sri Lanka, India, South Africa, England, Zimbabwe and Kenya; Group B: Australia, West Indies, Pakistan, New Zealand, Bangladesh and Scotland. Each team will play the others in its group. The first match, England v Sri Lanka at Lord's, will be preceded by a short opening ceremony.

Following the group matches, the top three teams from each group will progress to the next phase, the Super Six, taking with them only the points scored against the other successful teams in their group. Nine Super Six matches will be played at the Test match grounds, with each progressing team in Group A playing the three progressing teams in Group B. The top four teams in the Super Six league will qualify for the semi-finals.

The Final will be played at Lord's on Sunday June 20.

· OVERALL STATISTICS ·

Highest total

1996 398 for 5, Sri Lanka v Kenya

Highest total
by side batting second

1992 313 for 7, Sri Lanka v Zimbabwe

Lowest total

1979 45, Canada v England

Highest winning margin

1975 10 wickets, India beat South Africa
1983 10 wickets, West Indies beat Zimbabwe
1992 10 wickets, West Indies beat Pakistan
1975 202 runs, England beat India

Closest winning margins

1975 1 wicket, West Indies beat Pakistan
1987 1 wicket, Pakistan beat West Indies
1987 1 run, Australia beat India
1992 1 run, Australia beat India

Overall World Cup table

	P	W	L	N/R	Win Rate
South Africa	15	10	5	0	66.67%
West Indies	39	25	13	1	65.38%
England	40	25	14	1	63.75%
Pakistan	37	21	15	1	58.11%
Australia	38	22	16	0	57.89%
New Zealand	35	19	16	0	54.29%
India	36	18	17	1	51.39%
Sri Lanka	34	12	20	2	38.24%
Kenya	5	1	4	0	20.00%
UAE	5	1	4	0	20.00%
Zimbabwe	25	3	22	0	12.00%
Canada	3	0	3	0	00.00%
East Africa	3	0	3	0	00.00%
Holland	5	0	5	0	00.00%

Highest aggregate

1996 652 for 12, Sri Lanka v Kenya

Highest total for

Sri Lanka	398 for 5 (50 overs) v Kenya 1996
West Indies	360 for 4 (50 overs) v Sri Lanka 1987
Pakistan	338 for 5 (60 overs) v Sri Lanka 1983
England	334 for 4 (60 overs) v India 1975
South Africa	328 for 3 (50 overs) v Holland 1996
Australia	328 for 5 (60 overs) v Sri Lanka 1975
Zimbabwe	312 for 4 (50 overs) v Sri Lanka 1992
New Zealand	309 for 5 (60 overs) v E Africa 1975
India	289 for 6 (50 overs) v Australia 1987
Kenya	254 for 7 (50 overs) v Sri Lanka 1996
Holland	230 for 6 (50 overs) v England 1996
UAE	220 for 3 (44.2 overs) v Holland 1996
Canada	139 for 9 (60 overs) v Pakistan 1979
East Africa	128 for 8 (60 overs) v New Zealand 1975

Aravinda de Silva scored 145 in Sri Lanka's highest total of 398 against Kenya in 1996

Highest total against

Kenya	Sri Lanka 398 for 5 (50 overs) 1996
Sri Lanka	West Indies 360 for 4 (50 overs) 1987
India	England 334 for 4 (60 overs) 1975
Holland	Pakistan 328 for 3 (50 overs) 1996
New Zealand	England 322 for 6 (60 overs) 1983
UAE	South Africa 321 for 2 (50 overs) 1996
Zimbabwe	Sri Lanka 313 for 7 (49 overs) 1992
East Africa	New Zealand 309 for 5 (60 overs) 1975
Pakistan	West Indies 293 for 6 (60 overs) 1979
Australia	West Indies 291 for 8 (60 overs) 1975
England	Sri Lanka 286 (58 overs) 1983
West Indies	Australia 274 (58.4 overs) 1975 (final)
South Africa	West Indies 264 for 8 (50 overs) 1996
Canada	Pakistan 140 for 2 (40.1 overs) 1979

Lowest total for
(completed innings only)

Canada	45 v England 1979
Pakistan	74 v England 1992
Sri Lanka	86 v West Indies 1975
England	93 v Australia 1975
West Indies	93 v Kenya 1996
East Africa	94 v England 1975
UAE	109 for 9 (50 overs) v Pakistan 1996
Australia	129 v India 1983
India	132 for 3 v England 1975
Zimbabwe	134 v England 1992
Kenya	134 v Zimbabwe 1996
Holland	145 for 7 (50 overs) v Pakistan 1996
New Zealand	158 v West Indies 1975

Lowest total against (completed innings only)

England 45 (40 overs) Canada 1979
West Indies 86 (37.2 overs) Sri Lanka 1975
Australia 93 (36.2) England 1975
Kenya 93 (35.2) West Indies 1996
Pakistan 109 for 9 (33 overs) UAE 1996
India 120 (55.3) East Africa 1975
Zimbabwe 125 (49.1) England 1992
New Zealand 128 for 8 (60 overs) East Africa 1975
South Africa 136 (38 overs) West Indies 1992
UAE 216 (50 overs) Holland 1996
Holland 279 for 4 (50 overs) England 1996
East Africa 290 for 5 (60 overs) 1975
Canada n/a

· BATTING ·

Highest career runs

1,083 at 43.32 Javed Miandad, Pakistan
1,013 at 63.31 I V A Richards, West Indies
897 at 44.85 G A Gooch, England
880 at 55.00 M D Crowe, New Zealand
854 at 37.13 D L Haynes, West Indies

Highest scores

188 n.o. G Kirsten, South Africa v UAE 1996
181 I V A Richards, West Indies
v Sri Lanka 1987
175 n.o. Kapil Dev, India v Zimbabwe 1983
171 G M Turner, New Zealand
v East Africa 1975
161 A C Hudson, South Africa
v Holland 1996

Most runs in a tournament

		M	I	NO	Runs	HS	Avge	100	50
S R Tendulkar	(Ind 1996)	7	7	1	523	137	87.16	2	3
M E Waugh	(Aus 1996)	7	7	1	484	130	80.66	3	1
G A Gooch	(Eng 1987)	8	8	0	471	115	58.87	1	3
M D Crowe	(NZ 1992)	9	9	5	456	100*	114.00	1	4
P A de Silva	(SL 1996)	6	6	1	448	145	89.60	2	2

Highest scores for

South Africa G Kirsten 188 n.o. v UAE 1996
West Indies I V A Richards 181 v Sri Lanka 1987
India Kapil Dev 175 n.o. v Zimbabwe 1983
New Zealand G M Turner, 171 n.o. v E Africa 1975
Sri Lanka P A de Silva, 145 v Kenya 1996
Zimbabwe D L Houghton, 142 v New Zealand 1987
England D L Amiss, 137 v India 1975
Australia M E Waugh, 130 v Kenya 1996
Pakistan Ramiz Raja, 119 n.o. v New Zealand 1992
Kenya S Tikolo, 95 v Sri Lanka 1996
UAE 84, Saleem Raza v Holland 1996
Holland K J van Noortwijk, 64 v England 1996
East Africa Frasat Ali, 45 v New Zealand 1975
Canada G R Seeley, 45 v Pakistan 1979

Most individual hundreds

3 I V A Richards, West Indies
3 Ramiz Raja, Pakistan
3 M E Waugh, Australia

Highest partnership for each wicket

1st 186 G Kirsten and A C Hudson
South Africa v Holland 1996
2nd 176 D L Amiss and K W R Fletcher
England v India 1975
3rd 207 M E Waugh and S R Waugh
Australia v Kenya 1996
4th 168 L K Germon and C Z Harris
New Zealand v Australia 1996
5th 145* A Flower and A C Waller
Zimbabwe v Sri Lanka 1992
6th 144 Imran Khan and Shahid Mahboob
Pakistan v Sri Lanka 1983
7th 75* D A G Fletcher and I P Butchart
Zimbabwe v Australia 1983
8th 117 D L Houghton and I P Butchart
Zimbabwe v New Zealand 1987
9th 126* Kapil Dev and S M H Kirmani
India v Zimbabwe, 1983
10th 71 A M E Roberts and J Garner
West Indies v India 1983

Below: Viv Richards, first man to score three centuries, including the second highest innings

· B O W L I N G ·

Most wickets in a tournament

	O	M	R	W	Ave	Best	5w	Econ
C J McDermott (Aus 1987)	73	3	341	18	18.94	5-44	1	4.67
R M H Binny (Ind 1983)	88	9	336	18	18.66	4-29	–	3.81
Wasim Akram (Pak 1992)	89.4	3	338	18	18.77	4-32	–	3.76
Imran Khan (Pak 1987)	49.5	6	222	17	13.05	4-37	–	4.45
A L F de Mel (SL 1983)	66	13	265	17	15.58	5-32	2	4.01

Highest career wickets

34 at 19.26   Imran Khan, Pakistan
30 at 25.40   I T Botham, England
28 at 27.42   Wasim Akram, Pakistan
28 at 31.85   Kapil Dev, India
27 at 22.18   C J McDermott, Australia

Hat-tricks

1987   Chetan Sharma, India v New Zealand

Best bowling

W W Davis   10.3-0-51-7
            WI v Aus, Leeds 11/6/1983
G J Gilmour 12-6-14-6
            Aus v Eng, Leeds 18/6/1975
K H MacLeay 11.5-3-39-6
            Aus v Ind, Nottingham 13/6/1983
A G Hurst   10-3-21-5
            Aus v Can, Birmingham 16/6/1979
P A Strang 9.4-1-21-5
            Zim v Ken, Patna 27/2/1996

Most economical bowling

B S Bedi   12-8-6-1
           India v East Africa 1975

Most expensive bowling

M C Snedden 12-1-105-2
            New Zealand v England 1983

Most wickets in a match for

West Indies	7-51	W W Davis v Australia 1983
Australia	6-14	G J Gilmour v England 1975
Zimbabwe	5-21	P A Strang v Kenya 1996
New Zealand	5-25	R J Hadlee v Sri Lanka 1983
UAE	5-29	S Dukanwala v Holland 1996
Sri Lanka	5-32	A L F de Mel v N Zealand 1983
England	5-39	V J Marks v Sri Lanka 1983
India	5-43	Kapil Dev v Australia 1983
Pakistan	5-44	Abdul Qadir v Sri Lanka 1983
South Africa	4-11	M W Pringle v W Indies 1992
Kenya	3-15	M Odumbe v West Indies 1996
Holland	3-48	S W Lubbers v N Zealand 1996
East Africa	3-63	Zulfiqar Ali v England 1975
Canada	2-27	C C Henry v Australia 1979

· F I E L D I N G ·

Most World Cup dismissals by a wicketkeeper

22   (18 ct, 4st)   Wasim Bari, Pakistan
20   (17ct, 3st)   I A Healy, Australia
20   (19ct, 1st)   P J L Dujon, West Indies
18   (12ct, 6st)   K S More, India
18   (17ct, 1st)   R W Marsh, Australia

Most World Cup catches by an outfielder

12   C H Lloyd, West Indies
12   Kapil Dev, India
12   D L Haynes, West Indies
11   C L Cairns, New Zealand
10   I T Botham, England
10   A R Border, Australia

Most appearances

33   Javed Miandad, Pakistan
28   Imran Khan, Pakistan
26   Kapil Dev, India
25   A R Border, Australia
25   D L Haynes, West Indies
25   A Ranatunga, Sri Lanka

**Is it a bird? Is it a plane? No, it's Jonty Rhodes
– most exciting fielder in a World Cup**

· MAN OF THE MATCH ·

Man of the Match award winners in Finals

1975	C H Lloyd, West Indies
1979	I V A Richards, West Indies
1983	M Amarnath, India
1987	D C Boon, Australia
1992	Wasim Akram, Pakistan
1996	P A de Silva, Sri Lanka

Top Man of the Match award winners

5	G A Gooch, England
5	I V A Richards, West Indies
4	D C Boon, Australia
4	P A de Silva, Sri Lanka
4	S R Tendulkar, India

Right: David Boon, Man of the Match in the 1987 Final after scoring 75 runs

· FINALS ·

Totals over 250 in a Final

1975	West Indies 291 for 8
1975	Australia 274
1979	West Indies 286 for 9
1987	Australia 253 for 5

Totals under 150 in a Final

1983	West Indies 140

Hundreds in a Final

1975	102	C H Lloyd West Indies v Australia
1979	138 n.o.	I V A Richards West Indies v England
1996	107 n.o.	P A de Silva Sri Lanka v Australia

Four wickets or more in a Final

1975	5-48	G J Gilmour, Australia v West Indies
1979	5-38	J Garner, West Indies v England

Captains winning toss and fielding first in a Final

1975	I M Chappell, Australia v West Indies
1979	J M Brearley, England v West Indies
1983	C H Lloyd, West Indies v India
1996	A Ranatunga, Sri Lanka v Australia

Man of the Match award winners by country

PAKISTAN

3	Abdul Qadir
3	Imran Khan
3	Aamir Sohail
2	Zaheer Abbas
2	Javed Miandad
2	Salim Malik
2	Mushtaq Ahmed
1	Sarfraz Nawaz
1	Sadiq Mohammad
1	Asif Iqbal
1	Mohsin Khan
1	Salim Yousuf
1	Inzamam-ul-Haq
1	Wasim Akram
1	Waqar Younis

ENGLAND

5	G A Gooch
3	A J Lamb
2	I T Botham
2	C C Lewis
2	G A Hick
1	D L Amiss
1	K W R Fletcher
1	J A Snow
1	C M Old
1	M Hendrick
1	D I Gower
1	G Fowler
1	R G D Willis
1	A J Stewart
1	N M K Smith

WEST INDIES

5	I V A Richards
3	C G Greenidge
3	B C Lara
2	C H Lloyd
2	A I Kallicharran
2	P V Simmons
2	R B Richardson

1	B D Julien
1	W W Davis
1	S F A F Bacchus
1	A C Cummins
1	C E L Ambrose

AUSTRALIA

4	D C Boon
3	M E Waugh
2	G R Marsh
2	S R Waugh
2	S K Warne
1	D K Lillee
1	A Turner
1	G J Gilmour
1	A G Hurst
1	T M Chappell
1	C J McDermott
1	D M Jones
1	T M Moody

INDIA

4	S R Tendulkar
3	Kapil Dev
2	M Amarnath
1	F M Engineer
1	Yashpal Sharma
1	Madan Lal
1	R M H Binny
1	S M Gavaskar
1	M Prabhakar
1	A Jadeja
1	N S Sidhu

NEW ZEALAND

3	M D Crowe
2	G M Turner
2	M J Greatbatch
1	G P Howarth
1	B A Edgar
1	R J Hadlee
1	J V Coney

1	J J Crowe
1	K R Rutherford
1	A H Jones
1	N J Astle
1	R G Twose
1	C M Spearman

SOUTH AFRICA

2	P N Kirsten
2	A C Hudson
2	W J Cronje
1	K C Wessels
1	M W Pringle
1	J N Rhodes

SRI LANKA

4	P A de Silva
2	S T Jayasuriya
1	L R D Mendis
1	A L F de Mel
1	A Ranatunga

ZIMBABWE

2	D L Houghton
1	D A G Fletcher
1	A Flower
1	E A Brandes
1	P A Strang

KENYA

1	M Odumbe

UAE

1	S Dukanwala*
1	Saleem Raza*

*shared award against Holland, 1996

For the Tigers -
Noah, Will, Tim and Antonia
~JS and TW

LITTLE TIGER PRESS
An imprint of Magi Publications
1 The Coda Centre, 189 Munster Road
London SW6 6AW
First published in Great Britain 2001
Text © 2001 Julie Sykes
Illustrations © 2001 Tim Warnes
Julie Sykes and Tim Warnes have asserted their rights
to be identified as the author and illustrator of this work
under the Copyright, Designs and Patents Act, 1988.
Printed in Belgium by Proost NV, Turnhout
All rights reserved
ISBN 1 85430 722 3
1 3 5 7 9 10 8 6 4 2

Wait for me, Little Tiger!

by Julie Sykes

illustrated by Tim Warnes

LITTLE TIGER PRESS

London

Little Tiger had lots of friends.
They liked to play exciting games.
Each time he went out to look for
them his little sister would say,
"I'm lonely. Can I come with you,
Little Tiger?"

And Little Tiger would answer,
"No you can't, Little Sister. You're
much too small."

One day, Little Tiger said, "Can I go out to play?"
Mummy Tiger was very busy, so she told him to take Little
Sister along, too.
"I don't want to!" cried Little Tiger. "She's much too small
to play with me."
But Mummy Tiger wouldn't change her mind. "She's not
too small, if you lend her a paw now and then," she said.

Crossly, Little Tiger ran off into the jungle.
"Wait for me!" cried Little Sister,
scampering after him.

Little Tiger took Little Sister to visit Little Bear.
They played skittles, but Little Sister couldn't
roll the ball straight.
She missed the skittles, and hit Little Bear instead.

"Ouch!" cried Little Bear, nursing her paw. "Perhaps you should find somewhere safer to play."
Little Tiger thought so, too.
"Wait for me!" cried Little Sister, as he hurried towards the trees.

Very soon Little Tiger came across
Little Monkey. They both climbed
up trees and swung down vines.
But Little Sister couldn't climb
trees. She reached the first
branch, then fell and landed
on top of Little Monkey.

"Ouch!" he squeaked.
Little Tiger sighed. He didn't
want to leave his game with Little
Monkey, but it wasn't safe enough
for Little Sister. He would have to
take her away from the trees.
"Wait for me!" cried Little Sister,
bouncing after him.

Little Tiger went to find Little Leopard. His spotty friend was running in the grass. Little Leopard started a chase, but Little Sister didn't look where she was going. She tripped on a stone, hurtled forward and knocked Little Leopard flat on his face.

"Ow!" cried Little Leopard. "That hurt!"
Little Tiger was worried he would have no
friends left, if Little Sister kept causing accidents.
"Come along," he said. "We'd better go
somewhere else."

Little Tiger trotted off to the river, where he found Little Elephant on the bank. Little Sister couldn't wait to learn how to swim. "It's easy," said Little Tiger, jumping in. "You kick your paws and off you go!"
Little Sister didn't find swimming easy. The water splashed in her eyes and she couldn't see where she was going. Suddenly . . .

SPLASH!

Little Elephant jumped in . . .

and Little Sister swallowed a mouthful of water.

"Help!" she spluttered.

Little Tiger towed her safely to the bank.

"Swimming is too dangerous for you," he said.

"You'd better sit and watch."

"I don't *want* to watch. I want to play with you," she shouted crossly. "You're much too little to play my games," said Little Tiger.

Little Tiger jumped back into the water. It was
fun splashing around with Little Elephant. Soon
he forgot all about Little Sister on the bank.
He only remembered her when the game
was finished. "That was fun, wasn't it,
Little Sister?" he called.
There was no answer.

When Little Tiger jumped out of
the water, the riverbank was empty.
His little sister had gone!

Little Tiger felt really awful. He should not have left Little Sister on her own. What if she had fallen into the water and been swept away?

Little Elephant helped him search along the riverbank, but they couldn't see her anywhere.

Little Tiger looked everywhere.
He searched the plains,
but she wasn't there.
He hunted in the trees,
but she wasn't there.

He peered inside Little Bear's cave, but she wasn't there either. Now Little Tiger was frightened. Mummy Tiger would be so angry that he had lost Little Sister. Sadly, he ran home to tell her.

He was almost there when . . .

"BOO!"
Little Sister leapt down
at him from the trees.

"See, Little Tiger," she cried.
"I've been practising and
now I can climb trees, too!"

Little Tiger was so pleased that Little Sister was safe.
He wanted to make it up to her for being unkind.
"I'll help you practise at skittles next," he offered.
"And running?" asked Little Sister.
"And running," Little Tiger agreed.

"Good," she said. "And after all that, will you help me to swim?"

"Maybe," said Little Tiger. "But for now, Little Sister, it's time I helped you home."